St Albans
1455

The medieval clock tower at St Albans around which most of the intense fighting took place on 22 May 1455. (Courtesy of Geoffrey Wheeler)

St Albans 1455

The Anatomy of a Battle

A.W. BOARDMAN

First published 2006
This paperback edition published 2023

The History Press
97 St George's Place, Cheltenham,
Gloucestershire, GL50 3QB
www.thehistorypress.co.uk

British Library Cataloguing in Publication Data.
A catalogue record for this book is available from the British Library.

ISBN 978 1 80399 278 5

Typesetting and origination by The History Press
Printed and bound in Great Britain by TJ Books Limited, Padstow, Cornwall.

Trees for LYfe

Saint Albans battle won by famous York
Shall be eternized in all age to come.
Sound drums and trumpets, and to London all:
And more such days as these to us befall.

William Shakespeare
Henry VI, Part 2

Contents

Introduction

For many years, the battle of Bosworth was regarded as the final encounter of the 'Wars of the Roses' purely because some commentators found it a convenient place to mark the end of one historical period and the beginning of another. This same reasoning also claimed that Bosworth signified the end of Richard III's rule and the creation of a new age under Henry VII, the first Tudor king. Shakespeare, among other writers, appropriated this symbolism and made it common currency in his history plays, and thus the above timelines have featured in popular tradition ever since. However, today most historians accept that the 'Wars of the Roses' continued into the reign of Henry VII, and the final pitched battle of the conflict was fought not at Bosworth in 1485, but at Stoke Field two years later. So, if the battle of Stoke signified the end of the wars, where did York and Lancaster first cross swords?

Before I wrote the first edition of this book in 2006, I firmly believed that the civil wars known persistently as the 'Wars of the Roses' began at the battle of Blore Heath in 1459, when

Neville contingents led by the Earl of Salisbury successfully beat a Lancastrian army under Lord Audley. Suffice to say I have changed my opinion since. This book claims that the first battle of St Albans was not merely 'a short scuffle in the street', as Sir Charles Oman and several other historians have suggested. Instead, it was a significant battle of the 'Wars of the Roses' along with the battles of Heworth Moor and Stamford Bridge, fought in 1453 and 1454, which extend the wars further back in time, thereby challenging established history.

It is well known that civil disorder, rebellions and pitched battles had long been endemic throughout the fifteenth century, and when I wrote in 2006, even I accepted that a recognisable civil war had been avoided. However, by accepting this, I, like most historians, fell into a trap and it is not surprising that earlier battles of the 'Wars of the Roses' have been forgotten – until now. To declassify is to essentially forget these encounters remain central to our understanding of how the all-important blood feuding aspects and polarisation of the 'Wars of the Roses' began. Thus, a more measured exploration of the battles of Heworth Moor, Stamford Bridge and first St Albans is worthy of investigation, as is the thorny issue of who was responsible for provoking the wars in the first place.

Walking and exploring a battlefield is the only way to appreciate the ground over which armies fought, and this is essential when dealing with a medieval battlefield like St Albans. The archaeology of battlefields is an ongoing preoccupation in the twenty-first century, but the evidence of first St Albans is not easy to appreciate, given the sprawl of urban life that has almost erased it. Unlike a pitched battle fought somewhere in the English countryside, a town or city changes over time. Although thankfully, the epicentre of St Albans still conforms to its medieval footprint. Therefore, it could be said we are lucky, in one respect, that the existing street layout is the only place where the battle could have been fought in 1455. The main areas of interest are set in stone, and so are many period buildings that medieval inhabitants would have recognised in their day. However, the new science of conflict archaeology is fairly limited at St Albans. Predictably, little in the way of artefacts relating to the first battle have been found, unlike at the second battle, fought in 1461, where a medieval cannonball was recently discovered close to Bernards Heath.

How, then, do we unlock what happened at St Albans in 1455? The answer has spawned some debate over the years, although not an in-depth military and topographic study until now. In 1960, C.A.J. Armstrong wrote 'Politics and the Battle of St Albans 1455' for the *Bulletin of the Institute of Historical Research*, and this was the only serious study of how the battle came about. Other books, biographies and papers touched on the battle and the politics, but no military history had been written to enlarge Armstrong's work. History is constantly evolving, and even I have revised my work on the battle since 2006, the results of which are presented here.

Today the wealth of information about the 'Wars of the Roses' is staggering, but to reveal the obvious conclusions about the civil wars is to discount the not so obvious. Stripping down the military aspects of the period to the bare minimum is one way of telling the story. Another is to see what remains on the ground or can be proven by modern research methods. However, as M.A. Hicks points out, any new research depends heavily on contemporary sources, and according to him, we should always listen to these closely:

> Records seldom offer overt avowals of motives: their significance is not always or often beyond dispute. Even the perusal of vast quantities of second-rate material can add relatively little to what is known. Our attempts to answer the major questions by oblique approaches and with reference to an ever-wider range of sources has seldom borne the direct fruits that were once hoped.[1]

To investigate the first battle of St Albans it is, therefore, essential to analyse the words of those who lived at the time and were witness to what occurred there. This must be our principal compass. Such testimonies mark the start of any journey into history's looking glass, then follows interpretation by other means. In fact, St Albans was quite a unique town in the 'Wars of the Roses' as it was the only place in Britain where two battles were fought over similar ground in the space of only a few years. The first battle was also the site of at least three assassinations that affected how English chivalry was viewed from then on. It was the place where a significant blood feud began, where indiscriminate pillaging of an English town occurred, and where a king was abandoned and almost killed in the street. Even the phrase the 'Wars of the Roses' is directly associated with how historians have viewed the St Albans story. Therefore, I feel the only productive way to investigate the battle as it appeared to those living at the time is to forget the title was ever coined.

It is well known that the term 'Wars of the Roses' was not recognised during the conflict or in the fifteenth century. In contemporary chronicles, we only hear about the 'civil wars', and no contending roses are mentioned. Therefore, we may wonder how people viewed the battle of St Albans and the events that came before it. Considering the uncertainty of the times, it seems safe to assume writers did not try to pigeonhole the battle and that it was not considered part of a particular phase or division of military history at all.

In 1964, the eminent historian S.B. Chrimes wrote in his acclaimed book *Lancastrians Yorkists and Henry VII* that the 'Wars of the Roses' as a title should be dropped from every history book. In his lifetime, he examined the conflict between York and Lancaster from various academic viewpoints, and to achieve a broader perspective on the wars, it is worth reiterating his introductory words in full:

> It deserves to be made quite clear at the start that there is no historical justification for the term 'Wars of the Roses'. We need to grasp firmly that no contemporary ever thought of the civil wars in such terms, nor indeed ever used the expression at all...The men who fought those battles from 1455 onwards certainly knew nothing of such flights of literary fancy, and for that reason the present writer has avoided using the term at all, even though he can scarcely hope that others will readily follow his example in this perhaps, by now, pedantic renunciation.[2]

My renunciation of the term 'Wars of the Roses' is not done lightly. However, my decision bears no similarity to that condoned by Professor Chrimes. In all previous books about the civil wars, historians have traditionally endeavoured to stylise the period due, in part, to its complexity. As I have said, no contemporary writer or chronicler ever mentioned a 'series' of wars. Instead, they only recorded what they saw or heard, not how the wars fitted into a specific time frame. Therefore, in this work about the first battle of St Albans, I have entirely divorced this well-worn cliché from the late fifteenth century and assimilated the viewpoint of a person living at the time. My aim is to give a new perspective on the military and topographic aspects of St Albans, without the romanticism, supported and referenced by contemporary or near-contemporary sources. Where possible, I have only used reliable evidence, official documentation, letters, and foreign authorities that can be verified. I have discounted the later Tudor chroniclers, and other commentators in their entirety, which may shock some readers as most of the detail about the civil wars comes from them.

To explain this, it is well known that the sixteenth-century chronicler Edward Hall invented the 'Wars of the Roses' although Sir Walter Scott first popularised the phrase in 1829. However, *Hall's Chronicle*, published in the first year of

Edward VI's reign (1548), was a masterpiece of Tudor propaganda, and on the title page of his book, Hall dedicated his work in grandiose style to,

> the union of the two noble and illustrious families of Lancaster and York being long in continual dissention for the crown of this noble realm with all the acts done in both the times of the princes, both of the one lineage and of the other, beginning at the time of King Henry the Fourth, the first author of this division, and so successively proceeding to the reign of the high and prudent prince King Henry the Eighth, the undoubted flower and very heir of both the said lineages.[3]

There is no doubt that Hall wrote factual history, but he also invented fictional scenes that Shakespeare later used for dramatic purposes. Crucially, Hall paints a mainly black-and-white picture of historical characters and their motives, with particular reference to the battles of the era, none of which referenced extensive resources or oral tradition.[4] The picture of a country wholly torn apart by conflict and blood feuding is the common theme throughout Hall's work. Unrest, inward war, unrighteousness, the shedding of innocent blood and the abuse of law and order were his blueprints to Tudor stardom. But more than this, Hall's story of the fifteenth century is more divisive and focuses on divine judgement, political morals, and the fear of unrest and usurpation rather than contemporary analysis. The simple fact is that a great deal of *Hall's Chronicle* is a dramatised account. The author loved to describe battles in graphic detail and put speeches into the mouths of principal characters. And later, Tudor writers and dramatists, including Sir Thomas More, Raphael Holinshed and Shakespeare, followed his example with stories of their own that distorted the reputations of even kings to please their benefactors. That Hall's grandfather Sir David had been slain fighting for the

Yorkists at the battle of Wakefield in 1460 was also a strong incentive to embroider the truth and charge certain individuals with murder.

It is well known that chroniclers saw morals and the hand of God in everything, while others claimed that history was the key to inducing virtue and repressing vice. Edward Hall was a lawyer, a great believer in justice, and his near contemporary Raphael Holinshed thought that most chronicles were next to holy scripture and packed with profitable lessons.[5] Famous battles were the pinnacle of his work, and later chroniclers wrote passionately about them partly to enhance the deep divisions and later 'perfect union' of York and Lancaster in 1486. The expected fame of Edward VI in 1547 was, according to Hall, a product of Henry VII's triumph over Richard III at the battle of Bosworth. And in his chronicle, you can almost hear the universal sigh of relief when Richard III is killed and Henry Tudor is crowned king. It was also the end of the medieval period for some writers, which takes us neatly back to the beginning and end of the civil wars and the 'Wars of the Roses' as a time frame.

As discussed, I take the viewpoint that the first battle of St Albans was a continuation of military activity in England rather than a commencement. And by this rule, we can safely say the battle was no different from the private wars that peppered the second half of the fifteenth century. St Albans, for this reason, was a battle and not a skirmish in the street. It is certain the Duke of York aimed to remove the Duke of Somerset, by force if needed. Thousands of men were ready to fight at St Albans and knew the consequences of the battle might cause political shockwaves for years to come. After hours of waiting in Key Field to the east of St Albans, York contemplated the dreaded crime of treason, and not for the first time. Furious that his many declarations of loyalty had not been heeded, he was determined to act against his political enemies or die trying. Henry VI's last message to York spoke

of severe punishment for him and all his followers, and rather
than act faithfully upon the words of a king who might be
constrained by false councillors, York was put in an incredibly
difficult position.

However, that morning in May 1455, the duke was supported by his brother-in-law, the Earl of Salisbury, and his
ambitious young son, Richard Neville, Earl of Warwick, later
to become known as the 'kingmaker' of 'Wars of the Roses'
legend. Both were itching for a fight with their northern rivals,
the Percys. Both Neville earls had swelled York's ranks with
their extensive retinues, mustered from those parts of England
where violence was an everyday fact of life. Add to this the fact
that their border levies were agitated after hours of waiting
for orders, and there was potential for violence even without a
political expedient.

But what if York failed in his attempt to remove the Duke
of Somerset from office peaceably? What would the kingdom
think of his decision to act forcefully against the king with
banners displayed? How might he explain such treasonable
action afterwards if, by some chance, the king was injured or
even killed in battle? Alternatively, if York's bid to capture
Somerset succeeded, how could he permanently remove his
rival from the king's inner circle once his Neville supporters
had disbanded their contingents? In short, what crucial decision might Duke Richard have to take to remove Somerset's
'seditious' hold over the king? York could step back from
the abyss, but the argument of who should rule England if
King Henry succumbed to another bout of mental illness was
unmistakably one-sided. The only course of action was for
York to try and extract Somerset by force and thereby cut a
new cloth of state with cold steel.

Intense local rivalry would open hostilities at St Albans, but
for both sides, the first blow struck would inflict a much deeper
wound that would overshadow political wrangling. The battle
would be brutal and merciless. A climax of all that had gone

before. One side would display its rebellious proclivity, the other its need for a competent military leader. And no one that day could have anticipated the long-term effects of the battle, nor prophesy how the bloodletting at St Albans would eventually sign the death warrants of a substantial portion of England's nobility by the end of the fifteenth century.

Andrew Boardman
2023

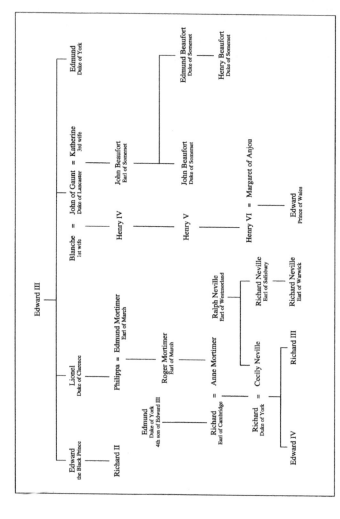

1 *A simplified genealogical chart of the contending houses of York and Lancaster. (Author's Collection)*

One

York and Somerset

Like most medieval nobles, Richard Plantagenet, third Duke of York, wanted to be liked by his contemporaries. Yet, this seemingly innocent ambition – to appear the perfect champion of law and order and the model protector of England – was never fully realised in his lifetime.

Despite several attempts at political mediation, not to mention various bouts of what might have been termed treasonable activity, York was destined to fail time and time again in his efforts to remove his political rivals from office, chiefly because his noble and impetuous character always got in the way of sound judgement. Chivalric pride was a quality that most fifteenth-century nobles understood and would readily die for if the cause benefited themselves or their family. Therefore, it comes as no surprise that York's self-righteous and reckless ambition would eventually lead to a copybook chivalrous death at the hands of those injured by his rise to power. We may question York's rash paladin nature, ambition and pride, but was this noble reckless-ness the chief cause of his downfall, as some historians suggest? In short, was the Duke of York completely loyal to the crown during his lifetime, even after the watershed battle of St Albans in 1455, or was he, in fact, a rebel opportunist whose aim was to usurp the throne in place of Henry VI, who was clearly unfit to rule the kingdom.

A considerable body of written evidence remains concerning the Duke of York's vast inheritance, official correspondence and military appointments. However, as with so many other historical figures, no accurate character assessment of York is possible other than to say that, at face value, his sense of nobility far outweighed his recklessness. Many times, in his letters and petitions to the king, we are reminded of York's apparent loyalty and determination to prove he was 'the king's true liegeman and servant ... to advise his Royal Majesty of certain articles concerning the weal and safeguard of his most royal person, and the tranquillity and conservation of all this his realm'.[1] However, as part of this loyalty York also wished to remove the king's enemies, including Edmund Beaufort, Duke of Somerset and his supporters, all of whom, in his own words, 'laboureth continually about the King's Highness for my undoing' – an opinion that can be taken both ways if York was in any way paranoid.[2] Therefore, in the absence of an impartial character witness, much of Richard of York's temperament and character must remain hidden from view.

It is also a matter of great frustration that no full descriptions or faithful images survive of medieval personalities other than in character sketches, manuscripts and statues, which often contain misinformation and portray invented images. In York's case, the most famous of these is the stained-glass window at Trinity College Cambridge, which shows him wearing full armour, while another similar depiction in Cirencester parish church reveals the face of a rather weak-looking character, clearly not in keeping with one so powerful. However, in written evidence, York's immediate family provide the best clue to the duke's outward appearance. It was evidently well known to later contemporaries that York resembled his youngest son (later

Richard III), who, during the defamatory campaign aimed at bastardising his brother Edward IV in 1483, was noted by the Italian writer Dominic Mancini:

> Edward, said they, was conceived in adultery and in every way was unlike his father the late Duke of York whose son he was falsely said to be, but Richard Duke of Gloucester *who altogether resembled his father* [York], was to come to the throne as the legitimate successor.[3]

Richard of York was born on 21 September 1411 into an infamous family who inherited its royal blood from the patriarch of all late medieval kings, Edward III, through his two sons, Edmund, Duke of York and Lionel, Duke of Clarence. Richard was an only son, and his renowned claim to greatness and dynastic right to the English throne can be explained on two counts. His mother, Anne Mortimer, was the sister of Edmund, Earl of March, whose family had been the focus of so many political intrigues and threats against the crown in the past, including

2 *Richard, Duke of York.*
Fifteenth-century glass in Cirencester
Church. (Courtesy of Geoffrey Wheeler)

3 *Richard III, 'Altogether like his father'*
the Duke of York, according to sources.
Engraving of a Society of Antiquaries
portrait. (Courtesy of Geoffrey Wheeler)

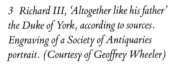

Henry Bolingbroke (later Henry IV), whose usurpation of 1399 later formed part of Yorkist propaganda. On the paternal side of York's family, his father, Richard Earl of Cambridge, was executed for high treason in what later became known as the Southampton Plot against Henry V in 1415. This terrible association was one that Richard of York had to bear throughout his life, and, indeed, it may have been a psychological stigma that weighed heavily on his character in adulthood. However, apart from the apparent antipathy he may have felt against such treasonable behaviour against the crown, York was never openly tainted with his father's crime. Also, Richard's uncle, Edward, Duke of York, had died loyal to the Lancastrian cause at the battle of Agincourt in 1415, and thus York's family, at least on the ascendant branch, had redeemed itself in blood.

Soon after Henry V's brilliant victories in France, the young Richard of York was placed with trusted mentors, like most noble offspring of his age, to learn the 'gentle' arts of nobility and chivalry. In Richard's case, this was with Sir Robert Waterton, an old Yorkshire knight and veteran of the French Wars. No better-skilled campaigner could have been chosen for York, but in 1423 it was decided that the young duke should be transferred to the Earl of Westmoreland's care for nine years. And it was here that he learned much about the Neville family and their Beaufort connections from Joan, Westmoreland's second wife.

However, on the death of the Earl of March in 1425, significant changes began to shape Richard's life, and soon the vast Mortimer inheritance of his uncle, the earl, became the focus of his attention. In May 1426, York was knighted, along with the new king Henry VI at the Leicester parliament, and in November 1429, he was summoned to attend Henry's lavish coronation at Westminster Abbey. Not long after this, York began to take up his rightful position at court as Duke of York, and he was present at Henry's other crowning as King of France in Paris – a notable achievement for any English monarch, although a legacy left by the new king's warrior father that his infant son could never hope to equal.

As for the Duke of York's future, a bride had been found for him when he was only thirteen. In 1426, he married into the respected and powerful northern family where he had spent much of his youth. The Nevilles were equally pleased with their daughter Cecily's marriage into the house of York. And like many other large and ambitious medieval dynasties before them, they doubtless saw Duke Richard as a lucrative way to advance their position at court and in northern England.

By 1445, the Duke of York had become acquainted with his vast lordship. He had secured the services of many notable knights and retainers as befitted his position, including Ralph Lord Cromwell, Thomas Lord Scales, Sir John Falstolf, Sir Andrew Ogard, Sir William ap Thomas and Sir William Oldhall, the latter knight figuring in the critical political events which followed his master's enforced exile to Ireland in 1450. Also prominent among Richard's many connections at this time were members of the powerful Bourchier family, Viscount Bourchier being recorded as York's chief councillor in 1448. More significantly, regarding St Albans, Duke Richard was also related to Thomas Bourchier, who became chancellor and Archbishop of Canterbury in 1454 and recieved York's letters of fealty prior to the battle. The Bourchiers were the powerful half-brothers of Richard's aunt, the countess of March, and York's only sister Isabel was married to Henry Bourchier, connections that would prove crucially important to the duke later in his career.

As might be expected, the Duke of York's links to these and several other important baronial houses made him an extremely wealthy man in his own right. And by the time he finally gained his Mortimer inheritance, provided he honoured the outstanding obligations of his two dead uncles, he could boast vast landholdings in almost every English county. He also owned properties and estates in the Marches of Wales and Ireland, while on his maternal grandmother's side, he benefited from being known as the Earl of March and Ulster, the Lord of Wigmore, Clare, Trim and Connaught, the latter titles providing him with a foothold in Ireland and, by coincidence, a place of refuge where he might find shelter in times of trouble or personal crisis.

Like most men of his age, York had already seen military service in France, but it was not until 1436 that he formally agreed by indenture to serve as the king's lieutenant-general in Normandy, an appointment that was to lead to several dismissals and recalls, all resulting in a vast personal debt that was never repaid in full by the crown. Richard Beauchamp, Earl of Warwick, was appointed to succeed York as lieutenant in 1437, but when he died two years later, the chief command of English armies in France devolved to John Beaufort, then Earl of Somerset. As a nephew of the extremely powerful and politically minded Cardinal Beaufort, the Earl of Somerset could, like York, trace his royal blood back to Edward III through John of Gaunt and his second wife, Catherine Swynford. However, Somerset's line of descent had been barred from the succession, and so was no threat to York at this time, although if this claim was legitimised, it could provide an heir to the throne should Henry VI remain childless.

Somerset was an unconvincing military leader, but when York's bid to provoke Charles VII into fighting pitched battles failed, the king's council decided that Somerset should take York's place as lieutenant – a decision that was to result in the duke's distrust of the entire Beaufort family and, most notably, his dread of a possible competitor for the throne if Henry should die. Advanced by his uncle, the wealthy cardinal, and given a dukedom to enhance his authority by the king, Somerset crossed the English Channel in August 1443 and proceeded to pillage La Guerche, a town belonging to the friendly Duke of Brittany. Incurring not only the anger of York but also the great displeasure of the English government, Somerset's appointment proved to be a complete disaster. However, given that the war was slowly turning in favour of the French anyway, Somerset

4 *Seal of Edmund Beaufort, Duke of Somerset. (Courtesy of Geoffrey Wheeler)*

was not the first to suffer a severe reprimand from those who had appointed him. Recalled to England, he died the following year, leaving the new duke, Edmund Beaufort, in direct competition to York's supremacy.

As for the Duke of York, he continued to command in France despite a lack of financial help, but his ambitions to emulate the English successes of Crécy, Poitiers and Agincourt were ingloriously dashed on several occasions. Instead, he was given more commercial and civil duties, and in 1445 he accompanied Margaret of Anjou, his future enemy, to the French coast before she embarked for England to marry Henry VI. Evidently, more peaceable means were being contemplated in England to heal the wounds of war in the form of a truce. But soon, the political wheel of fortune was about to turn full circle against Duke Richard when he, like Somerset before him, was ordered to return home on the pretext that his presence was required at the coming parliament.

York's term of office in France had, in fact, expired, but Duke Richard obviously hoped to be recalled at some later date as, in theory at least, he was the obvious choice to command now that the Beauforts were discredited.

However, the Duke of York had no idea what the court party was planning against him at this time, or he would have acted against the threat immediately. The essential mechanism that brought about York's recall and later 'banishment' to Ireland was clearly the design of a group of unscrupulous nobles who sought to control the king and, in so doing, enhance their own positions at court. It is also apparent that broader politics and a complex web of retainers and 'well-willers' added fuel to the political fire when England's finances began to suffer because of the Hundred Years War.

It is no accident that the politics which brought York into direct opposition with Edmund, the new Duke of Somerset, were initially manufactured by the ambitions of lesser courtiers hoping to carve out a career at the expense of an ineffective king. However, King Henry must also bear a significant portion of the blame, and to appreciate this further, it is essential, as far as possible, to understand the king's complex character. In his fulsome assessment of Henry's 'saintly' nature, John Blacman, the king's confessor, makes plain the absurdity and complexity of his sovereign's monkish kingship:

> He was like a second Job, a man simple and upright, altogether fearing the Lord God, and departing from evil. He was a simple man, without any crook of craft or untruth, as is plain to all. With none did he deal craftily, nor ever would say an untrue word to any, but framed his speech always to speak the truth ... The lord king complained to me once in his room at Eltham, when I was alone with him and working with him on his holy books, and hearing his serious admonitions and devout observations, one of the most powerful of the English dukes knocked on the door. The king said: 'See how they disturb me!'[4]

This depiction of Henry's devout and other-worldly nature is contrary to what other commentators thought of him, as there is no contemporary evidence to suggest the king was uniquely addicted to prayer or private meditation. Indeed, Henry could be both spiteful and vindictive, and his apparent failure to appreciate what was going on in the real world was, in fact, one of the main causes of the civil wars. All his life, apart from faint glimpses of adroit kingship, others controlled him to the extent that one biased chronicler later described him as 'of small intelligence'.[5] However, this character assassination of the king formed later anti-Lancastrian propaganda, and during his youth, there was no reason to suppose that Henry might not turn out to be a replica of his formidable father. Among the chroniclers who lamented the passing of Henry V was John Hardyng, a northern chronicler and former soldier, who wrote at about the same time as the first battle of St Albans. His eulogy in praise of the victor of Agincourt is interesting, considering that Hardyng fought for Harry Hotspur against the young Henry V in 1403, and it compares the rule of both father and son:

O good Lord God, why did you let so soon to pass
This noble prince [Henry V], that in all Christianity
Had then no peer in any land, no more nor less,
So excellent was his happy truth.
In flourishing age of all freshness of youth,
That might have let him live to greater age
Till he had wholly gained his heritage.

The peace at home and law so well maintained
Were root and head of all his great conquest,
Which exiled is away and foully now disdained
In such degree that north and south and west
And east also enjoys now little rest,
But by day and night in every shire throughout
With sallets bright and jacks make fearful rout.[6]

Such was the contempt levelled at Henry VI in adulthood, at a time when many men must have known first-hand how lawless some parts of England had become. Clearly, Hardyng's scathing but veiled words about Henry VI did not express his propaganda alone, and this, aside from the obvious bias, points to a weakness in both the king and his administration. However, this was not the only reason for the steady decline mentioned above by Hardyng. From as early as September 1422, the government of England had been carried on in the name of Henry VI by a select council of peers, the infant king then being a minor and not yet old enough to rule the kingdom alone.

It was common medieval practice for the king's uncles to take precedence during a minority, but Humphrey, Duke of Gloucester, Henry V's younger brother, had reluctantly become part of a ruling council in which the Beauforts were his most quarrelsome enemies. With the crown virtually out of commission for a time, one would have expected that these two factions

5 A young Henry VI from an original dated c. 1450 in the Royal Collection at Windsor Castle.

might have come to blows on more than one occasion, but this was not the case, and business was carried on as usual in the name of the king. However, the political history of the next ten years disclosed an underlying conflict, established in 1437, which brought about factionalism and division when King Henry emerged from his minority a less forceful monarch than medieval England deserved. Thus, it was only a matter of time before the most dominant court faction took control of the king, and as the war with France turned unmistakably sour against the English, this inner circle became headed by William de la Pole, later Duke of Suffolk, and a group of clerics guided by bishops Ayscough of Salisbury and Moleyns of Chichester.

The public denunciation of these three men leaves no doubt that they were chiefly responsible for the disasters that followed, both at home and abroad. After Gloucester's mysterious death in 1447, Suffolk succeeded in making Henry VI his puppet while at the same time removing many of the enemies who stood in his way. This process of control and indoctrination was, of course, a gradual development, but in July 1446, the Duke of York was involved in a violent quarrel with Adam Moleyns, then Henry's keeper of the privy seal, who he accused of bribing his troops so that they would charge him with embezzlement. The result had been a serious breach with the court party who, during their machinations, caused York's recall to England and the appointment of Edmund Beaufort, Duke of Somerset, to the lieutenancy of France.

The Duke of York's punishment was clearly galling and even more so when he was appointed Lieutenant of Ireland for the unusual term of ten years. However, it is apparent that Suffolk and the court party wanted York out of the way for purely selfish reasons, and by using King Henry's pliability and power to impose their will, they largely succeeded in achieving their aim.

However, soon, from his enforced 'exile' in Ireland, York had the dubious satisfaction of hearing that yet another Beaufort was leading English armies to disaster in France. It is significant that at the end of York's term of office in Normandy and his removal to Ireland in 1447, Henry's dwindling exchequer owed him £38,666, an enormous sum of money at the time, part of which the duke renounced and the remainder of which he aimed to recover in the future. The resulting French losses, caused by the well-financed Somerset, therefore injured York on two counts at a time when he was both physically and politically constrained abroad. By the tone of his later letters denouncing Somerset's conduct in France, it was a personal humiliation that cut York to the core.

But was there yet another reason why the Duke of York was being excluded from the king's council? Abbot Whethamstede, the opinionated chronicler who recorded the first and second battles of St Albans, had no doubt that York's dynastic claim to the throne was the true source of his arrogant and uncontrolled quest for power in the 1450s. Whethamstede asserted that York's vendetta against Somerset was unmindful, and that revenge was wrong. Duke Richard, as Henry's heir apparent, had every reason to fear Somerset's ambitions, especially when his rival came to entrench himself deep within the king's inner council. In fact, the fear that Somerset might be officially recognised as the Lancastrian heir if Henry VI should die childless was probably the main reason for Whethamstede's scathing remarks about York's ambitious nature. While another motive could be that the abbot probably harboured intense feelings against the Duke of York because his men pillaged the town of St Albans in 1455 and almost sacked his abbey.[7]

However, it is clear that York could not afford to overlook the Beaufort claims to the throne, and doubtless this was the main reason for his feud with Somerset. As for the Duke of Suffolk, the chief instigator of all York's troubles, he did not live long enough to see his political intrigues come to fruition. In January 1450, the commons, awakening to the frightening losses in France as well as the tides of discontent and lawlessness at home,

6 *Edmund Beaufort in Rouen. (Chronique de Jean Chartier. © Bibliothèque Nationale de France)*

conveniently placed the blame for the current misfortunes on Suffolk's ambitious head. Clearly, the court party needed a scapegoat, and it was undoubtedly to Somerset's benefit that someone else was available to take the blame. The exclusion and death of Suffolk was a travesty brought about by an ineffective king and a series of events that were undoubtedly arranged by other ambitious courtiers. When the commons tried to impeach Suffolk, the king's merciful intervention backfired and only helped to delay the inevitable. A term of banishment was placed on the duke, and consequently, when his boat pulled away from the Kentish coast, there was already a plot to kill him:

And one of the lewdest of the ship bade him lay down his head [so] that he might be fairly dealt with and die on a sword; and

[he] took a rusty sword and smote off his head with half a dozen strokes, and [he] took away his gown of russet and his doublet of velvet mailed, and laid his body on the sands of Dover; and some say his head was set on a pole by it.[8]

Banishment for five years was clearly a sentence that a man like Suffolk could have easily survived, but, as fate would have it, the duke was considered a worthy sacrifice for England's troubles. The kind of unrest that was virulent in the kingdom, and the general disorder that was rife, especially in Kent, only added to the mounting problems that King Henry and his corrupt government had to overcome. Indeed, their troubles went from bad to worse. The insurrection and rebellion led by Jack Cade in May-July 1450 was symptomatic of the growing dissatisfaction against many of the king's chief ministers. Once more, the cry of 'Mortimer' was used to signal popular rebellion in English shires, and by the time hundreds of southern insurgents reached the gates of London, news of Cade's murderous rampage had spread far and wide. The volatile situation could only have added to York's unease in Ireland, especially when news reached him that his name was being used in the rebel's manifesto as the man most likely to bring about reform. The rebel petition was adamant that the king should,

take about his noble person his true blood of his royal realm, that is to say, the high and mighty prince, the Duke of York, exiled from our sovereign lord's person by the noising of the false traitor the Duke of Suffolk and his affinity.[9]

It was a situation that York, and his enemy Somerset, could not fail to ignore, even though Cade's rebellion was soon put down and its ringleaders executed for treason. With characteristic blindness, the final act of the king's council was to recall Somerset from France and duly appoint him Constable of England to help deal with any further disturbances at home. Despite failing dismally in Normandy, Somerset was given every opportunity and assistance to establish law and order in the country, including the power and finances to coordinate resistance against the problematic return of Duke Richard, who, due to Cade's slanderous manifesto, had already taken alarm and landed in North Wales. But characteristically, Somerset's appointment only added fuel to the fire.

At first, York's threatened return caused a great deal of panic among the court party, although, according to the letter he sent before he arrived in England, he was not aiming to cause trouble in the king's council. Waiting jealously in Ireland for a message to recall him to England can hardly have soothed the feelings of injustice and frustration that York must have felt at this time. He, therefore, took the initiative even though Somerset and his friends wanted the duke permanently exiled, a fact that must have crossed York's mind when he managed to avoid several ambushes on his way to London. After these attempts on his life, Duke Richard had no choice but to protect himself, and he soon raised an army of some 4,000 men, an act guaranteed to raise the stakes in the York and Somerset feud. In fact, very soon their rivalry entered a new and dangerous phase of animosity.

Forcing his way into the king's apartments may have been one way for York to convey his point to King Henry. But the king's 'kindly' demeanour dampened Duke Richard's hot-headedness and ultimately postponed all the inevitable questions still surrounding his unreasonable treatment. A rash petition in parliament for the recognition of Duke Richard as Henry's heir, made by the member for Bristol, Thomas Young, was yet another personal presumption that York could have done without at this time. However, even as Young was conducted to the Tower for his impulsive behaviour, it was apparent to all present, including York's enemies, that others might raise the same dynastic question if King Henry's marriage remained unconsummated.

On the face of it, Duke Richard's first attempt to bring about reform had failed miserably. Somerset retained his position as Henry's chief councillor and York was forced to retire peaceably. However, York's rash behaviour was a taste of things to come. In the autumn of 1450, the duke took a different course of action and used the petition he had previously brought before Henry to try and enlist the help of parliament. Of course, York could count on his many tenants and followers for additional support in his bid to overthrow the government, but such personal adherents were useless in matters of state. What York needed was political muscle in the right quarter at the right time and, if necessary, bows and bills on hand if his petitions failed to have the desired effect. But ironically, while York was trying to pursue a policy of peace to remove his enemy Somerset, other lesser ministers were yet again exploiting his name and his famous dynastic claim by promoting political unease.

As early as March 1450, William Oldhall, York's chamberlain, had been associated with cries to remove Henry VI and have his

7 *Seal of Sir William Oldhall.*
(Courtesy of Geoffrey Wheeler)

master York, acclaimed king. He spread the rumour that Henry, by the advice of Suffolk, had sold the realm of England to the King of France, a claim that was ludicrous in the extreme but nonetheless a lie of sufficient substance to make any of York's petitions aimed at political reform appear utterly worthless. In fact, the appointment of the Duke of Somerset to the captaincy of Calais in 1451 gives credence to the theory that York's appeals and constant petitioning were becoming tiresome to all but a minority. Somerset's appointment to command the largest permanent military establishment at the king's disposal also indicated that, even after his previous failures in France, Henry still had every confidence in Somerset's abilities.

Finding himself more politically isolated than ever, the Duke of York now sought to remove Somerset by force. He was in a very dangerous position, but despite his reckless reputation, he was, on this occasion, prudent in his preparations. He had previously sought support in the Welsh Marches to protect himself from his enemies, and now that support was called upon again in the form of an armed demonstration, he was confident of victory. However, York was careful not to alienate himself from King Henry, and on 9 January 1452, he signed and sealed a declaration protesting his loyalty. On 3 February, from his castle at Ludlow, he also wrote to the town of Shrewsbury, stressing the danger to the country now that the Duke of Somerset was in command of the Calais Garrison:

Right worshipful friends, I recommend me unto you; and I suppose it is well known unto you, as well by experience as by common language said and reported throughout all Christendom, what laud, what worship, honour, and manhood, was ascribed of all nations unto the people of this realm whilst the kingdom's sovereign lord stood possessed of his lordship in the realm of France and Duchy of Normandy; and what derogation, loss of merchandise, lesion of honour, and villainy, is said and reported generally unto the English nation for the loss of the same; namely unto the Duke of Somerset, when he had the command and charge thereof ... Wherefore, worshipful friends, to the intent that every man shall know my purpose and desire for to declare me such as I am, I signify unto you that, with the help and support of Almighty God, and of Our Lady, and of all the Company of Heaven, I, after long sufferance and delays, [though it is] not my will or intent to displease my sovereign lord, seeing that the said duke ever prevaileth and ruleth about the king's person, and that by this means the land is likely to be destroyed, I am fully concluded to proceed in all haste against him with the help of my kinsmen and friends.[10]

York further warned that 'the said Duke of Somerset ... laboureth continually about the king's highness for my undoing',[11] and urged several other English towns to help him restore good governance to the realm – a clear indication that he not only feared for his own safety but also the safety of the kingdom.

Despite the winter season, York was successful in raising a large force and, with the help of the Earl of Devon and his henchman Lord Cobham, his army was soon on the march, taking a route towards London that allowed him to muster further support in the South Midlands and along the Severn valley. On 22 and 26 February, he was met by a delegation of lords sent by the king, wishing to know his intentions. York stated that his aim was not to harm the king's person, but he explained that certain 'traitors' who had brought about the country's ruin would answer for their crimes. However, when news of his claims reached King Henry and his ministers, orders were dispatched for London to close its gates, forcing the duke's army to divert across Kingston Bridge into Kent, where, at least in theory, the 'Yorkists', as we now must call them, hoped to gather more support.

Meanwhile, the royal army, including retinues supplied by the earls of Salisbury and Warwick along with the Duke of Buckingham, had marched south from Northampton. In fact, by the time York encamped his army at Dartford in Kent, Henry's forces had been substantially augmented and were comprised of York's friends and relatives, including the Duke of Norfolk, who had previously supported his cause.

With the prospect of little or no Kentish support forthcoming, York suddenly found himself trapped between an angle of the River Thames and the royal host with banners displayed for war. Fate had dealt him another cruel hand it seemed. With neither hope of reinforcement nor the prospect of retreat open to him, he had no option but to fortify his position near Crayford at a place called Sandhill, where, according to sources, 3,000 gunners fronted his army. The *London Chronicle* gives an account of what happened next:

And the Duke of York pitched his field about Dartford with great ordnance. And whilst the king lay still at St Mary Overey's, bishops rode between the king and the Duke of York to set them at rest and peace. But the Duke of York said he would have the Duke of Somerset, or else he would die therefore. And on Wednesday next following [1 March], the king with his host rode to Blackheath, and forth over Shooters Hill to Welling, and there lodged that day and the morrow. And on Thursday at afternoon there was made an appointment between the king and the Duke of York by the mean of his lords. And on the morrow, that was Friday, the king assembled his host on the Blackheath afore noon; and there abode the coming of the Duke of York.[12]

Both sides were now in a position to fight, despite offers to parley. However, whether the Duke of York or the royalists desired to pursue military action is questionable. The next few hours were to have a critical impact on the way York and his Neville in-laws would conduct themselves at the first battle of St Albans, but contrary to the events of 1455, where battle was joined after protracted negotiations, it was the earls of Salisbury and Warwick, along with Thomas Bourchier, later Archbishop of Canterbury, who were charged with opening discussions, to avert the shedding of English blood.

York at first stood by his original purpose of accusing Somerset of high treason and stated that only if his rival was immediately detained and put on trial would he disband his army. The Nevilles ostensibly agreed with these aims, and when the king was advised of York's rebellious stance, he apparently gave his verbal consent to a formal inquiry. However, when the Yorkist army stood down, trusting Somerset would be confined and questioned, Duke Richard found to his dismay, that he had been tricked in the worst possible way. In fact, when he and the Nevilles arrived at the king's tent with a small escort, Somerset was found to be at liberty and in his accustomed seat beside the king. It was evident that with or without the Nevilles' collusion, York had walked into a trap and that soon he would be forced

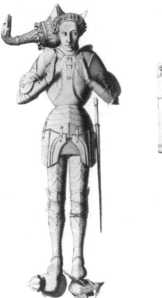

8 *Armour of the period. Richard Beauchamp, Earl of Warwick (d.1439), taken from his monument in St Mary's Church, Warwick. (© The Board of Trustees of the Armouries)*

to answer charges of treason. York had no other option than to submit, and he was first confined to his house in London, then later was forced to swear an oath of loyalty to King Henry at St Pauls. It was a victory that Somerset no doubt relished to the full and one that York would remember at St Albans in 1455 when he was cornered again.

York's quarrel with his rival had yet again backfired it seemed, and he returned to Ludlow a bitter man. He had shown his hand openly, first by petitioning the king and then by force of arms, but it was now the turn of the court party to strike back, which they did by punishing several of Duke Richard's adherents and 'co-conspirators', including the Earl of Devon and Lord Cobham, who were both imprisoned awaiting trial. Sir William Oldhall was also indicted for his treacherous behaviour, and later was attainted for spreading unrest in the shires. Thus, in the summer of 1453, Richard of York was yet again forced into exile – this time on his own estates – while abroad, against all the odds, the English army in France had seized Bordeaux and was expected to recover it, led by the renowned captain John Talbot, Earl of Shrewsbury.

At home, to add insult to injury, York's lieutenancy of Ireland was stripped from him and instead given to the Earl of Wiltshire, a courtier who, as we will later see, was conspicuous for his cowardice and aptitude for battlefield survival. The reversals meant that York had no other option but to bide his time and wait for Somerset's position to become more vulnerable. In July 1453, this opening seemed highly unlikely, but when John Talbot was killed, and his army routed at the battle of Castillon in France, there was a complete reversal of fortune. When the king received this terrible news at his hunting lodge at Clarendon, he suddenly went mad from the shock. Somerset was in attendance, and this association, along with the total loss of Aquitaine, caused a tide of popular anger against the duke that he would never be able to shake off, although it cannot be proven that he had anything directly to do with either event.

However, apart from the disasters in France, a king who was mentally and physically inert was something that could neither be hidden nor tolerated. Something had to be done, and the protracted debate as to whether Henry could ever stay sane for a reasonable period of time came to a head when the king's council were put in the unenviable position of assessing the nature of Henry's inertia:

> [But] they could get no answer nor sign [from the king] no prayer nor desire, lamentable cheer nor exhortation, nor anything that they or any of them could do or say, to their great sorrow and discomfort.[13]

King Henry remained unresponsive and in a catatonic state until Christmas 1454, and in the interim, Queen Margaret's anxieties became so pronounced that she laid claim to the regency, which, in the end, failed to gain widespread support among the king's ministers and nobles.

Margaret's drive and ambition were to later figure predominantly in the civil wars between York and Lancaster, but all the evidence suggests that her famous 'she-wolf' image was not apparent before King Henry's madness. Margaret's position and exercise of power as queen was always fraught with difficulty. As a woman, her authority was restricted to a place behind the throne and secondary to the all-consuming mightiness of her husband, the king. Over the years, some historians have given Margaret a bad press, and her supposed adulterous behaviour with Somerset has never been proven. Instead, she managed to survive extremely well in a male-dominated world, and nothing sinister or partisan can be attributed to her as the country dived into political meltdown. One of the things that a medieval queen was not supposed to do was rule in place of her husband. However, Margaret was later forced to assume a more aggressive position to protect her son's inheritance when faced with nobles (like the Duke of York and his heirs) who were intent on usurpation. Even though the problem of the succession had been solved in October 1453 by natural means, namely the birth of her son, Edward Prince of Wales, the king's ministers were still at a loss who should rule the kingdom while the king was ill. Therefore, it was a credit to Margaret's willpower that she made a bid for power in January 1454 when the king failed to recover, and personal rivalries were not set aside to help her rule the kingdom:

> The queen hath made a bill of five articles, desiring those articles to be granted; whereof the first is that she desireth to have the whole rule of this land; the second is that she may make the Chancellor, the Treasurer, the Privy Seal, and all other officers of this land, with shire reeves and all other officers that the king should make; the third is, that she may give all bishoprics of this land, and all other benefices belonging to the king's gift; the fourth is that she may have sufficient livelihood assigned her for the king, the prince and herself. [14]

The fifth of these articles was unknown to the author, but as discussed, Margaret's attempted regency was not widely supported, even though some unnamed nobles thought her worthy to rule in Henry's place. Therefore, Margaret resumed a subordinate role again and several months passed before anything constructive was done to solve the problem of a vacant throne.

Clearly, the political wheel of fortune was turning again, and its workings placed Duke Richard in a perfect position at its central axis despite everything that had gone before. Due to Henry's infirmity (probably catatonic schizophrenia), York found himself recalled to London and appointed back onto the king's council. Secondly, he was nominated as Protector of the Realm, and thirdly, he put a plan in place to rid himself of the Duke of Somerset by accusing him of treason.

As might be expected, York's newfound title as protector afforded him wide-ranging powers, and he immediately

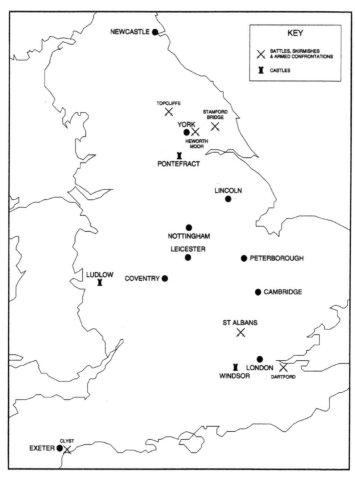

9　England 1452–55. (Author's Collection)

used them to the full by attacking Somerset from a position of strength. The unfortunate duke, weakened by the king's incapacity to rule, was immediately stripped of his captaincy of Calais, blamed for the reverses in France and confined to the Tower awaiting trial. The way was now open for York to appoint his own administration, and it was no accident that personal feuding in Wales and the north and southwest of England coloured his thinking.

In the 1450s, it is certain that none of the aristocracy or their adherents would have been known as either a 'Yorkist' or a 'Lancastrian' supporter, but certain divisions had already been formed due to Duke Richard's political and military demonstrations. Therefore, it is hardly surprising that after he was appointed protector, York gave prominence to his own supporters when filling the council chamber. In April 1454, he managed to secure the nomination of his own brother-in-law, the fifty-four-year-old Earl of Salisbury, as Chancellor of England. Salisbury, whose sons were engaged in a violent Yorkshire feud with the Duke of Exeter and the Percy family, was eager to lend the new protector a hand for reasons of his own. More local issues in the north prompted the Nevilles to seize the moment, and they received somewhat biased support from the government, and York, despite the problems favouritism could cause.

Also prominent in Duke Richard's council at this time were members of the Bourchier family, while neither the Duke of Exeter nor the mighty Earl of Northumberland played any part in York's administration. From now on, the question of loyalty to an anointed king would never have the same meaning, and factionalism was fast becoming a much more dangerous weapon to wield if a noble wished to survive.

But what did the Duke of Somerset think of York's recent victory? Had Edmund Beaufort consciously manipulated Henry VI to the point of no return? Had he, in fact, pushed him to the brink of insanity with his machinations? Apart from his failure in France (where others had failed before him), what other crimes had Somerset committed against the kingdom? Obviously, he had not displeased Henry VI in the slightest, and contrary to what the Duke of York had claimed in his many petitions, Somerset had not committed treason in the traditional sense of the word. His 'constant labouring' about the king's person may have given many courtiers cause for concern. Still, the king thought Somerset, and others like him, worthy councillors, or he would have immediately taken steps to remove him. As for Henry's mental health before his breakdown in 1453, there is every reason to believe that everything might have carried on as before. In fact, apart from several lapses in judgement, the king had single-handedly defused some challenging situations. Evidently, he had his faults, one of which was his misplaced trust and preferential treatment of others. However, before his mental illness, he had shown signs of kingship that were undoubtedly not the musings of a madman incapable of personal rule. After all, during his minority, Henry had been tutored by the best military and academic minds in the land, and his only failing seems to have been that he found it difficult, if not impossible, to equal the perfect portrayal of medieval kingship seen in Henry V.

On the face of it, Somerset seems to have been guilty of gross mismanagement of the king, but how much of this image was a direct result of York's political pressure and personal ambition, not to mention his much-promoted dynastic aspirations before the birth of the Prince of Wales? As with all historical relationships, the line is hard to draw with any certainty. Richard Duke of York was, above all, an honourable man, but he was also a fifteenth-century nobleman who had to secure his position on a daily basis, even to the point of rebellion and, if necessary, treason. This was also true of his contemporaries, including Somerset and all those other English nobles who sought to enhance their power and positions at court, sometimes at the expense of others. Aristocratic power had to be maintained at all costs, and the Neville and Percy families fit this description so perfectly that, to analyse further what occurred in the streets of St Albans on 22 May 1455, it is essential that a great northern feud must be examined, the effects of which one chronicler blamed for the 'beginning of the greatest sorrows in England'.[15]

Two

The Beginning of Sorrows

Any study of the first battle of St Albans must also consider the effects of local feuding that had become widespread in several parts of England during the early 1450s. Indeed, it can be said that St Albans was primarily a continuation of the feud between the Neville and Percy families and that the dukes of York and Somerset were drawn into this conflict purely by association.

This hypothesis holds weight regarding how the battle began, but it can also be argued that other nobles and their adherents paved the way for factionalism on a broader scale. In particular, the two lords chiefly responsible for the Yorkshire risings of 1453–54 – Henry Holand, Duke of Exeter, and the violent and highly unpredictable Thomas Percy, Lord Egremont – fuelled the fires of aristocratic division before St Albans that few were able to control. Historians generally agree that these two nobles brought about the alliance of Neville and York, which proved so dangerous to the royalists and the Duke of Somerset in 1455. But it is also my opinion that it was their actions, and the reactions of the Nevilles, that sparked civil warfare in England two years earlier than historians think.

As will be explained later, neither the Duke of Exeter nor Lord Egremont fought at the first battle of St Albans. Still, it was chiefly their actions in the north of England (and how York overprotected the Nevilles in his official capacity as protector) that caused the 'Yorkist' alliance to occur following the release of Somerset from the Tower in February 1455. However, it was not the case that the Nevilles automatically sided with their cousin York against Somerset or that the Percys supported the king purely out of loyalty or hatred of the Nevilles. Instead, it was a series of complex connections and events that brought about the Yorkist coalition and, in time, the formation of the 'Lancastrian' party, which later opposed it.

Rekindled immediately after the war with Scotland in 1448, the relationship between Neville and Percy slowly deteriorated when the balance of power was influenced, not for the first time in history, by those in command of the northern Marches. However, the real danger came from an unexpected quarter, and this accelerated wave of local violence originated from the younger members of the Neville and Percy families. Contrary to popular opinion, the resulting northern blood feud only erupted after 1453, chiefly because of Neville aggrandisement and how it outstripped the Percys' wealth, power and favouritism in Yorkshire. In short, the Percys had to resort to violence to survive. Before this date, local rivalry between the families had existed for several generations, but actual armed resistance had been rare, due to the demise of Percy autonomy in the reign of Henry IV. But this situation changed noticeably in the 1450s and progressively worsened when the Percys and their adherents instigated a supreme bout of violence against the Nevilles, which was finally repaid at St Albans in 1455. Indeed, the resulting vendetta and civil war proved so intense that the family quarrel was not fully settled until Richard Neville Earl of Warwick was killed at the battle of Barnet in 1471.

However, before 1450, both families and their retainers had been forced into cooperating against Scottish raiding. On numerous occasions, local rivalries had been set aside in favour of joint action against the common foe. Warfare of this kind was intermittent and primarily seasonal. Still, full-scale battles with the Scots had been fought throughout the medieval period with significant loss of life. Therefore, members of the northern aristocracy had been periodically appointed Wardens of the Marches to combat this threat to the border. Ever since the time of 'Hotspur' and his overmighty father, Henry Percy, the first Earl of Northumberland, peace treaties with the Scots had rarely been taken seriously. But the warden's office, permanently instigated in the reign of Richard II, was coveted by the gentry to establish power not only in the north but also in the king's council. It was crucial that the reigning monarch could count on his northern lords and their retainers to support the existing infrastructure of border recruitment whenever Scotland threatened to invade England. However, the disgrace of the Percys in 1403 and 1405, along with the disaster of Northumberland's death at the battle of Bramham Moor in 1408, crippled Percy fortunes significantly. In short, it was some years before Hotspur's son, another Henry Percy, could achieve anything like his grandfather's supremacy in the north. And by the time he recovered his title as the second Earl of Northumberland in 1416, the Nevilles had equalled, if not surpassed, the Percy achievement in every respect.[1]

Ralph Neville, Earl of Westmoreland, was the chief instigator of this rise to power in the early 1400s. But when he died in 1425, the quest for land and titles had become not only a Neville and Percy issue but also an internal power struggle which Richard Neville, Earl of Salisbury, set about pursuing within his own family. In fact, while the Nevilles were at odds with each other from within, Northumberland was also busy making enemies elsewhere in Yorkshire. For example, Archbishop Kemp was determined to extend his secular rights into Percy territory, and in 1441 and 1447, fighting broke out between the retainers of both sides and lives were lost. The irony of these bouts of violence was that during the 1440s, not only did the Nevilles

*10 Seal of Henry Percy,
Earl of Northumberland.
(Courtesy of Geoffrey
Wheeler)*

and Percys pursue each other in Yorkshire, but also other nobles wished to capitalise on their instability.

All this changed in 1453, when the Percys, still struggling to reha-bilitate themselves after the attainder and disgrace of the first Earl of Northumberland, were irreverently pushed aside by a sudden bout of Neville expansion. A rapid deterioration in relationships, caused by a disparity in wealth, plus the fact that the Nevilles had far stronger connections, had an enormous effect on Percy for-tunes, and this forced the younger members of Northumberland's family over the edge. How had the Earl of Salisbury created all this hostility in such a short space of time? Evidently, he had been extending his northern domains at the expense of others and pro-curing several lucrative marriages and positions for his relatives and retainers. In short, the Nevilles had succeeded where the Percys had failed. They had entered the medieval property and marriage market in a big way, and once established, they began to extend their hold over their rivals with unforgiving precision.

George Neville, for example, married the wealthy Elizabeth Beauchamp and succeeded to the barony of Latimer, which boasted extensive lands in Richmondshire and Cumberland. Neville was later certified as insane, but the Earl of Salisbury succeeded in acquiring his brother's estates to augment his own in 1451. This, in turn, led to his reappointment as Warden of the West March, which he received for a term of twenty years. Another of Salisbury's brothers, William Lord Fauconberg, a notable veteran of the French wars, had also married an heiress who held estates in Cleveland, and this became another important area of Neville influence in the northeast of England.

However, Salisbury's younger brother, Robert Neville, attained the most important position of power. He was installed as Bishop of Durham in 1438, which put the resources of his Palatinate at Salisbury's disposal whenever the need arose. Add to this the fact that Edward Neville, Lord Abergavenny, through his marriage into the Beauchamp family, had also secured a foothold in Wales, and it only remained for Salisbury to manufacture for his son the grand prize of the Warwick inheritance to make the Neville achievement complete. By 1449, when Richard Neville gained his earldom, Salisbury's family owned vast tracts of land between the Pennines and the east coast that extended 50 miles northwards, from Wensleydale to the Tyne. No wonder the Percys stood in fear of their hegemony.[2]

As might be expected, along with all these new lucrative titles and estates came an extensive network of dependants and retainers, all willing to give faithful service to a good lord who could maintain them in the law courts and, if need be, on the battlefield. With such territorial advantage and willing manpower at his fingertips, it was evidently Salisbury's intention to make the wardenship of the West March hereditary and thereby control the Scottish border and the Percys. It was a situation that was bound to cause conflict. And in answer to this overmighty behaviour, the younger Percys lashed out in a spate of organised guerrilla warfare that took the Nevilles completely by surprise. The local anarchy that resulted was to have far-reaching effects, especially when the most menacing of the Percy 'pride of lions' was let loose on his unsuspecting prey.

11 Garter stall plate of Richard Neville, Earl of Salisbury. (Courtesy of Geoffrey Wheeler)

Born in 1422, Thomas Percy epitomised the problem of a younger son with no lucrative heiress to enhance his wealth and status. The result was that he had become a burden on his father's estates with little or no chance of advancement. Wild, troublesome and violent, Egremont was nonetheless determined to shake off his father's yoke by setting himself on a course of reckless self-aggrandisement, like that pursued by his grandfather, Hotspur, at the turn of the century. Soon after returning home from the war with Scotland, he began to assemble a band of ruffians to hasten conflict with the Nevilles, and to annoy further the younger members of Salisbury's family, he began to distribute his livery of red and black to anyone willing to help him. According to later official documents, the Percy brothers were out of control:

Forasmuch as Thomas Percy, Lord Egremont, and Richard
Percy squire, brother to the said lord, diverse and many times
have raided assembled and gathered, your people in the shires
of York, Cumberland, Westmoreland and Northumberland,
in great number together, and daily draw unto them great
numbers of people and great misdoers, with many other
idle men of great riotous rule and misgovernance, and great
affrays and riots have heinously [been] committed within the
said shires, and many wrongful entries as well forcibly and
otherwise have made, for maintenance of other men's quarrels, in lands, tenements and possessions, of your true and
well ruled liege people of the same shires, against your peace
and laws, as it is supposed: Whereof your people of the same
shires have been, and yet be, hurt, vexed and troubled, and
dare not [take] lawful action against them, for fear of death,
to their likely destruction.[3]

In direct opposition to the Nevilles' authority in the West
March, Egremont soon set up his headquarters at Cockermouth,
and in 1447 he and his retainers rode south into Neville territory;
the result being he was flung into York prison for disturbing the
peace. When he was released, on two separate occasions, both
feuding families deliberately ignored summonses by the king to
muster for service in France in favour of challenging each other's authority in Yorkshire. Not surprisingly, Sir John Neville,
Salisbury's younger son, rose to Egremont's bait, and in 1453 he
raided the Percy lordship of Topcliffe in North Yorkshire on
the pretext of apprehending his opposite number. In reply, Sir
Richard Percy, Egremont's brother, attacked the Neville manors
of Halton and Swinden in Craven, and the resulting spate of *quid
pro quo* raiding caused a complete breakdown of law and order
in the county. Troublemakers from all over Yorkshire began to
abuse the law while the government was undecided, and King
Henry was insane. However, the next affront to Neville ascend-
ancy was aimed directly at the Earl of Salisbury and the leading

members of his family. In fact, it is almost certain that Egremont intended to assassinate the earl and his sons in a frenzy of blood-letting that would leave the Percys in control of the north.

Heworth Moor

On Friday, 24 August 1453, the Earl of Salisbury, his countess, Sir Thomas Neville and Neville's new bride Maud Stanhope, a niece of Ralph Lord Cromwell, were on their way north from Tattershall Castle in Lincolnshire where Thomas and Maud had been celebrating their wedding. Sir John Neville was also among Salisbury's impressive riding retinue, and Egremont intended to stop its progress somewhere beyond the gates of York. To this end, he and his brother, Sir Richard Percy, had gathered an army to block the road at Heworth Moor – a route the Nevilles must take to reach Sherriff Hutton, one of their many castles in North Yorkshire.

Lord Cromwell's willingness to settle the Yorkshire castle of Wressle on the young Neville couple was yet another insult to the Percy family and a probable cause of Egremont's action. Wressle had formerly been a possession of the Percy family in the reign of Henry IV and was clearly a property they sought to recover as part of their rehabilitation programme. Doubtless, the Earl of Northumberland hoped the castle would someday return to his family by peaceful negotiation. He may not have bargained on two of his sons trying to settle the property dis-pute by force. However, the annalist at Whitby Abbey was sure the disagreement concerned the whole family, and he was well placed to report what happened next:

> And there arose, for diverse causes, a great discord betwixt him [Northumberland] and Richard the Earl of Salisbury, his wife's brother, insomuch that many men of both parties were beaten, slain, and hurt.[4]

Heworth is now a suburb of York situated on the Roman road east, about a mile from the city centre. The name of the original village is Anglo-Saxon in origin, meaning 'high enclosure', but in 1453 Heworth was likely a small settlement with an open heath (moor), much like Monk Stray is today. The road turns north at Heworth to Sherriff Hutton and it was likely here or on Monk Stray that Egremont embattled his troops on 24 August, waiting for the Nevilles to pass through the City of York.

Several months after the battle at Heworth Moor, the Duke of York launched a full-scale inquiry into the incident. Therefore, an accurate picture of a noble's 'private army' before the first battle of St Albans can be reconstructed. Names, occupations and an indication of where the accused lived are recorded in the indictment, while a more detailed reading of the document gives the impression that Egremont's antagonism towards the Neville family was well supported from elsewhere in the

12 *Monk Stray, York. Where the battle of Heworth Moor was fought in 1453.*
(Author's Collection)

north. Yorkshiremen formed ninety-four per cent of his force. Approximately 15 per cent of the 710 indicted men were free-men and tradesmen from the City of York, and some willing partisans had come from Doncaster, Scarborough and Hull. As might be expected, most of the Percy manors were well repre-sented in Egremont's muster, half of those men named being described as yeomen farmers – some from the Percy honour of Cockermouth in Cumberland, who had followed Egremont's since 1447. Outside the Percy sphere of influence, a handful of sympathisers from Lincolnshire, Westmoreland and Lancashire had decided to join him, while mariners and chapmen had been recruited from Scarborough, Hull and Whitby, the result being that a diverse and largely untrained army was at Egremont's dis-posal. Some of these men had been given Egremont's livery of red and black as early as February and May 1453, while there was a respectable array of six knights, thirty-two esquires, twenty-six gentlemen and twenty-four clerks to command them. Clerics also formed part of the Percy muster, and men like Thomas Colvel, vicar of Topcliffe, and William Wood, rector of Leathley, along with seven others were on hand, although pre-sumably not for spiritual guidance.

Egremont's levies may have been ill-disciplined, but they were not an unruly band of thugs spoiling for a fight.[5] The knights and gentry commanding them were professional sol-diers, including Lord Clifford of Skipton, who later fought at St Albans and had been loyal to the Percys for many years. Most of those named in the indictment were retainers of the Earl of Northumberland, and no doubt Egremont was eager to prove himself in arms. However, the purely mercenary decision to assassinate all the leading members of Salisbury's family was most likely Egremont's brainchild, which is probably why the attack on the Nevilles failed.

Although it is recorded that some casualties were sustained before the Earl of Salisbury and his entourage pushed on through Egremont's ranks, it is not known how serious the

battle became. It is recorded that Sir William Buckton personally
fought with the Earl of Salisbury at some point in the struggle,
therefore, Heworth was not an insignificant encounter. The
various attacks may have been skirmishes, but at what point does
a skirmish become a battle when thousands of men are involved?

In his paper on the local rivalries of the Percys, the Nevilles
and the Duke of Exeter, R.A Griffiths makes clear that 'the
Heworth incident was the most serious to date of a number of
clashes between Percy and Neville...It threw the citizens of
York into a veritable paroxysm of alarm, and the civic authorities spent the ensuing weeks in vain attempts at mediation
between Salisbury and the Percys'.[6] In his *The End of the House
of Lancaster,* R.L. Storey states, 'There were altercations and
threats, doubtless a fair amount of rough play, but the Nevilles
reached home without bloodshed'.[7] But none of these remarks
can be substantiated, and, in this instance, I am inclined to agree
with the *Whitby Chronicle* that Heworth was a 'battle' where men
were either beaten up, killed, or seriously injured. Indeed, this
was civil warfare where Englishman had fought Englishman.

The Neville entourage may have been too strong for Percy's
liking, or another theory could be that Egremont's levies began
to fight only to withdraw, fearing the consequences of their
action or through cowardice. It is known that the Bailiff of
Pocklington, Peter Lound, the instigator of the coming Percy
rout at Stamford Bridge in 1454, was involved in the fighting
and was later indicted for his part in the battle. Therefore, this
may have been a cause for some of the Percy contingents to flee
at Heworth. However, whatever the real reason for Egremont's
change of heart, Neville and Percy had crossed swords for the
first time in their history, and this was a situation that needed
a firm hand in the absence of royal intervention. But none was
forthcoming until June 1454.

Despite vain attempts at mediation between the Nevilles
and the Percys, the autumn of 1453 was punctuated by several
renewed outbursts of violence and raiding, each side turning a

deaf ear to royal commands and civic pleadings. Further raids on Percy manors, houses and even churches took place. The Nevilles responded in turn, and as far as both sides were concerned, nothing had been settled at Heworth. Swords had been drawn, and men had confronted each other, willing to kill or be killed, but no advantage had been gained. It may have been irresponsible for Lord Egremont to act so foolishly against the Nevilles in the first place, but what if much larger political ideals had prompted the Percys to act so confidently at Heworth Moor? In short, had the machinations of Henry Holand, Duke of Exeter, been at work in the north much earlier than historians think?

Earlier that year, Lord Cromwell (Neville's recent benefactor) was involved in a dispute with Lord Grey of Ruthin and the Duke of Exeter, which proved crucial to how Egremont and the Percys would conduct their war against the Nevilles from then on. Exeter was another noble descended of royal blood, and it is certain that he had ambitions far beyond his means, not to mention his intellect. In 1452, he claimed two of Cromwell's manors, also pursued by Lord Grey, who had a similar entitlement to the estates. Grey had reached a temporary agreement with Cromwell, but Exeter was not a patient man, and he forcibly dispossessed the latter of his manor of Ampthill in Bedfordshire in 1453.

The result was a stern reprimand from the crown and orders to appear immediately before the king. However, when the respective factions finally arrived in London, their presence was backed by force, each having armed retinues hoping to overawe the court, and all three men suffered a spell of imprisonment before being dismissed back to their respective estates. No further action was taken, but it was no accident that the browbeaten Exeter later sought out Lord Egremont and the Percys in a bid to topple Cromwell, their common enemy. Proof of this pact was recorded in an official London newsletter, which reported that on 19 January 1454, Lord Egremont and the Duke of Exeter met

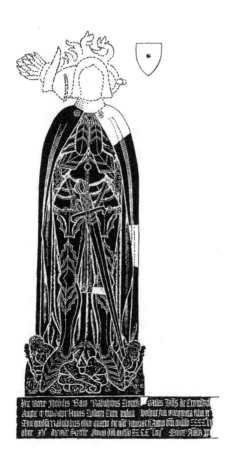

13 *Brass of Ralph, Lord Cromwell, Tattershall, Lincolnshire. (Courtesy of Geoffrey Wheeler)*

near Doncaster to further their aims against the Nevilles and anyone else who opposed them. The *Paston Letters* records what measures and countermeasures all the interested parties put in place to protect themselves:

> Item, the cardinal hath charged and commanded all his servants to be ready with bow and arrows, sword and buckler, crossbows, and all other habiliments of war, such as they can meddle with, to await upon the safeguard of his person. Item, the Earl of Wiltshire and the Lord Bonville have [proclaimed]

at Taunton in Somerset shire, that every man that is likely will go with them and serve them shall have [6d] every day as long as he abideth with them. Item, the Duke of Exeter in his own person hath been at Tuxford beside Doncaster, in the north country and there the Lord Egremont met him, and the two [were] sworn together, and the duke has come home again. Item, the Earl of Wiltshire, the Lord Beaumont, Poynings, Clifford, Egremont, and Bonville have [assembled] all the puissance they can and may come hither with them. Item, Thorpe of the exchequer articulated fast against the Duke of York, but what his articles [are] it is yet unknown. Item, Tresham, Joseph, Daniel, and Trevilian have made a bill to the Lords, desiring to have a garrison kept at Windsor for the safeguard of the king and of the prince, and that they may have money for wages and other that shall keep the garrison. Item, the Duke of Buckingham hath made [2,000] bends with knots [livery badges] to what intent men may construe as their wits will give them. Item, the Duke of Somerset's harbinger hath taken up all the lodging that may be gotten near the Tower, in Thames Street, Martin Lane, Saint Katherines, Tower Hill, and thereabouts.[8]

The historian G.M. Trevelyan remarked that 'the Wars of the Roses were to a large extent a quarrel between Welsh Marcher Lords, who were also great English nobles, closely related to the English throne'.[9] This opinion was endorsed by R.A. Griffiths but modified by a more valid observation that if Trevelyan had looked northwards, especially to Yorkshire, 'he might well have described the Wars of the Roses as in part a quarrel between great Yorkshire magnates who were also involved in the campaign to reform and ultimately displace the Lancastrian government'.[9] Certainly, the opening skirmishes between the Nevilles and the Percys, which culminated in the first battle of St Albans, were the model for all confrontations to come. Local feuding and rivalry had caused division in the past, and with no forceful king to quell the instability at source, this behaviour was causing widespread unrest. In fact, even before the above escalations of January 1454, on 20 October 1453, further risings had been staged in Yorkshire, and the northern feud reached a new and dangerous climax, chiefly because so many men were in a rebellious mood.

As for the Neville and Percy feud, before the 'official' alliance between Lord Egremont and the Duke of Exeter, another major battle was almost fought near the Percy manor of Topcliffe. With Neville and Percy armies numbered in thousands rather than hundreds, the stage had been set for a bloodbath which might have been described, had it occurred, as the first major battle of the civil wars. Some sources say as many as 10,000 men lined up, ready to fight. However, both sides agreed to a truce instead, even though most of the key protagonists had arrived in force, including the Earl of Warwick, who had accompanied his father, Salisbury, for the first time. Lord Egremont, who had been supported by Henry Lord Poynings and Lord Clifford, was undoubtedly mortified that the confrontation had been inconclusive. At Heworth Moor, there had been casualties, but the fact that the armies at Topcliffe were made up of professional soldiers rather than ill-organised levies may have caused commanders to dismiss their men without major bloodshed. In short, moderation and discipline likely saved the day, but the final confrontation between the Nevilles and Percys had merely been postponed to a later date.

With the king still incapacitated, the Duke of York's responsibility as protector was to bring order to the disturbances. And the massive concentration of Percy strength at Spofforth Castle in Yorkshire on 21 May 1454 (not to mention the appearance of the Duke of Exeter in the north) prompted him to march from London in force. However, Exeter and Egremont had already anticipated York's move against them. After claiming the Duchy of Lancaster as his own and distributing liveries of red and white to anyone who would follow him, Exeter embarked on a highly dangerous campaign that directly threatened York's authority.

With Egremont at his side, Exeter marched on York, then Hull, to extend his control over Yorkshire. However, it was an enterprise doomed to failure, primarily due to a lack of foresight. Turning west after a failed attempt to seize Hull, the rebels soon dispersed, although a force led by Robert Mauleverer tried to organise opposition against the Duke of York when he entered the county.

Caught between Duke Richard with an army in the east and Sir Thomas Stanley in the west, Exeter had no choice but to flee into sanctuary at Westminster, where he was advised to submit his 'grievances' directly to the king – undoubtedly a petition that he could not uphold. Therefore, it was left to York, the Nevilles and the justices of the City of York to conclude the disturbances by indicting the main culprits. And by placing the blame on the Duke of Exeter and the Percys, the Nevilles moved one step closer to an alliance with the protector.

On 4 June 1454, the 710 Percy men who had fought at Heworth Moor the previous August were finally brought to trial, and most were punished for their crimes against the Nevilles. Of the 710, 446 were condemned to forfeiture, 144 to outlawry, nine were pardoned, one was dead by 1454 and 110 were not convicted.[10] Some men had previously been found guilty of causing other affrays and received harsher punishments. Still, the Nevilles were no doubt pleased with the outcome, although they probably knew the feud was far from over.

Lord Egremont was still at liberty, and it is hardly surprising that when the Duke of York returned to London on 4 July 1454, one of his first tasks was to have the Duke of Exeter and his bastard brother, Robert, forcibly removed from sanctuary. Immediately conveyed into the north, the renegade duke was imprisoned in Pontefract Castle, where the Earl of Salisbury was tasked with keeping a watchful eye on him. And as further punishment, Exeter's manors of Ampthill and Fanhope, which were fought over so vehemently by Lord Cromwell, were granted to Lord Grey of Ruthin instead.

Stamford Bridge

For a while, it seemed that York's intervention had calmed the north. However, the Duke of Exeter's reckless accomplice was not deterred from causing trouble. In late October or early November 1454 (probably 1 November), Lord Egremont decided to attack the Neville manor at Stamford Bridge near York, hoping to renew the conflict. The *Whitby Cartulary* recorded what happened when Lord Egremont, his retainers, and 200 Pocklington men clashed with the Nevilles on ground well acquainted with warfare:

> And in the Year of Grace [1454] at Stamford Bridge besides York, there was a battle set betwixt Thomas Lord Egremont and Richard his brother, the sons of the said Earl of Northumberland on the one party, and two sons of the said Earl of Salisbury on the other party, that is to say, Sir Thomas Neville and Sir John Neville, but through the treason and withdrawing of Piers [Peter] of Lound, the said Lord Egremont and his brother were taken.[11]

Stamford Bridge is situated on the River Derwent but mainly on the east bank, 8 miles from York. Here the main road to the east coast crosses the river over a stone bridge of three arches, but the original medieval crossing, thought to be made of wood with stone piers, was about 150 yards further downstream. Therefore, if the battle was fought near the bridge, as indicated by one chronicler, the latter crossing may have been where Egremont and the Neville brothers met.

The manor house at Stamford Bridge (and the Percy one at Catton) are both long gone, as is the layout of the original settlements. But the Catton property was a moated site and ancient by all accounts, therefore, this may be the reason why Egremont chose to restore Stamford Bridge to his family. Thomas Percy had clearly not yet had enough of feuding with his opposite numbers, and

14 Mail shirt of the type worn by soldiers during the Wars of the Roses. (© The Board of Trustees of the Armouries)

according to a manuscript at Trinity College Dublin, Egremont and the Nevilles had again managed to gather sizable forces considering the number of casualties inflicted during the fight.[12]

According to the manuscript above, Egremont led the Percy faction against Sir Thomas and Sir John Neville 'and hundreds of men were killed and many wounded', making this battle more significant, in fatalities at least, than St Albans the following year. It was certainly remembered in Yorkshire, although not well recorded by chroniclers. We have next to no information about what happened at Stamford Bridge other than the battle led to the capture of Lord Egremont by Sir Thomas Neville somewhere near York and Richard Percy was arrested soon after. What part the Earl of Northumberland played in the feud is hard to prove, but the capture of his two sons must have weighed heavily on his mind. After Stamford Bridge, the balance of power had once more tipped in favour of the Nevilles and their ally, the Duke of York, and Northumberland knew he must seek support from the king against them, or his family might once again be threatened with extinction.

As described in the above *Whitby Cartulary*, at some point during the battle of Stamford Bridge, the renowned Bailiff of Pocklington, Peter Lound, treacherously fled the field with his men, leaving Egremont at the Nevilles' mercy and his reign of terror at an end.[13] At a court of oyer and terminer[14] at York, the Percy brothers were ordered to pay Salisbury damages of £11,200, an enormous sum of money that Egremont was unable and unwilling to pay. His own income was only £100 per year, and so he and his brother were first conveyed to Middleham Castle and then transferred to London, where they were confined by the Duke of York to the debtor's prison at Newgate for the next two years.

It was a lenient sentence considering Egremont and his allies could have faced a more serious trial at the King's Bench for felony and treason. But it seems Thomas Percy's previous letters of a general pardon were enough to dissuade the authorities, and maybe others, from pursuing that course. As discussed, central government was extremely disorganised, and King Henry was still unresponsive and confined to quarters. Therefore, it is no surprise that Egremont managed to escape from Newgate the year after St Albans and the Nevilles once again put their trust in the Duke of York to close ranks against a common threat.

As for events at court, the English disasters in France and the battle of Castillon were probably the main reasons for the king's breakdown in August 1453. But when Henry suddenly recovered his senses at the end of 1454 and blessed his son Edward Prince of Wales, all hell broke loose in London. The Duke of York was immediately dismissed as protector, and the speed at which his enemy Somerset was restored to power was a move on the part of King Henry that was bound to cause a renewed sense of anxiety in the 'Yorkist' camp. The correctness of discharging York from his duties can be understood. But the blatant and imprudent restoration of his rival, rather than the transfer of authority to a third party, suggests an unscrupulous guiding hand behind the throne. York knew that once released, Somerset would seek his downfall as quickly as possible. Only the establishment of a friendly government could ensure York's survival, and if the king ever suffered a relapse again, then might not Somerset react with force rather than submission?

However, when the Duke of Somerset was finally conducted from the Tower on 5 February 1455, York, Salisbury and Warwick seemed totally unaware of what plans had been put in place to ensure his return to politics. Indeed, York and Salisbury were listed among the attendees of a Great Council meeting that accompanied Somerset's 'strange' release from confinement. At first, there was no hint of anything underhand, and Somerset agreed never again to involve himself in national politics. He also promised not to approach within 20 miles of the king. However, one month later, against all the odds, Somerset's sureties were formally discharged, and far from being constrained or cast out, he once again resumed his former place as Henry's chief minister.

Did the Duke of York anticipate the king's flagrant breach of faith? Evidently not. In fact, soon after resigning his office as protector at Greenwich, York and his friends believed that Somerset was actually about to step down from political life. However, the significant change of heart in favour of Somerset on 4 March immediately reversed the fortunes of York and the Nevilles. It also made them fear for their lives. The grounds for this sudden apprehension became abundantly clear when two days later (after all charges against Somerset had been dropped), the Duke of York was relieved of his captaincy of Calais and Somerset was reinstated in his place. The next day, Salisbury resigned the Great Seal to Henry VI, and on 15 March, the Earl of Wiltshire, who coincidentally had his own grievances against York, was appointed as Treasurer. The royalist coup was concluded with the surprising release of the Duke of Exeter from Pontefract Castle on 19 March – a development bound to cause unease in the Neville camp.

Once again, York and the Nevilles had been side-lined by a king who had succumbed to gross manipulation by others. But who was pulling Henry's strings while Somerset was incarcerated in the Tower? Before becoming regent, York assumed that only his rival was labouring about the king for his undoing. But who had arranged for Somerset to be released early from the Tower? Who had canvassed royalist support while King Henry was incapacitated? In short, who had everything to lose if York used the king's illness to assume the protectorship permanently? Clearly, Queen Margaret and her son would suffer if the young prince was ever subjected to a long minority under 'Yorkist' rule, and now that the Duke of York had allies against Somerset, there was no telling where his ambitions might lead. All these accusations of manipulation formed part of later Yorkist propaganda.

Still, the question of the queen's guiding hand behind the throne is inescapable and validated by her later dogged and resourceful involvement in the civil wars. That the newborn prince had to be protected against any ambitious claimants to the throne was a natural stance for any mother to take, and Margaret now clearly regarded York as a threat to her child's succession. Indeed, the fact that the queen tried to wrest control of the kingdom from the Duke of York immediately after King Henry became insane was undoubtedly a clear signal of her intentions.[15]

According to the rebuff of her five bills recorded in the *Paston Letters*, Queen Margaret could do no other but work secretly for Somerset's release. When Henry showed signs of improvement (although there is no confirmation that the king was ever completely sane again), the support for Somerset was so overwhelming that it is hard to believe that Margaret had not been active behind the scenes. At a Great Council meeting on 5 February 1455, only York and the Nevilles were overtly hostile to Somerset's release, which supports the claim that a great deal of preparation had gone into promoting his freedom. Indeed, Somerset's release from the Tower dated 4 February 1455 had been achieved by someone before the 'actual' day of its legal termination. According to *Bale's Chronicle*:

[And on] the xxvi day of January the Duke of Somerset was strangely conveyed out of the Tower by the Duke of Buckingham the Earl of Wiltshire and Lord Roos. Wherefore the Duke of York gave up the king's sword and no longer occupied [the role of] protector.[16]

With the battle lines now drawn in anger and blood, and King Henry once more back on the throne, only one course of action presented itself to York and his Neville allies – Somerset had to be permanently removed from politics. Having withdrawn into the north rather than to Ludlow or another of Duke Richard's many English lordships, the Yorkists immediately began to muster an army. This recruitment likely took place in and around Sandal Castle, near Wakefield, and at Middleham, one of the Nevilles' premier castles in Yorkshire. The court party apparently had no idea of Yorkist preparations at this time, but after the dispersal of York and the Nevilles from London on 7 March, it is plausible that Somerset and his supporters immediately closed ranks around the king (and queen), forming an inner circle that much resembled the buttress to Henry's throne that had existed in the 1440s.

15 Sallet or kettle hat, c.1450, made in Italy for export to western Europe. (© The Board of Trustees of the Armouries)

But was anyone prepared to fight a civil war? Clearly, York and the Nevilles were if the court party saw the abrupt disappearance of the Yorkists as a military threat. Instead of a swift campaign to rid the kingdom of northern discontent, the official reaction was to summon a council at Leicester, the declared purpose being to provide for the personal safety of the king, the Prince of Wales and, as it was rumoured, Somerset. Messengers were sent out to various shires, carrying letters bidding only certain lords and knights to attend the meeting. However, York and the Nevilles were not excluded. Therefore, it is assumed that the 'Yorkist' lords must have been alerted to either being exposed as traitors or, worse, being sought out and assassinated before the meeting by their enemies. Proof of a plot to undermine the Yorkist lords at Leicester was later confirmed when news soon reached them that another covert meeting had taken place previously, at Westminster, immediately after they had left London, to which neither York nor his allies had been invited. In a letter written by the Duke of York, Salisbury and Warwick to the Chancellor, Archbishop Bourchier, on 20 May 1455, immediately before the first battle of St Albans, the reference to a secret meeting is abundantly clear. Their 'mistrust of some persones'[17] was a feature of the suspicions that York and the Nevilles felt at this time and the main reason they set about protecting themselves by mustering a northern army and preparing a carefully worded petition of loyalty meant for the king.

As it transpired, the Leicester council never met due to the ensuing battle of St Albans. Still, the covert plan was clearly intended to wound York and perhaps even designed to force him, yet again, into acting inappropriately. The lords and knights invited may even have been brought together to witness yet another humiliating scene of York swearing oaths of loyalty to Henry, like at Dartford in 1452. However, there is no doubt that York and Somerset had already decided what action should be taken. Although the royal reaction was somewhat remiss, the 'Yorkist' lords had decided to capture Somerset before the Leicester meeting could take place.

While York and the Nevilles were recruiting their forces in the north, there was an element of popular unrest in the south, leading to the belief that Somerset, at least, was preparing for a hostile reaction. According to the *Dijon Relation*, Somerset had become highly unpopular in London due to his reputation and fearing that the journey north to Leicester with the king might prove hazardous to his life, he set about making plans to protect himself. Both the *Dijon Relation* and a letter to the Archbishop of Ravenna in the *Calendar of State Papers in Milan* allude to the fact that the royalists, and Somerset, were fearful of what York might do next to regain credibility:

> When the Duke of Somerset and those who were of his party then being in the City of London, heard that the Duke of York and many other lords in his company were advancing against them with a force of five thousand men, and when he considered what he had done against the Duke of York, and that he was also in very bad odour with the people of London, he came to the conclusion that he should not remain in the City of London for fear that the people would fall on him the moment [York] arrived. For which cause, he [Somerset] persuaded the king to sally forth against the said Duke of York and his other enemies.[18]

This threat of personal danger caused Somerset, as Constable, to immediately send out summonses for military aid in the king's name, although he must have known that to recruit substantially would be an impossible task, given the timing of the meeting at Leicester. However, commissions to raise troops were dispatched from Westminster on 18 May, and all these hastily raised contingents were likely called upon to concentrate at St Albans, although the wording of one document alludes to an immediate convergence upon the king's person, wherever that might be:

Whereupon the said mayor [of Coventry] let call to come
afore him the counsel of this city with his brethren afore
whom this letter is [to be] read, and they having tenderness
of the welfare and also of the preservation and safeguard of
our sovereign lord the king, as every true liegeman oweth,
to ordain that a hundred of good-men defensibly with bow
and arrows, jakked and saletted, arrayed, should be made
ready in all haste possible to go to our sovereign lord at Saint
Albans, and to abide with him, and to do him service such
[as] it should please his highness to command them to do.
And the mayor and the afore-rehearsed worthy-men ordain
that William Tybeaudis should be captain to the afore named
[hundred] men.[19]

The Coventry summons for military support may be typical of
what was expected from town militia and noble retinues at this
time. The urgency to send forces 'in all haste possible' likely
indicates that Somerset was desperate for support from almost
anywhere in the kingdom, although on receipt of the royal
summons, time was running out. The council of Coventry
were eager that their men should be made ready and equipped
for war, and a list of coloured cloth was requisitioned so that
liveries and jackets could be made, which would have all taken
time to complete. Therefore, the commission to muster troops
speedily was slightly ambitious by Somerset. Other noble retinues, including those commanded by the Duke of Norfolk,
the earls of Oxford and Shrewsbury, Lord Cromwell and Sir
Thomas Stanley, were also summoned at roughly the same
time. But these men were similarly either too slow to react or
did not heed the call due to wavering loyalties. Also, the royalists may not have known precisely where York's army was on
18 May, although if this were true, then surely someone was
guilty of gross negligence.

In support of this latter theory, it is recorded that emissaries
from King Henry had been sent north to the Duke of York soon

after he and the Nevilles had quit London on 7 March. Since this deputation included such worthies as the Bishop of Coventry, the Earl of Worcester, and the Prior of St John's, York's approximate location must have been known to someone in authority. Indeed, the official attitude to the abrupt disappearance of York and the Nevilles from court was highly charged and wholly in keeping with Somerset's worst fears. Therefore, the duke should have been concerned. The outcome of the Dartford affair may have caused Somerset not to worry unduly, but the circumstances that now presented themselves should have been enough to cause him a great deal of panic, given that York now had Neville backing in the north.

Therefore, it seems Somerset and his allies spent at least two months unaware of what York was doing. However, warned of this threat, on 19 May, the Chancellor, Thomas Bourchier, was finally directed to prepare letters addressed to the dukes of York and Norfolk and the earls of Warwick and Salisbury, forbidding them to array the king's subjects illegally. York was ordered to dismiss all but 200 followers as befitting his position, and all the other named lords were restricted to 160 men each or risk forfeiture. Evidently, Somerset took what precautions he could at such short notice by using the king's authority to issue the necessary documents. Apparently, the Duke of Buckingham, who was later to replace Somerset as Constable at the king's request before St Albans, thought the Yorkist threat not overtly hostile. Therefore, this indecision may have been widespread at court. As the senior commander of what soon would transform itself from a king's household into a royal army, Buckingham may have thought Somerset's urgent letters of 18 May to recruit far and wide slightly paranoid. How wrong he was. The Yorkists were at that moment marching south with an army of northerners, hell-bent on Somerset's capture.

The evidence for the Yorkist march south is imprecise, but, like all other medieval marches and recruitment drives, its course is peppered with correspondence. Therefore, it can be traced by where messages were initially drafted. While the king and his household were still preparing to leave Westminster, the Yorkists had already gained a great deal of ground; hence an element of surprise was achieved. They had mustered their northern contingents in only a few days and marched down the Great North Road to Royston. Here, on 20 May, York, Warwick and Salisbury signed and sealed a long letter to the Chancellor, Thomas Bourchier (then also Archbishop of Canterbury), that not only protested their continued loyalty to the king, but also declared that they understood his predicament and had brought a company of armed followers expressly for Henry's protection:

> Laying therefore apart our own particular quarrels, which we shall never prefer before the duty, truth, love and affection, that we owe unto our said sovereign lord [and] his said realm of people ... we understand the calling and establishing of the King's Council at his town of Leicester, [and] take ground by such as we conceive caused the appointment thereof there, for surety of his most noble person, which of common presumption implies a mistrust of some persons. We therefore his true and humble liegemen, have accompanied us the better to th'intent to employ us in such devoir as accordant with our duty, to that may be the surety of his said most noble person, wherein we will neither spare our bodies nor goods, and also to know who be jealous of such mistrust, to th'intent that we must proceed to the subduing of them ... [therefore] we will be of power to keep ourselves out of danger.[20]

Couched in dutiful and loyal language, the Yorkists also stated to the chancellor that he, in his official capacity of archbishop, should publicly excommunicate at St Paul's Cross all those who intended harm towards the king. Protesting that they had received no invitation to the recent Westminster council, the Yorkists also questioned the summoning of another council at Leicester and asked why it was convened to provide for the king's 'surety'. If the council mistrusted 'some persons', the Yorkists demanded to know who had inspired the king with such mistrust in the first place. The signatories explained that their 'lords, knights, squires and all other people being with us'[21] wished the chancellor to deliver their message to the king, asking that another council of their own choosing be convened, where in return, they would undertake to do nothing to solve their private quarrels without proper consent. Bourchier was also asked to plead their cause with the king and instructed him to do his duty if he wished to avoid responsibility for anything 'inconvenient' that might result from failure to represent York and his followers fairly. Considering that his brother Henry, Viscount Bourchier, and the latter's son were probably among York's followers encamped at Royston, the anxious chancellor had no choice but to act as honestly and swiftly as possible.

Historians have never fully explained why the king never received or heeded the above communication from York or why the premier prelate of England did not act personally on receiving the letter when expressly asked to do so. However, when the Yorkist proposal eventually arrived at Westminster on 21 May, the court had already left on its progress north. Therefore, the chancellor was forced to dispatch a rider after them. This courier was Sir John Saye, keeper of the Privy Palace of Westminster and squire of the body to the Duke of York, who intercepted the royal progress at Kilburn, 4 miles distant. At ten o'clock that morning, he handed the letter to a royal secretary, Thomas Manning, but aside from this fact, it is not certain who then received it. It is probable that it was given to Somerset and that he withheld its contents from the king to protect himself, as claimed by the Yorkists thereafter. The *Parliamentary Pardon* issued after St Albans, clearing the Yorkist lords from all responsibility for the battle, stated that the king never saw the Yorkist statement and that 'certain persons' were to blame for

16 Brass of Sir John Saye. (Courtesy of Geoffrey Wheeler)

withholding it. However, aside from exposing the widespread opinion that York and Somerset were mortal enemies, what other harm could the Yorkist letter have done to Somerset, a man the king was protecting? It was essentially a repeat of York's previous petitions. Therefore, it is more likely that the dutiful Somerset delivered the letter to King Henry and that nothing whatsoever was concealed from him. It was already well known to the king that York and the Nevilles posed no threat to him and were willing to talk. Their retinues had, no doubt, been culled to a more appropriate level (on pain of forfeiture), and their movements south had been anticipated to coincide with the Leicester council meeting. King Henry also knew that the Duke of York's prime objective had always been to be a loyal subject. In short, as far as Henry was concerned, nothing sinister could be attributed to York's movements at this time. But what is striking is that the king reserved his judgement on the contents of the Westminster letter. Instead, he ordered his progress to Leicester to continue, and this apathy and similar acts of dilatory behaviour the next day proved so disastrous to Somerset and the Percys that they were left completely open to attack.

Three

Faith, Allegiance and Duty

On the night of 21 May 1455, the king and his followers 'rested at Watford', while to the north-east, the Yorkists continued their march south from Royston to Ware.[1] By this time, the Duke of York probably knew that his first message to Archbishop Bourchier had missed the king by a matter of hours, prompting a rethink of his strategy. Clearly, York thought King Henry should be informed of Yorkist intentions before they met him, or it might be construed as committing treason. Therefore, with time running out, York and his allies composed another letter to the king, complaining of the 'ambiguities' surrounding their 'faith, allegiance and duty' fraudulently spread by their enemies.[2] This second Yorkist letter, again declaring loyalty to Henry, was immediately dispatched by a trusted courier. And although it was embellished with all the courtly formalities of the period, it bid the king,

> not to give trust [or] confidence unto the sinister, malicious, and fraudulent labours and rapports of our said enemies unto our coming to your said most noble presence; where unto we beseech humbly that we may be admitted as your liege men,

to th'entent to show us the same, whereof yesterday we wrote
our letters of intent to the right reverend father in God, the
Archbishop of Canterbury, your Chancellor of England, to be
shown to your said Highness, whereof, forasmuch as we [are]
not certain whether our said intent be by his fatherhood showed
unto your said good grace or not. We send thereof unto [you]
this closed copy of our said letters of our disposition toward
your said High Excellence and the honour and weal of the land,
wherein we will persevere with the grace of our Lord.[3]

Like their first letter, this second from the Yorkists should have
prompted a reaction from Henry. But instead, there was no
answer to their demands against Somerset nor, more importantly, about the prickly issue of their loyalty – a rebuff that
could only have been galling to York's pride. According to the
biased *Parliamentary Pardon* that later absolved the Yorkists from
their actions at St Albans, both letters dispatched to the king
were concealed by the Duke of Somerset and two other court
officials named Thomas Thorpe and William Joseph. However,
it is far more likely that circumstances other than the above
caused the resounding silence from Henry and, secondly, that
the atmosphere in the royal camp had suddenly changed due, in
part, to the proximity of the Yorkist host.

It is recorded that the second Yorkist letter was carried post-
haste from Ware to the king by William Williflete, the Duke of
York's confessor, and that it was passed to the Earl of Devon at
two o'clock in the morning on 22 May. Given the early hour,
a reply from the king may not have been possible. But a more
likely reason for the king's silence is that Henry had not changed
his stance regarding York's remonstrations and that complacency
had taken the place of urgency in his mind. However, another
matter may have also prompted a dilatory reaction from the king,
and this was due to a change of command in the royalist camp.
Fearing that the mounting feud between York and Somerset
might hinder the king's progress to Leicester, Henry, either

through merit or mismanagement, chose to strip the Duke of Somerset of his command and transfer the office of constable to the more military able Duke of Buckingham.

Humphrey Stafford was a man particularly well suited to command Henry's retinue since he held the position of Constable of England by hereditary right. Before moving on to St Albans and a confrontation with York and his allies, this sudden change of approach marked a revolution in royal policy that is highly interesting, especially if we consider King Henry and Somerset's supposed lack of military foresight. However, in the wake of this decision, it may be safe to assume that the substance of the second Yorkist letter was not concealed or ignored but acted upon in more ways than one. Either way, the king's progress did not falter. St Albans was the planned concentration point of all the king's forces commissioned on 18 May, and Buckingham's appointment as commander-in-chief must have brought renewed confidence to those in his company. On the other hand, Somerset must have felt somewhat distanced and subordinated by Buckingham's new promotion, not to mention highly vulnerable to any actions that York might take against him. It also follows that considering everything that had happened in the past between the two nobles, Somerset must have now felt like an outsider.

Historical personalities are never easy to fathom, and writers are almost always unfavourable to Edmund Beaufort and his manipulative tendencies. It is also easy to see why he might be viewed as a military incapable noble bent on controlling the king for purely personal reasons. But is this a fair description of Somerset, whose Beaufort roots were firmly embedded in history and descended from Edward III? In France, the Duke of Somerset had failed miserably, just like other nobles (including the Duke of York) before him. However, the difference was he was taken back under Henry's wing several times and re-appointed to office, much to York's chagrin. After Queen Margaret gave birth to a son, Somerset was earmarked for later

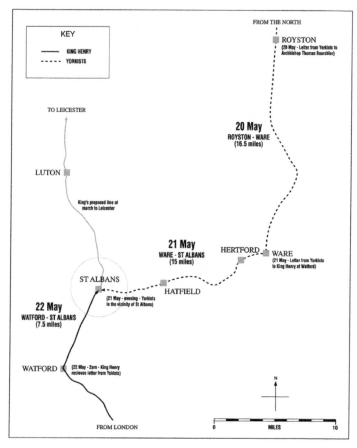

17 *The first battle of St Albans, 1455. Movements of the opposing forces 20–22 May.
(Author's Collection)*

scandalous Yorkist propaganda that had little substance other than hearsay. But Beaufort was undoubtedly a resilient individual, and with his royal bloodline legitimised, he could have taken steps to usurp the throne during the king's madness on more than one occasion. That he did not act treasonably suggests Somerset was completely loyal to the king but feared York, and his connection with Queen Margaret likely stems from this and not the bedchamber. The queen and Somerset had a mutual distrust of the Duke of York and viewed his veiled attacks on the crown personally. Therefore we may forgive Somerset for trying to curb the duke's rash efforts to reform the government and his central position. Margaret feared York's power even more. By her reckoning, he was an overmighty noble, and because he had committed treason before, she no doubt considered him a rebel bent on usurpation. The hostility she held for York and later his sons directly resulted from her experience in France torn apart by political infighting. However, in the 1450s, Margaret's main preoccupation was the vital issue of the succession, and the ways King Henry could be coaxed into fathering a child. She may have felt powerless at the time of the battle of St Albans, but by 1459, according to one biased writer, she had thrown caution to the wind:

> The queen with such as were of her affinity ruled the realm as she liked gathering riches innumerable. She was defamed and slandered that he that was called prince was not her son, but a bastard gotten in adultery; wherefore she, dreading that he should not succeed his father to the crown of England, allied unto her all the knights and squires of Chestershire for to have their benevolence, and held open household among them.[4]

Apart from the apparent slander, in 1455, Margaret could only act against York by assembling an affinity of nobles behind the throne, of which Somerset was the most prominent. Her promotion and grooming of Somerset likely caused the king to also support him, despite his failures in France. But had his support for the duke taken a different turn in May 1455? Immediately before the first battle of St Albans, the king (or others) decided that the Duke of Somerset's reputation for command was questionable. This decision was, no doubt, challenged but assented to by Henry, a fact that may prove that the king fully appreciated Somerset's limitations.

Meanwhile, York's reaction to the king's whereabouts was characteristic. He had already decided to march west at once to consult with Henry in person. Acting upon news from his scourers and those couriers that had returned from Westminster and Watford with news of the king's departure, the Yorkists marched first through Hertford, then Hatfield. According to *Davies' Chronicle*, York's army executed this manoeuvre secretly and, after a day's march, he 'gathered privily a power of people and kept them covertly in the villages about the town of Saint Albans',[5] where the king intended to dine the next day.

By the late evening of 21 May, both armies were encamped within a few miles of each other, with the Yorkists in sight of the great Benedictine abbey of St Alban. But what did the Yorkists hope to gain from their armed demonstration? Did they intend to attack the king's entourage and openly commit treason? If York and the Nevilles did propose violence to capture Somerset, how could they control who was attacked in the royal party and who was not? How did they know the calibre of the royalist troops and who might command them? In fact, would the king listen to another petition slandering Somerset and his 'evil' council? On the other hand, if the king failed to release Somerset into York's custody, would his allies be prepared to attack Henry, considering their enemies were protected by his entourage?

Evidently, Somerset had no option but to await his fate. He was not only the reason for York's hatred, but, according to sources, he had also been shunned by the people of London, an unenviable position to be in, to say the least, if he ever meant to return to politics. However, Somerset knew that the monarch afforded him the best protection in the kingdom, and he was shielded by an array of formidable men at arms and knights of the realm, some of whom were kinsmen of York and the Nevilles. Somerset was also aware that other contingents were marching to his aid, but how sure was he that the king's men would uphold his position if York launched an attack?

To begin with, the king's party that marched the 7 miles from Watford to St Albans on the morning of 22 May was, in fact, not an army at all in the traditional sense of the word, although it could transform itself into one if it chose to do so. In essence, the march to Leicester was like a royal 'progress', made up of the king's household, his baggage train and the multitude of servants who provided for his every need. Complementing this unwieldy entourage, there was also a select group of magnates and gentry, each with their own riding retinues, personal baggage and several of their servants who were duty-bound to accompany their masters on their journeys from place to place. Naturally, these nobles wished to be seen on the right side at the council meeting at Leicester, and clearly, their contingents were not greatly enlarged in accordance with royal proclamations. However, a letter existing in the *Calendar of State Papers of Milan*, written after the battle of St Albans on 3 June, claims that 'they [the royal entourage] went armed because they suggested that the Duke of York would also go there with men at arms'[6] which had been standard practice when nobles felt there might be trouble and they might have to present a show of force.

Although a royal progress from one place to another was generally a peaceful affair of political influence rather than military might, it was generally accepted that men at arms accompanied the king. Therefore, the above letter, written by an Italian correspondent to the Archbishop of Ravenna, suggests normality rather than aggression, and we can be sure that, due to the noticeable absence of archers and large contingents of shire levies armed with bills, the retinues accompanying the various nobles to Leicester were not armed more than usual.

The king's household consisted of his personal administration, his entourage, and those who provided for his everyday needs 'above' and 'below' stairs. In 1445, precise regulations were promulgated in parliament to restrict the numbers included in the king's following, but ordered magnificence was expected in the royal household, and that of Henry VI was no exception. Aside from the plethora of domestic offices, which included the king's stables, mews, kitchen and pantry, along with the 'above'-stairs departments of the chapel, hall, wardrobe, counting house and chamber, Henry's entourage was headed by his confessor (usually a bishop); next came the chamberlain's office, then the keeper of the household, the keeper of the great wardrobe, the household chamberlain, the king's carvers (usually two or three knights of the chamber), the master of the horse, the controller, the cofferer, the dean of the chapel and the royal almoner. Add to this list of offices a whole host of other select esquires and yeomen of the body and the hall, plus those administrators known as 'sovereigns' who ruled all the household departments, and it is easy to see why the medieval household in the mid-fifteenth century had become the largest single institution in the land.

The number of knights, squires and yeomen doubled in Henry's years of personal rule to a staggering 550 by 1451, not counting those who were ordered only to come to court at the five principal feasts of the year. The appointed officers were expected to travel with the king on a royal progress and, if need be, accompany him abroad to war, as they were not merely servants and providers in the traditional sense of the word. Indeed, apart from scribes and churchmen, these men constituted Henry's personal bodyguard: a select company of trained soldiers who had attained their positions through military service to the crown. Men like John Brecknock, controller of the king's household, Sir Richard Harrington, clerk of the household,

Roger Morecroft, the king's messenger, Ralph Babthorpe, the king's second sewer, and the lesser servants, such as 'Halyn', the king's porter, 'Gryphet' (Reginald Griffith), the usher of the hall, and 'Harpour' (Thomas Harper), a yeoman of the crown, these men were all probably with Henry when he raised his standard at St Albans in 1455. All were trained in the use of arms, and along with other recognised knights and esquires who also fought at St Albans, every man in Henry's household, without exception, was duty-bound to protect the king's royal person. It is, therefore, no accident that many of Henry's immediate and more personal adherents died in the streets of St Albans doing their duty.[7]

If the king's household was an institution and model for the kingdom, the riding retinues of the nobles mirrored its opulence. In terms of manpower, this similarity exceeded the king's magnificence on several occasions during the civil wars, but generally, even peers such as the Duke of Somerset and the Earl of Northumberland commanded limited personal riding retinues. When transferring their household from one manor to another, there was no need to employ private armies, an act which made a political statement of power to their rivals and drained their purse. Unless they were threatened personally, the reverse was more usual for financial reasons. However, several times during the fifteenth century, this military façade was made real by augmentation and by calling upon liveried retainers, extraordinary retainers and 'well-willers' to provide support on the battlefield.

Efforts were made to curb inflated personal retinues on many occasions before 1455. Still, it is doubtful whether the nobles in the king's party on 22 May had had the time to recruit additional troops to supplement their households. The fact that the Earl of Northumberland, and others like him, had not expected to fight a battle so far away from his northern powerbase gives credence to the theory that military action, at least at the outset of the march to Leicester, was not expected. Indeed, the fact that the Duke of York and his Neville allies had recently been instructed

18   A medieval army on the march as depicted in the Hausbuch. (© The Board of Trustees of the Armouries)

not to exceed the required number of personal followers proves that the united strength of King Henry's party was not enhanced in any way. The evidence that Coventry was instructed to raise a company of men to march south to St Albans cannot be taken as proof that a general commission of array succeeded in providing additional recruits. Indeed, they all did not arrive in time to fight. Therefore, we can safely assume that the 2,000 men who eventually fought at St Albans at Henry's behest were made up essentially of the king's household (approximately 500 men), with the remaining manpower being supplied by the nobles and the gentry that accompanied him.

As circumstances would have it, some of these lords and gentry can be identified due to them being named after their deaths and burials in and near St Albans. The peer presence is obvious, but to single out other individuals, it is necessary to consult contemporary chronicles, newsletters, and personal correspondence for clues. The resulting cross-section of nobility provided the nucleus of a typical army of the period. However, for the balance of troop types that supplemented a noble's retinue in times of war, only the Yorkist army resembles a conventional force armed with its share of bows and bills. If the *Rotuli Parliamentorum* is to be believed, the Yorkists also had rudimentary artillery pieces with them (which were not used), as the evidence states that the Duke of York's forces, assembled them together with great multitude of people harnessed, and other habiliments of war, as guns and other, and [they came] to the town of Saint Albans in your Shire of Hertford, where you, Sovereign Lord, were present, and your banner displayed there, and there they falsely and traitorously reared war against you.[8]

That the king's men were ultimately forced into fighting a battle to uphold their sovereign's wishes is self-evident, but it is surprising how far from knightly virtue some of these royalist men at arms were prepared to risk their own safety. Two men, the Earl of Wiltshire and Sir Phillip Wentworth, were both accused of deserting their posts at St Albans. Other nobles, namely William Lord Fauconberg (Salisbury's brother) and John Lord Berners (a brother of Viscount Bourchier), probably took no part in the battle while the men of the king's household and other leading nobles fought it out with their relatives in the street. The Earl of Devon may also have fought faintly due to his past allegiance and sympathy with York's cause at Dartford in March 1452. Of the main protagonists, the Duke of Somerset, the Earl of Northumberland and anyone associated with them were the ones who had the most to lose at St Albans. Somerset was undoubtedly York's primary target, but, considering that the Nevilles had old scores to settle with the Percys (that were still fresh in their memory), this vendetta had a significant bearing on how the battle of St Albans was ultimately fought.

Of the fathers and sons who were present at the battle, the Duke of York's eldest son Edward, Earl of March, may have been present. Somerset's son, the Earl of Dorset, was seriously wounded during the fighting, and it is known that Ralph Babthorpe and his son were killed, according to the *Phillipps Relation*.[9] Sir Ralph Percy, along with Lord Clifford, the retainer of Northumberland and adherent of Egremont, was also a prime target of the Nevilles in the ensuing battle in St Peter's Street, even though intermarriage amongst the nobility meant that most men on opposite sides were distantly related in some way. Even Humphrey Stafford, Duke of Buckingham, the new military commander of the royal army, was unusually complacent regarding his Yorkist in-laws. *Giles' Chronicle*, the only royalist source of the battle, records that immediately before the fighting, Buckingham disapproved of the first suggestion (probably Somerset's) that the king should stand and fight where he was at Watford rather than continue his journey to St Albans. Buckingham defended his proposal to follow their proposed route because he apparently *knew* the Duke of York would prefer to negotiate rather than fight a battle. Apart from his ties with the Nevilles (he had married Ann Neville in 1424), the confidence with which Buckingham asserted his authority and the trust he placed in York to negotiate is characteristic of a man who genuinely believed that familiarity would save the day – how wrong he was. Probably considered the veteran of the nobles (he was fifty-three in 1455), his belief that York would cooperate and stand down, as he did at Dartford in 1452, was doubtless the view of an ill-informed optimist. Buckingham may have had some inside information regarding York's temperament, especially his attitude concerning the sanctity of King Henry's rule. Still, he obviously did not bargain on York's current mindset and the local ambitions of his Neville allies, who were now not prepared to stand by and let the Dartford fiasco, or worse, repeat itself.

Like other great nobles of his age, Buckingham would have had a large riding retinue accompanying him, many of whom would have been retained by indenture to 'do him service' in return for money and 'preferment'. Indeed, ninety-nine men from Surrey and Kent were paid *6s 8d* a head for being with him at St Albans in 1455. The use of indentures was nothing new in the fifteenth century; indeed, the system had evolved out of the older landed feudal relationship through the *fief-rente*. Money and mutual need were the foundation of an indentured relationship, but 'bastard feudalism' (the later form of recruitment by indenture) was slightly different and certainly was not as binding as mutual household service. By the time the *fief-rente* disappeared in England about 1450, retaining was so widespread that the king had to rely on his nobility to raise his armies by contract to fight at home and abroad. Indeed, using more efficient non-feudal contractual agreements between the king and his military captains (the nobles) was the only way to raise a substantial force. A captain agreed to muster a specified number of troops, who would be paid wages ultimately drawn from the royal coffers or a noble's landed incomes, and they would serve for an agreed period. Some indentured retainers were bound to their masters for life but were also free to make highly lucrative connections of service with other nobles. Other men were retained purely for household or administrative duties, yet others gave favour and support in return for livery (usually the noble's livery jacket) and a fee (maintenance for a specific period), the latter being the source of great outcries in the fifteenth century and a danger to the crown. It was customary for nobles to retain others, and controls were introduced to curb all forms of livery and maintenance throughout the period, although retaining itself was too useful and well-established to be abandoned, and thus it flourished in every walk of society.[10]

Buckingham's large following was not dissimilar to most fifteenth-century retinues in that it contained men who had contracted for all kinds of service. For example, the indenture of John Gresley esquire, retained in 1450–51 for £10 during his life, recorded that he should ride with the duke 'this side the sea' (English Channel) with three yeomen, two pages and five horses, and 'beyond the sea' with as many men as the duke should think fit. The wording on most indentures was very similar, but some had modifications depending on a retainer's status. The subservient nature of the lesser indentured retainer is made clear from the wording that he would provide service 'before all other men' while the indentures of some knights could include clauses such as the one below:

The indenture of retinue of William Feins knight Lord Saye
of Sele for £10 fee during his life out of the revenues of the
office of Constable of the Castle of Dover and warden of
the five ports and the said Lord Saye to do the duke service
[before] all other except our sovereign lord the king and his
heirs in [the] manner following, viz he shall ride with the
duke [to] all places this side of the sea with competent fellowship according to his estate or such as the said duke shall assign
him to do him service etc.[11]

Lord Saye's primary loyalty to his sovereign ultimately provided the perfect defence if the king called his devotion into
question. And considering the circumstances of his father's
demise in Cade's Rebellion, it is highly likely that Fiennes was
particularly astute regarding his connections. As an asset to
Buckingham's retinue, he could reap the rewards of contractual
service with a great lord, but only if his lord's actions were parallel to the king's.

Evidence of a different kind of service is also seen in the
collection of Buckingham's extant indentures taken from the
so-called 'Red Book of Caurs Castle'. Probably retained in 1448
at an annual fee of £10, Thomas Edmund was contracted to be
always ready to ride at Buckingham's side with three horsemen,
a yeoman and a page. Similarly commanded to do him service at home and abroad 'afore all other', it is probable that the
duke relied on his retainer's invaluable expertise in more ways
than one, especially at St Albans when he was injured. Thomas
Edmund was useful with a different kind of blade on this occasion and, as the duke's personal physician, it is highly likely
that after the battle, he treated Buckingham's wounds (which,
according to the report that found its way into the *Paston Letters*,
were potentially life-threatening).

Historians have variously evaluated the recruitment of feed
retainers, and as a force for stability in society, bastard feudalism
was invaluable to the crown. However, under the weak rule of

Henry VI and as a long-term cause of civil war, some historians have taken a retrograde view of the system. W.H. Dunham, in his *Lord Hasting's Indentured Retainers,* viewed bastard feudalism in a favourable light, obviously leaving room for human inconsistency, while on the other side of the fence, the system has been called 'a parasite institution ... cut off from its natural roots in the soil, and far removed from the atmosphere of responsibility, loyalty and faith'[12] owed by a subject of the king. In his book *The End of the House of Lancaster*, R.L. Storey suggested that if Henry VI had ruled competently, the quarrels among English magnates might have been kept within tolerable limits, and Lancaster need not have given way to York in 1461. It is, therefore, safe to conclude that bastard feudalism did not cause the civil wars, as some historians have claimed; it only provided the manpower to fight them.

In tracing those who fought at the battle of St Albans, the lists of the royalist dead and wounded give a clear indication that all the named yeomen, esquires and knights were ultimately bound by the connections mentioned above. Thomas Pakington, for example, was the sword-bearer to the Earl of Northumberland and, thus, his personal retainer. Ralph Babthorpe and his son were both members of the king's household, Ralph being the Constable of Scarborough Castle and sewer (server) to the king. Sir Bertine (Bertram) Entwistle was born in Lancashire and

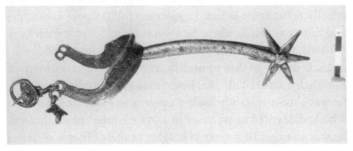

19 Long-necked six-pointed rowel spur for the left leg, English, c.1460. (© The Board of Trustees of the Armouries)

had been appointed Viscount of Bricquebec in Normandy, Lord of Hambye and Bailiff of Cotentin. He was present at the barriers at St Peter's Church when Mowbray herald delivered his final message to the king and was more than likely retained by Lord Clifford, who in turn was indentured to ride with the Earl of Northumberland.

Entwistle is typical of those knights who regarded war as a lucrative way to enhance their status. His career can be followed a little further, and it is worthwhile tracing this to appreciate what most knights experienced in the 1450s, when the English were finally ousted from France and forced to return home to England, with practically nothing to show for their labours. In Bertram's case, he was already well furnished with property and titles in Normandy when the rot set in. Born in 1396 and knighted at the battle of Agincourt in 1415, he had served in Normandy since 1429 and had fought with the redoubtable English captain John Talbot, Earl of Shrewsbury, in France, where he was later captured and held to ransom. To help pay the excessive amount demanded of him when in the hands of the French, it is recorded that he was licensed to sell wool to Calais for his own profit in 1445. However, when Talbot was killed at the battle of Castillon in 1453 and the English were finally expelled from France, Entwistle, like many of his comrades, returned home to find little or no employment in the trade he knew best. Evidently, in Bertram's case, he was not to be made wholly redundant; in fact, he returned to his native Lancashire and Entwistle Hall, where he soon took up service with Lord Clifford, who held lands in Yorkshire and Westmoreland.[13]

Like many of his contemporaries, little is known of Entwistle's actual daily life, but at the age of fifty-nine in 1455, he was almost certainly looked upon as an experienced soldier who had devoted many years of service to the crown. Indeed, he was among many veteran knights in their fifties and sixties who were called upon to travel north to Leicester with the king. As discussed, the Duke of Buckingham was fifty-three in

1455; William Lord Fauconberg was fifty-four; Lord Dudley was fifty-five, and the Earl of Northumberland was probably considered ancient at sixty-three. Sir John Wenlock (later Lord Wenlock), who later became a Yorkist and fought for Edward IV (York's eldest son), was also in his fifties. Dudley, among others, was named as the king's standard-bearer during the battle, although others were similarly employed until Henry's banner was finally abandoned against a house end in St Peter's Street.

It is, therefore, not the case that the royalist army was inexperienced or faint-hearted during the battle. Furnished with the best equipment in Europe and commanding the staunchest of retainers, all willing to die for their masters if need be, the nobles and gentry who fought for the king in 1455 were definitely a force to be reckoned with if they were attacked. They had the power of the throne behind them and were able to strike fear into even the most stubborn subjects by merely displaying the royal standard. In short, it would take an extremely determined man, or a complete fool, to dare contest the king's authority on the battlefield.

But what price Yorkist intentions, confronted with such an array of imperial might? The question is difficult to answer when considering who commanded the contingents of York's northern army. Even with contemporary letters and chronicles recording the battle to guide us, only a handful of York's captains can be clearly identified. Admittedly, this is because St Albans was a Yorkist victory and their overall casualties were light. However, it is essential to document the variation between the contending armies and show the differences between the two sides to trace the battle. At first glance, this comparison is particularly one-sided. It favours the royal army both in terms of equipment and troop quality, but it is apparent that several other factors suggest that the Yorkist army had an edge, and these advantages were noted in some contemporary chronicles.

Firstly, on a psychological note, the Yorkist commanders had a point to prove. They verged on the terrible crime of treason if their strategies ran out of control or were resisted by the king. Secondly, feuds existed between the two sides, and personal issues undoubtedly shaped what occurred in the streets of St Albans when fighting broke out. Thirdly, the Duke of York had already experienced a measure of humiliation in the field before, and was clearly not about to do so again. His admonishments in the council chamber against Somerset, not to mention his failed coup at Dartford, must have seriously affected York's political and psychological outlook. The duke no doubt saw himself as the mouthpiece of the common people in more ways than one, although we cannot prove this conclusively. Lastly, the psyche of the Yorkist soldiers was dissimilar to that of the king's men. The northerners who had marched south with the Nevilles were used to garrison duty and border warfare and were undoubtedly more than ready to fight for their masters without question. However, contrary to the picture painted of Henry's shining professional force ranged against a 'rag-tag' band of moss troopers culled from the north, the real strength of the Yorkist army was not their leaders' determination or advantage of numbers, which were admittedly greater and more constant than the kings, but in their local outlook. According to reports and most chroniclers, the Neville army's reputation as hardened fighters was driven by the fear of their overmighty neighbours, the Percys, and their extensive network of retainers.

As we have seen, Neville and Percy's feuding caused infighting among the nobles and gentry in the north, and quite naturally, it had polarised many tenant farmers and local townsmen who owed them allegiance. Richard of York was the most senior Yorkist commander at St Albans, but at the age of sixty, his 'prudent' brother-in-law, Richard Neville, Earl of Salisbury, was ten years older than York and by far the more influential captain in his army. Regarding manpower and the command of their trained bands of retainers and border levies, it is highly likely that the greater authority was also demanded by Salisbury, who, along with his son, the Earl of Warwick, had recruited most of York's men from their northern domains. This fact does not, however, belittle the overriding influence of the Duke of York, nor does it underestimate his ability to recruit from his own areas of influence, but merely suggests that York's willingness to act was nothing without Neville accord. After all, this political alliance had made York's army more notable as a fighting unit than at Dartford. Judging by the king's orders to restrict Neville retinues before St Albans, he feared widespread recruitment. The Duke of Somerset knew the danger of this and the Nevilles' ability to recruit border levies, not to mention plenty of archers armed with the warbow.

With a host of other more personal issues burning in the Nevilles' minds, the chance to accomplish what they had failed to do in the north against the Percys was probably a good enough reason for Salisbury to accord with York's wishes. Freeing the king from the influence of an unjust minister likely came secondary to more urgent matters in the north. In short, the overriding feud of Neville against Percy may not have impinged on the will of York to act against Somerset but instead on the mutual understanding between the Yorkist commanders that they would combat more enemies than one under the smokescreen of a noble cause.

Although sources do not fully document the organisation of the Yorkist army, we can identify at least some of the men who accompanied York in 1455 and thereby describe what troop types they may have commanded. Aside from the three most senior commanders – York, Salisbury, and Warwick – we know that Sir John Neville, Salisbury's other son, was present at St Albans, given that his long-standing feud with the Percys was ongoing and not yet settled. John Neville was probably more eager than most to renew the conflict with his rivals, and although his brother, the Earl of Warwick, had not yet suffered the direct effects of Percy hostility first-hand, clearly John and

20 Richard Neville, Earl of Salisbury depicted in the Salisbury Roll. (Author's Collection)

his brother Thomas still harboured a grudge against the Percy family since Lord Egremont's attack at Heworth Moor in 1453. Therefore, it is possible that Sir Thomas Neville also fought at St Albans, considering that Egremont's assassination attempt was still fresh in the mind of the Neville family and the fact that the Earl of Northumberland had stood idly by while his renegade son had not only planned the deed but also given him leave to terrorise Neville estates in Yorkshire. Evidently, Salisbury and his sons could not see the folly of continuing their feud with the Percy family due to an ingrained and ancient prejudice on both sides. Family and chivalric pride had to be upheld, and no doubt the Earl of Warwick felt the same pangs of family hatred for his blood enemies, the Percys. However, the overriding reason for Warwick's fervent involvement at St Albans was undoubtedly territorial disagreements in other parts of the country.

On 21 July 1453, Henry VI had presided over a meeting to settle the differences between the Duke of Somerset and the Earl of Warwick regarding the possession of the lordship of Glamorgan and Morgannock in South Wales. The conflict had arisen due to Henry's willingness to grant Somerset the keeping of these lands, which had been held by Warwick since 1450 as part of the Beauchamp inheritance through his wife, Anne. Due to Henry's mismanagement, Warwick had been forced to hold the principal strongholds there by force of arms against Somerset, who was quite clearly willing to accept his king's munificence as favouritism. The attempt by Somerset to dispossess Warwick and the Nevilles of their rightful inheritance was, of course, deplorable. Still, the fact that a loophole had been found and exploited by Somerset caused Warwick to mistrust his rival's intentions on a much broader scale, even to the extent of causing him to side with the Duke of York in a bid to punish his enemy. As a result, the royal meeting of 21 July was a chance for King Henry to make amends. However, the decision of the council to order Warwick to disperse his armed followers and to give the lordships over to Lord Dudley until Henry had decided what proper action should be taken was a dismal failure. Indeed, there is no evidence that Warwick ever surrendered his lands to Dudley or Somerset, and, in the author's opinion, this same territorial quarrel was finally settled in the streets of St Albans, where Warwick had the ideal opportunity to deal with both men at once.

As for the Earl of Salisbury's forces, there are numerous indentures detailing his retainers to call upon, and these are described by historians such as A.J. Pollard and K. Dockray. Most of these documents date to the 1440s, and all the families below were likely represented at St Albans in 1455:

[Salisbury] could confidently expect backing from an impressive line-up of fellow northerners, ranging from baronial houses such as the Greystokes of Greystoke, the Fitzhughs of Ravensworth and the Scropes of Bolton to greater gentry families such as the Strangeways of West Harlsey, the Pickerings of Ellerton, the Harringtons of Hornby (in Lancashire) and the Conyers of Hornby (in Richmondshire).[14]

Aside from the Neville contingents, other disgruntled nobles had also decided to join York in his effort to oust Somerset from power. That John Lord Clinton fought with the Yorkists at St Albans is certain, although his death there, according to the *Paston Letters*, is doubtful. Clinton, an impoverished Yorkshire magnate who had been induced by an act of royal patronage to sell his claim to the title of Lord Saye in 1448, later fought for the Yorkists at Ludford Bridge, the second battle of St Albans and the battle of Towton. His death in 1464 strengthens the case that he was a staunch Yorkist sympathiser to the last, more than ready to face attainder and, if necessary, death to regain his former position.

Edward Brooke, Lord Cobham, also joined York's army, as he had done before the Dartford affair in 1452. Indeed, it will be remembered that he and his master, the Earl of Devon, had been imprisoned in Berkhamsted Castle for two years for their part in York's failed coup, and although 2,430 other rebels had received a pardon for their treasonable actions at Dartford, Lord Cobham was likely marked out for special treatment by the king's councillors. The result was that Devon joined the king's army at St Albans and Cobham, his former henchman, sided with York, doubtless nursing a measure of resentment for his incarceration.

The Bourchiers had also decided to follow their cousin York against Somerset. Their family were represented by Henry, Viscount Bourchier, later created the Earl of Essex, and his son Humphrey, afterwards Lord Cromwell – although a degree of uncertainty exists about Humphrey's participation in the actual battle. According to the *Paston Letters*, a 'Lord Crumwelle'[15] was in the vicinity of St Albans on 22/23 May 1455, but this must not be confused by the fact that Ralph, the current bearer of the title, and other nobles were advancing on, or near, St Albans on the day of the battle. Henry Bourchier had been created viscount in 1446 and was now aged fifty-one. He was married to York's sister Isobel; thus, his connection to his brother-in-law's cause was assured, although this recent militancy was founded more on embarrassment than commitment. Even though his own brother, John Lord Berners, was with the king at St Albans, he had probably chosen to adhere to York's cause for a more personal reason. At Dartford, Henry Bourchier had been among the group of nobles and clergy who had advised York to negotiate with the king and Somerset, and it will be remembered that on this occasion, the duke had been tricked into dispersing his army under the pretence of fair treatment. Bourchier had therefore been party to York's capture and his resulting dressing-down in London, and this was doubtless the reason for his backing at St Albans – Somerset quite clearly being the one who had manufactured the Dartford betrayal.

As for the other leading Yorkist captains at St Albans, we can only hazard a guess as to their identities based on who was retained by the leading nobles at the time and who was later rewarded by York after the battle. Regarding the latter, there were precious few rewards after St Albans, due to the likelihood of an act of resumption in the forthcoming parliament, when a list of York's favourites would have created a bad impression on all those present. In view of this, only six rewards were distributed to lesser men who gave service in the field. These men were Sir William Oldhall, York's former Speaker and activist, Sir Henry Retford, Sir Thomas Lumley, John Denston esquire, Henry Unton and Robert Burton.

However, as discussed, it is certain that a good proportion of Neville retainers fought at St Albans, and as regards the Earl of Salisbury's knights, two indentures still survive that were still in

21 *John Denston esquire, who fought for the Duke of York at St Albans. (Stained glass at Long Melford Church. Courtesy of Geoffrey Wheeler)*

force in 1455. These documents belong to Sir Henry Threlkeld, who served with Salisbury in France in 1431 with eight men at arms and twenty-two archers, and Sir Walter Strickland of Sizergh, who, in return for a pension of £6 13s 4d, was retained by Salisbury 'for the term of his life, against all folk, saving his allegiance'.[16] Strickland could muster a total of 290 armed men and was, therefore, a valuable Neville adherent in the north when harnessing manpower. His indenture to Salisbury and his muster of 1448/9 'in the twenty-seventh year of King Henry's reign' gives a good idea of his capacity to call out his tenants at a moment's notice. The extract below also provides the names and equipment of some of the local soldiers from Hackthorpe (Westmoreland) who owed him faith, allegiance, duty, and their lives:

This indenture made between Richard Earl of Salisbury on the one party, and Walter Strickland's son and heir of Sir Thomas Strickland knight on the t'other, beareth witness, that the same Walter is behest [retained] and withholden with the said earl, for the term of his life, against all folks, saving his allegiance. And the said Walter shall be well and suitably horsed, armed, and arrayed; and always ready to ride, come, and go with [him], to and for the said earl, at all times and into all places on this side and beyond the sea, as well in time of peace as of war, that he be warned by the said earl on his behalf, at the wages and costs reasonable of the same earl. Taking the said Walter yearly for his fee of the said earl ten marks of money of the issues and profits of the lordship of Penrith, with th'appurtenances, giving by the hands of the receiver there being for the time, at the feasts of Martin mass and Whit Sunday by even portions...

In Hackthorpe:
Thomas Willen; a horse, a jack, and a spear.
Henry Danson; a horse, a jack, and a bow.
John Chappelhow; a horse, a jack, and a bow.

Bills:
Christopher Willen; a horse harness and a bill.
Richard Mylne; a horse, a jack, and a bill.
Robert Taylor; a horse, a jack, and a bill.
Christopher Chappelhow; a horse, a jack, and a bill.
John Bank; a horse, a jack, and a bill.
John Dobson; a horse, a jack, and a bill.
William Hudson; a horse and a bill.

Footmen, with part harness:
Thomas Chappelhow; a jack and a bow.
Renald Water; a jack and a bill.
Thomas Stevenson; a jack and a bill

Footmen, without harness:
Richard Willen, a bill.
Hew Sands, a bill.

Young men:
Henry Sawkelt; a bow.

Rolland Wyllen; a bow.
John Taylor; a bow.
Robert Milne; a bow.
Edward Ayray; a bill.

The whole number [of Strickland's lands]:
Bowmen horsed and harnessed, 69
Billmen horsed and harnessed, 74
Bowmen without horse harness, 71
Billmen without horse harness, 76

Total: 290 men.[17]

The totals above represent the approximate combined strength of Strickland's force overall when all his lands were counted in. Soldiers horsed and harnessed [meaning a man with horse and armour] are obviously marked out as the better sort of recruit, whilst the widespread use of the quilted 'jack' as upper body protection is an outstanding feature of those levies able to serve their lord with arms and equipment. It is also worth noting the percentage of bows and bills in Hackthorpe at the time, which suggests a more even spread of bows to polearms, like the bill, and unlike an English army abroad where the ratio was usually tipped exclusively in favour of the former. Looking closer, we can also appreciate the family connections in Hackthorpe and how some soldiers were younger men, probably sixteen (or even less), who were expected to fight alongside their relatives under commissions of array. Men from sixteen to sixty are mentioned in other extant documents of the fifteenth century, some ages can be calculated from the analysis of bones in war graves, and most soldiers would have been paid for their service, usually lasting forty days or thereabouts.[18]

However, aside from common levies, one man, who was most definitely at the battle of St Albans, and who can be clearly iden-tified as a retainer of the Earl of Salisbury is the largely unsung hero of the hour – Sir Robert Ogle, later Lord Ogle of Bothal, Northumberland. Although Ogle was raised to the peerage later in his career, his involvement as a knight at the first battle of St Albans, and especially the winning of it, has been overshadowed by what historians deemed to be a much better-publicised tactic and decision by the Earl of Warwick. This supposed manoeuvre by Warwick (which won the battle) did not help him acquire any immediate honour or title in his lifetime, but since then, historians have credited the 'kingmaker' with the master stroke that achieved victory instead of identifying who was responsible for turning the tide of battle.

Born in 1406 and aged forty-nine at St Albans, Ogle was descended from a long line of Northumberland gentry and soldiers, most of whom had devoted their lives to defending the border against the Scots. In 1423, Ogle married Isobel Kirkby and set about forging a career in the northern marches by replacing John Lord Greystoke as Constable of Roxburgh Castle, one of the more critical border strongholds and strategic focal points of Scottish 'fay' or pride. The reward for keeping the Scots at bay was incredibly lucrative and amounted to £1,000 per annum in peacetime and £2,000 per annum if war should occur. Particularly coveted by several other northern lords, any military redeployment to the northern border was highly dangerous. However, the other hazard, apart from the threat of Scottish attack, was the winning and keeping of such official positions, and Ogle, like many of his northern neighbours, was keen to extend his offices and land ownership. Jealous of others and their acquisition of property and eager to obtain more at any price, he was no different from most northern lords of the period, and he soon entered into a landed dispute with Sir William Elmeden at Newcastle. As a result, the two became embroiled in what can only be described as another local feud, which in the end, merited the nomination of a panel of arbitrators to help resolve the issue. The dispute was still unresolved in 1435 when Sir Ralph Grey replaced Ogle as the keeper of Roxburgh, the latter being appointed to the wardenship of Berwick, which he shared with Grey in 1437. Berwick was another primary focus of Scottish raiding and a highly prized border stronghold, but this appointment proved to be a short-term contract for Ogle. After serving as the joint warden of the East March in 1438, he appears to have sought a more permanent position within the Neville family, hence his involvement as a retainer of the Earl of Salisbury at St Albans.[19]

Despite being constable of several other important northern border strongholds, and holding the captaincy of Norham Castle, Ogle had been receiving a fee of £20 from the Earl of Salisbury since 1436. Therefore, he was an obvious choice to captain a contingent of men at arms and archers at St Albans. His close relationship with the Neville family and especially with Bishop Neville of Durham gives credence to the theory that the '[600] men of the Marches'[20] he commanded at St Albans were mustered through his official capacity at Norham. As a highly resourceful border fighter and a competent commander of men,

22 *Seal of Sir Robert Ogle, later Lord Ogle. (Courtesy of Geoffrey Wheeler)*

the contribution of Sir Robert Ogle to the winning of St Albans has been lost to history. Still, it is highly plausible that during the night of 21 May, when the Yorkist army was encamped close to the town contemplating what might occur if battle was joined, one Northumbrian knight was already preparing to impress his superiors, no matter what the cost.

Four

St Albans

To understand the anatomy of a battle, it is necessary to appreciate the ground over which the action was fought. Investigating various battlefield terrain features provides the military historian with vital clues as to how armies manoeuvred, fought, and pursued the strategies envisaged by their commanders. The terrain, whether chosen or happened upon by chance, could be either hazardous or favourable to soldiers once they had begun to move and engage the enemy. Therefore, topographical evidence, linked with contemporary sources, proven weapon mechanics and archaeology, provide the essential elements needed to flesh out a battle. As an alternative method, Colonel A.H. Burne, the author of *The Battlefields of England*, applied his famous Inherent Military Probability (IMP) to several historical sites in the 1950s. However, he concentrated more on putting himself into the minds of the rival commanders rather than appreciating the above techniques:

The fact is reliable records of our English battles are distressingly meagre. When one has discounted the exaggerations inevitable in a medieval chronicle, the distortions due to

misconception, the errors due to absence of maps, and sometimes even deliberate fabrication – there is not much pure
grain left. To complete the picture many gaps have to be
filled in … My method here is to start with what appear to
be the undisputed facts, then to place myself in the shoes of
each commander in turn, and to ask myself in each case what
I would have done. This I call working on Inherent Military
Probability.[1]

When measured against the information supplied in contemporary chronicles and newsletters, the workings of IMP are
significant where topographical evidence is lacking. However,
IMP is flawed on several counts, simply because Burne's 'personal' twentieth century understanding of warfare cannot
be applied to the mind of a medieval commander, or for that
matter, any other general who followed a completely different
set of rules, aims and values. In short, IMP is just the first of
many traps that ensnare the student of medieval warfare in a
paradigm of thought. Understanding how a battle was fought is
clearly best met with evidence, and an appreciation of the medieval mindset, given that a given battlefield will always have its
unique set of problems and ambiguities, no matter what method
of modern detection is applied.

Soldiers and commanders of any era, all anxiously seeking
victory (or survival) amid the fog of war, rarely know that a
given acreage of land may contain some diabolical surprise
or that pure chance may cause their best-laid plans to falter,
due to an unforeseen obstacle. Many such battlefield hazards
have ultimately led armies to disaster, and all prove conclusively that tactics and strategy in any age are useless against the
unknown perils of terrain. For example, how could a medieval
commander employ sound tactics in a built-up area such as
St Albans in 1455 or make his next move decisive if his men
were crowded together in a restricted area? What were his best
chances of communication if his troops were blindly fighting

in a maelstrom of flailing weapons and falling arrows? What price their manoeuvrability when hindered by mounting piles of dead and wounded? How might his captains communicate faced with hazards, not to mention how they might combat the ever-present threat of fatigue and disorientation experienced in crossing broken ground or ploughed fields in war armour? Therefore, it is the more physical and largely hidden factors of warfare, coupled with the practical aspects of terrain, that provide a formidable challenge to the battlefield detective, and prove to all who undertake the challenge, that a 'typical' battlefield does not exist, considering the diversity of land masses and agriculture throughout the ages. Indeed, the shock of a completely unfamiliar battlefield is the great thrill of the work. Walking the ground and searching the written evidence for clues is the only way to solve the problem, and this is certainly true of the first battle of St Albans. Indeed, establishing where and how this unique battle was fought necessitates a complete change in measurement. Therefore, it is essential to plot the ground over which the armies moved to separate fact from fiction.

In medieval England, rolling countryside, water meadows, ridge and furrow field systems, rivers and tributaries, hills, valleys, wooded escarpments and moorland can all influence the course of a battle, or at least this is how we might first envisage it. Two contending medieval armies ordered in three 'battles' (or divisions) opposing each other across a no-man's-land separated by perhaps no more than 300 yards, is how we have come to view the great battles of the period. However, the reality of St Albans is far from conventional or straightforward, and the *modus operandi* gained from understanding other battles of the same era cannot be applied in this case. In fact, St Albans, according to some historians, was described as a non-battle, a prequel to the civil wars and a sideshow to the main event that followed. The battle has even been dubbed a 'short scuffle in a street' by one eminent critic.[2] However, most historians have not considered that no less than 5,000 men were involved in the street fighting and that a large proportion of the English nobility were present at the battle, with others either waiting to engage or marching to the king's aid. As we will see in the next chapter, this so-called 'brawl in the street' was neither small nor insignificant. And its final phase, resulting in the cold-blooded murder of prominent English nobles, ranks among one of the most interesting and disastrous events of English medieval history.

Today St Albans is a bustling and historic city boasting a varied architectural heritage, and beneath the modern façade of civic and retail opulence, its medieval character is never far away. To begin with, the layout of the modern city follows the medieval blueprint established soon after the construction of its great abbey, now a cathedral, founded by Offa, King of Mercia, in AD 793. However, the origins of St Albans as an urban centre date back much further, to when the Roman town of Verulamium occupied the banks of the River Ver in AD 49. Sacked by Boudicca in AD 61 and burned to the ground during the reign of Antoninus Pius, ancient Verulamium was a thriving

23 The great Benedictine abbey at St Albans. (Author's Collection)

centre when Alban, formerly a Roman soldier, was executed for
his conversion to Christianity on the hill overlooking the settlement in the third-century AD. Alban became the first British
martyr, and the Benedictine abbey, built on the spot where he
died, soon attained great wealth and power, eventually becoming one of the most splendid abbeys in medieval England.

The Norman abbot Paul de Caen rebuilt the first Anglo-Saxon
church in the eleventh century, and the abbey soon prompted
the birth of a market town outside its precinct walls. Extended
and refurbished at various times throughout the medieval
period, the abbey achieved a licence to crenellate in 1357, considering many townsfolk of St Albans were its feudal tenants and
friction between peasant and churchman was not uncommon.
Much to the villeins' dismay, one of their most hated obligations was to be forced to have their corn ground at the abbot's
mill and, with few exceptions, the use of domestic hand mills
was forbidden. It was an ongoing feud that was animated by the
onset of the Peasants' Revolt in 1381. Thomas Walsingham, the
famous monastic chronicler of St Albans, records what occurred
in the aftermath of Wat Tyler's uprising:

> William Grindcobbe, William Cadington, John the Barber
> and other criminals to the number of fifteen were drawn
> and hanged for riot. Some leading townsmen like Richard
> Wallingford, John Garlick, William Berewick and Thomas
> Putor, were imprisoned among eighty others whom royal
> clemency later released. Meanwhile, the villeins spitefully
> accused the abbot, who had risked royal displeasure by his
> intercessions, of forcing them to join the London mob. Such
> malice shocked the justiciar [Robert Tresilian] who silenced
> them by asking why the abbot did so. Other slanders about
> the abbot's reduction of freemen to villeinage, compulsion to
> use his mill instead of grinding corn at home, and bribing the
> king were shaking most of the abbey's friends, despite pen-
> alties for slander, against the abbot, of hanging for men and
> burning for women.[3]

After eight days, the king, Richard II, met the townspeople's claims by sending a commission to see that the abbey's dues were rendered. However, when Richard had considered the overall disturbances in the kingdom, and particularly those riots caused by more serious offenders in London, he made the citizens pay a terrible penance. Firstly, he took the fealty of all the men of Hertfordshire between the ages of fifteen and sixty. Then, when he heard,

> that the bodies of those hanged at St Albans had been audaciously taken from the gallows [and buried] he sent a writ, dated 3 August, to the bailiffs, bidding them to be replaced in chains to hang as long as they lasted. This reduced to a revolting slavery the freedom-loving revolutionaries of St Albans, for none would do the work for them and with their own hands they had to hang up their fellow citizens whose decomposing bodies were full of maggots and stank.[4]

As for the beleaguered position of the abbey, the friction between villein and monk had two interrelated results: firstly, it made the friendship of influential people outside the abbey precincts hugely important, and secondly, it increased the abbey's burden of debt. Benefactors were anxiously sought out, and because St Albans Abbey was also a centre of intellectual activity, the works of art and literature produced within its confines vividly illuminated the ebb and flow of English politics.

Matthew Paris, Thomas Walsingham and John Whethamstede all exalted moral and social values in their histories while at the same time aiming to please a variety of wealthy benefactors with carefully chosen flourishes of propaganda. While the recurrent theme in Matthew Paris' chronicles was the wickedness of all the enemies of St Albans, Thomas Walsingham was more preoccupied with the abbey's patrons. His chronicles were strongly biased in favour of these friends, and God's divine intervention in all earthly matters was never too far away. However, the florid and rhetorical narrative of John Whethamstede (*alias* Bostock) is far more difficult to pin down. His boastful wordplay, set in a world of classical and biblical comparisons, provides few strategic details of the battle fought not a hundred yards from the abbey gateway. Whethamstede may have been an eyewitness to the fighting in 1455, maybe not, but without his history both battles of St Albans would be sadly lacking in the local detail missing from other contemporary chronicles.

The date when the son of Hugh and Margaret Bostock of Wheathampstead in Hertfordshire came to St Albans is unknown, but it was certainly before the death of Thomas Walsingham in 1422. After studying at Oxford, John Whethamstede became abbot of St Albans in 1420, a position he held for twenty years. In 1452 he was again elected abbot

24 Abbot John Whethamstede. (Courtesy of Geoffrey Wheeler)

and ruled until he died in 1465, four years after the second battle in his town. Whethamstede's chief historical works were two *Registers*, one for each of his abbatiates, which he wrote exclusively to record his own acts and present them in a favourable light to his benefactors. Therefore, justification of Whethamstede's work requires a measure of caution although some facts in his writings can be corroborated. As a friend of Humphrey, Duke of Gloucester, Whethamstede not only benefited from royal contact with a wide circle of friends and scholars engaged in classical studies, but he was also favoured by the duke's patronage. His flowery style of writing and boastful but elegant prose technique, his fondness for puns and biblical rhetoric, and his preoccupation with pleasing his benefactors, portray a man who wrote chiefly to persuade the reader to accept his own idealised view of people and events.

In general, his sympathies were with the Yorkists, and his eulogy on Humphrey, Duke of Gloucester, inserted in his *Register* for 1455, gives credibility to the enthusiastic support of Richard, Duke of York. He points an accusing finger at the Duke of Somerset for ousting York from the governorship of Normandy, and notes with approval, the duke's attempted negotiations for peace before first St Albans. However, Whethamstede tempers these remarks by straddling both sides of the fence when he condemns the Yorkists for plundering the town after the battle in 1455 and saying that York's vendetta against Somerset was morally wrong. His admiration of Henry VI is also intensified by a certain disapproval of him as a ruler and military commander. Henry was too gullible and easily led by his evil councillors, and this, according to Whethamstede, had brought about the demise and the murder of his benefactor and friend, Humphrey, Duke of Gloucester, in 1447. In short, Whethamstede's work is tarnished with a portion of egotism and self-preservation. Therefore, it is only useful to illuminate the battle of St Albans where other sources fail to deliver.

Apart from his digressions, Whethamstede knew his town intimately, and as will be shown in a later chapter, he spoke with the Duke of York immediately after the battle had ended. Therefore, it is likely that he did not actually witness the more violent events of the battle but probably did see the bloodstained streets he described so vividly. Local tradition, claiming that he viewed the fighting from the nearby abbey gatehouse or the church tower is unfounded, and this is clearly shown in his statement that the king and his men kept well clear of the abbey. In this way, Whethamstede states, his beloved enclave was saved from pillage, hinting at the possibility that before the battle the royalist position was much further north and closer to St Peter's Church than historians think. No doubt, Whethamstede was shocked by the carnage he saw in his home town after the battle and may have felt so helpless amid the violence (and murder) committed there that he was unusually silent about many of the more salient aspects of the encounter. In fact, while the battle was being fought, he was probably tucked away in the confines of his abbey, awaiting news from outside sources. Evidently, Whethamstede abhorred what occurred at the battle of St Albans, and he certainly took a different view on Yorkist politics thereafter. By criticising the Duke of York five years later for aspiring to the crown, calling it a sin of pride, he charged the duke with perjury because he had sworn to reform the government and not to usurp the throne. Whethamstede shows an avid will to survive amid the ever-changing political climate of the civil wars, and in this guise, he was no different to many people as the fighting intensified.

It is disappointing that Whethamstede's view of the first battle of St Albans cannot be precisely defined. Still, with the help of medieval documents, archaeology, cartography and modern survey methods, the medieval town he knew can be mapped out with great accuracy. However, due to the wealth of information available, we will only concern ourselves with the eastern part of the city and those areas directly linked to the battle. This locale can be narrowed down even further to describe the main roads into the town, the streets that converged on the marketplace, the buildings defining the eastern approaches, the 'town backsides', and the boundary field systems bordering the Tonman Ditch. In this case, conventional descriptions of battlefield terrain are hardly applicable; therefore, man-made features must be examined to trace the movements of the opposing armies. Field names play a significant role in defining the initial position of the Yorkist army, but houses, inns, ditches, barriers, narrow streets and lanes denote the killing zone. Similarly, the movements of the opposing forces cannot be traced by hundreds of yards but, in some cases, by only a few paces. Troop movements were made under limited conditions – essentially influenced by confined spaces between buildings and man-made objects. Major phases of the battle flowed through back gardens. Attacks were made across barricades, and more covert manoeuvres were judged by line of sight – conditions that would never be present on a more conventional battlefield. Indeed, as discussed, both the street battles of St Albans are unique to British history and the first, although smaller in both size and area, was more important in political terms than the second.

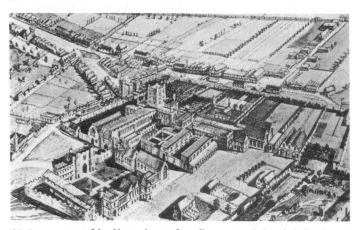

25 *Reconstruction of the abbey and town of St Albans as it might have looked in the fifteenth century. (Courtesy of Geoffrey Wheeler)*

The medieval town of St Albans was originally built on the southwestern extremity of a ridge that was, and is today, quite noticeably steeper in those areas falling away towards the River Ver and its extension, the Holywell Stream. If approached from the east, however, the ground rises more gently, and it is comparatively level where the first battle of St Albans was fought. In 1455, the abbey, with its great rectangular tower crowned by a spire, would have soared more magnificently over the clusters of half-timbered houses that swept back and forth along the main thoroughfares of the town. The outstretched arms of humble tenements and grander manor houses hugged the main streets and fanned out north, south and west of the marketplace, which was roughly triangular, and could be pinpointed in 1455 by a relatively new clock tower built between the years 1403–12. The abbey complex, with its great gatehouse and inner cloisters, was sealed off from the 'rebellious' town by a high precinct wall, while priories, religious houses and parish churches dotted both the town and the surrounding countryside. Between dense woods and open pastures accommodating grazing livestock, several fishponds broke the lazy continuity of the river, and these yielded fish and eels for the abbey kitchens. A multitude of inns provided accommodation and hospitality for those travellers who saw St Albans not only as a religious centre but also as a staging post on their journeys to and from London. At the heart of the town, the marketplace, like all economic centres, must have been a bustle of activity. Human cries, animal noises and intense aromas of foodstuffs would have emerged from both stalls and permanent shops. Square banners of fulled cloth were likely seen hanging out to dry in the 'tenter grounds' south of the town, close to its many water mills. All these and far stranger sights would have been familiar to both the medieval visitor and the town's residents on that fateful morning in May 1455. However, the populace could hardly have anticipated the appearance of two 'armies' converging on the town: a far cry from the intentions of pilgrims who regularly trudged their weary way towards St Alban's shrine and sought absolution for their sins.

Doubtless, that morning in May, Henry VI and his entourage of nobles and their retinues crossed the river, known in the fifteenth century as the 'Halywell Stream' over Holywell Bridge (built in 1143). After being appraised of the Yorkist position in Key Field to the east, they would have ridden into the town centre up the incline known as Holywell Hill or 'Halywell Street' in 1455, both variants of the word *haly* denoting 'holy' – the traditional site of a shrine or well, now lost to antiquity. Holywell Hill was the principal artery into St Albans after Watling Street (the Roman road into Verulamium) had been diverted by Abbot Ulsinus in about AD 860–70, and from the river, it was lined with houses and various inns on both sides of the street. On its western side, these dwellings were bounded to the rear by the abbey precinct wall, broken by the Holywell Gate, while to the east, the houses were backed by numerous garden 'backsides' and fields. Halfway up the incline into the town, again on the eastern side, Sopwell Lane, a road that was similarly lined with buildings and inns, formed a junction with Holywell Hill and eventually turned southeast to become the London road. This same road led to the Priory of St Mary, which Matthew Paris recorded as being founded in the twelfth century. However, regarding central St Albans, Sopwell Lane marked the first of three entry points into the town from the east and was thus of critical importance regarding access to the marketplace and St Peter's Street.

To the north of the lane mentioned above, all the medieval gardens and properties on the east side of Holywell Hill had medieval strip fields to their rear. These gardens and orchards were bordered by what was then known as the Houndspath, a track (previously thought to have been an early defensive ditch) that ran parallel to Holywell Hill and St Peter's Street. However, the strip fields and allotments that extended eastward from this path continued to the borough boundary and the defensive

26 Sopwell Lane, looking east from the junction of Holywell Hill. (Author's Collection)

entrenchment known as the 'Towneman' (or Monk) Ditch, beyond which larger fields were recorded on Benjamin Hare's 1634 map of the town. Although it is not known whether the Tonman Ditch defences were substantial in 1455, it is recorded in a survey of 1327, that a town ditch did exist during the Barons' War. A perambulation of St Albans, then said to be without bounds, established that the boundary ran from,

> Gonnerestone [Gonnerston] to the sheepfold of Kyngesbury [Kingsbury], and thence to the corner of Dounhegge [Down Hedge], and thence to the corner of Tonmandiche [Tonman Ditch], and from thence to the Grange of St Peter, and from thence to Barnatewode [Barnet Wood, Bernards Heath], and from thence to Stone Crouche [Stone Cross], and thence to the corner of the graveyard of St Peter towards the east, and from thence to the Grange of John, son of Richard Baldewyne, and from thence by Tonmandiche to Sopwellelane [Sopwell Lane], and from thence to the croft of John de Hamptone, and from thence to Grenelenehende

[Green Lane End], and from thence to Eyewodelane [Eywood Lane], and from thence to Halliwellebrugge [Holywell Bridge] and from thence to Gonnerestone by the stream of the river.[5]

Archaeological data proves the Tonman Ditch was quite substantial at some point during its history and may have originally been more than ten metres wide and two metres deep in some places. It undoubtedly consisted of a steep-sided entrenchment with an inner bank interspersed with crossing places protected by barriers to guard against attack. The archaeological evidence indicates that the defences were not insignificant. In fact, a section of the bank excavated and recorded near Key Field shows that the inner bank was more than eleven metres wide. According to the evidence above, the borough boundary of 1327 followed the course of the medieval ditch to some extent, and this entrenchment may have purposely breached the River Ver in the west and the Holywell Stream in the east, forcing the waters to flow into its channel creating a moat. If this conjectured line of the defences can be proved, then this would mean that the Tonman Ditch was almost certainly flooded in at least two places along its course. However, because St Albans occupies rising ground, the presence of water in the remainder of the ditch is doubtful. Moreover, in 1427 archery butts were built in what was then called Monk Ditch, which again points to the fact that the base was essentially a dry defensive earthwork by 1455, which had little practical use.

As for medieval field systems, spread out before the Yorkist host then encamped in one of the meadows beyond the Tonman Ditch known as 'the Key Field',[6] were large strips of extremely hazardous terrain. Admittedly, many of the Duke of York's men had previously fought in France and had undoubtedly encountered far worse obstacles in siege warfare than urban clutter. However, by the same token, if a battle was forced upon them at St Albans, it must be assumed that most of the Yorkist captains knew that the ensuing conflict would ultimately favour the defending army rather than those who made an assault. If the Yorkists took the initiative, their troops would have first crossed the Tonman Ditch and bank, which was bridged and barred in three places by temporary barriers. Many historians believe that the king's men guarded these before the Yorkist arrival, but as will be seen, this strategy was doubtful. The second hazard they would have to consider was a more general question of which narrow roads should be followed to arrive at the town centre. As already described, one of the roads that crossed the Tonman Ditch was Sopwell Lane (the medieval London road). To the north of this was Shropshire Lane, now Victoria Street (also known as Long Butts Lane in 1455), and further north was another road known as New Lane, now Hatfield Road (also later known as Cock Lane). The latter road entered St Peter's Street by the church of the same name. However, judging by the early occupation of Key Field by the Yorkists, at approximately seven o'clock in the morning, it is highly likely that all these roads into the town were occupied at the Tonman Ditch not by royalist soldiers but by Yorkists. Thus, the ditch (such as it was in 1455) was in the hands of the attackers. This obviously made the eastern approaches to the town passable, if highly dangerous to Yorkist troops, due to the 'funnelling effect' that any bridgehead or narrow road crossing would have had on masses of men with one purpose in mind.

Evidently, according to contemporary sources, the Earl of Warwick's contingents were not prevented from reaching the houses abutting the eastern side of St Peter's Street during the battle, therefore, even allowing for an early occupation of the defences by detachments of royalist soldiers, the Tonman Ditch was almost certainly crossable at most points along its length.

However, more difficult for the Yorkist troops to negotiate were the 'town backsides' and the strip fields beyond the Tonman Ditch. These were more than likely individual plots of land incorporating ridge and furrow and bounded by dykes,

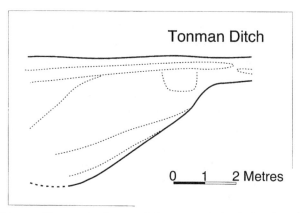

27 Diagram of the excavation dug across the Tonman Ditch. (Author's Collection)

drains and hedges that would have broken up the cohesion of any advancing body of soldiers. Similarly, beyond the second track or ditch known as the Houndspath, there was a maze of house gardens, and these were likely a veritable tangle of vegetation, outbuildings and obstacles, dividing up the properties and inns that lined the eastern side of St Peter's Street. That the numerous rows of jettied houses provided a complete defensive cordon around the king's forces and the marketplace is conjectural. However, it is certain that such dwellings were tightly knitted together, as sources claim that buildings frustrated the main Yorkist attack. Therefore, apart from some weak points (undoubtedly shored up by the king's men previously), the town, and especially the marketplace, was wholly defensible.

By the same token, any advancing Yorkist troops would have been screened by the frontages of the houses, and during an attack on the town, it was here, if anywhere, that a breakthrough might be contemplated and exploited. It was the same story all along the spine of the town, as far as St Peter's Church at the extreme northern end of St Albans. The eastern defences and the broken ground beyond the Tonman Ditch were hazards that any commander with the aim of occupation would have to navigate. It was a problem that could lead to stalemate, where the

larger army was only as formidable as the gap or frontage it tried
to assault. And this is likely what happened to the Yorkist army
when it was faced with a blockaded marketplace, with barriers,
and only certain areas where manoeuvrability was possible.

According to the sources, when the king and his entourage
reached the top of Holywell Hill on the morning of the battle,
there was no immediate alarm or orders to arm. No doubt,
a lookout was ordered to climb the narrow steps of the clock
tower to keep a watchful eye on the Yorkist army located in Key
Field, 'a cross-bow shot'[7] away, but apart from this, the king's
army was not embattled immediately. Indeed, most of Henry's
men were not 'harnessed' (in armour), either before or, to some
extent, during the battle. The complicated process would have
taken some time to complete. Still, given warning of York's
forces in the vicinity the night before, we cannot say the royal
entourage was caught napping, and most knights, including the
king, would probably have been armed by pages before they
marched that morning.

The clock tower at St Albans is a unique survival of the medieval period; consisting of five floors, it would have provided the
perfect observation post to view the approaches to the town.
The two staircases in the tower, one entered from the street
below and continuing the full height of the building, and the
second running from the ground-floor room and reaching the
second floor before joining the other, allowed its curfew bell,
called *Gabriel*, to be rung and the clock to be maintained independently. This meant that any attack by the Yorkists from the
east would have been instantly seen and acted upon by the king's
men, although at that time, and judging by the attitude of the
Duke of Buckingham, nothing was further from their minds.

The shambles (marketplace) below the clock tower was likely
a maze of structures and stalls in 1455, extending from High
Street to the base of St Peter's Street. Embracing an inner laby-
rinth of narrow alleys and some more permanent shops, the
area would have been the scene of much fighting and confusion

28 Clock Tower, St Albans (built in 1405). The only surviving medieval town belfry in England. (Courtesy of Geoffrey Wheeler)

during the battle. Market traders were encouraged to cram as many diverse products as possible into one relatively small area. Therefore, the main triangular plot of lean-to properties and wooden dwellings, which later evolved into modern alleys and lanes, was a hazard to all that entered except the townsfolk about their business. Critically, in 1455 this area directly affected troop movement and would have created great problems for those soldiers who chose to fight or were forced to flee.

Central to the marketplace, but at its southern end and in front of the clock tower, was situated an Eleanor (or Great) Cross, one of a series of impressive memorials built to commemorate the resting places of Queen Eleanor's body on its journey from Harby, near Nottingham, to Westminster, in 1290. One of twelve monuments erected by order of Edward I, the Queen's

Cross at St Albans had become a focal point of the town and
clearly served as a place for orators to speak and insurgents to
vent their anger on the political and religious matters of the day.

Clearly, on the day of battle, the more astute inhabitants of
St Albans would have vacated the town or chose to stay indoors.
Also, the sight of a large army close by, armed and ready for war,
would have been as much of a concern to the local population as
it was to the king's host when they arrived on the outskirts of the
town. There is no evidence of whether the Yorkists were supplied with food directly from St Albans, but it is highly unlikely.
What is recorded, however, is that the Yorkist lords succeeded in
keeping their men at a safe distance beyond the town's boundary
(as was usual practice while campaigning), which was to influence later how the armies were positioned and indeed dictated
how the battle began.

Further clues about the topography of St Albans can be found
in the *Paston Letters*, which mention that three inns were once
situated on the east side of what is now Chequer Street (then
an extension of Holywell Hill). These inns were called the
Chequer, the (Cross or Peter's) Keys and the Castle Inn at the
time of the battle, and it is these three ancient landmarks which
provide the most tangible evidence of links to the fighting. The
Castle Inn is famous for its link with the Duke of Somerset's
death. The Chequer and Keys for the place where the Yorkists
broke through into the marketplace, although there is some vari-
ance where these inns stood in 1455. F.G Kitton *c.*1895 described
them in *The Old Inns of St Albans*:

Behind the 'Key' was the famous Keyfield, where, in 1455,
the First Battle of St. Albans was begun, and that the inn itself
existed at this early period is proved by a document dated that
same year ... here we find the inn described as 'le Key in le
Hyghstrete opposite the Market where Wool is sold' while
mention is also made of 'a messuage called le Saryzynhede'
in the said street.' In a document, dated 1477, mention is

made of 'la Key' opposite 'le Rome Lande.' Perhaps the earliest reference to the inn with the sign of the 'Cross Keys' is
in a deed relating to a lawsuit which came before the Court
of Exchequer in 1485, where it is described as a tenement
called 'Le Cross Keys' ... The Chequers in Holywell-hill
originally comprised that portion of the ascent now familiar
to us as Chequer-street. The latter name was derived from
the Chequer Inn which was also known as 'The Chequers' or
'Exchequers'...What may be considered as the earliest reference to the 'Chequers' is to be found in the Marian Survey
of 1556...Concerning another ancient hostel that flourished
in close proximity to the 'Bell' and which bore the sign of
the 'Castle' there is but little recorded. I think there can be
no doubt that it stood either at the north or south corner of
the west end of Victoria Street (then called Shropshire Lane)
– that is, either on the spot where the business premises of
Mr Odell and Mr Kingham stand, or at the opposite corner –
Mr Hodding's offices. In Benjamin Hare's map, 1634, we find
the name of the inn written across the west end of what is
now Victoria Street, so this map (the only one, I believe, in
which the name appears) does not solve the difficulty. Expert
opinion, however, seems to favour the first-mentioned site
as that of the Castle, which Shakespeare has immortalised in
describing the incident of the death of the Duke of Somerset
(during the first battle of St. Albans), who fell early in the
fight, in the doorway of the Castle Inn. [8]

In the medieval period, much of present-day Chequer Street
was known as the Malt Market or Malt Cheaping, with the
upper end designated the Hay Market. The Keys then was situated at the top of Holywell Hill, but unfortunately, its site has
now been obliterated by the London turnpike road. However,
the location of the Chequer Inn can be accurately pinpointed.
Even though the original building was demolished, and its position was renamed several times, its location indicates where the

Yorkist troops broke into St Albans marketplace in 1455. Suffice to say that each of these inns had alleyways leading to the rear where stables were sited, and this evidence survives in more than one location in the modern city, especially on the east side of the present Chequer Street and the Christopher Inn in French Row. Therefore, it is apparent that there were several ways an enterprising commander might force his way into the marketplace if any of these 'alleys' were left unguarded or lightly defended.

Beyond the heart of the medieval town, with its marketplace and inns, the broad thoroughfare even now called St Peter's Street stretches north from the Moot Hall to the parish church of the same name. Between the rows of houses that flanked its perfectly aligned course, it is probable that some of the town's market stalls covered this entire area. Also, St Peter's Street was, like the rest of St Albans, not paved in the medieval period due in part to five ponds that existed somewhere along its length, the last one being filled in as late as 1849. These ponds were a significant feature of the medieval town and provided water for animals sold in the marketplace. Short of any verified documentary evidence to pinpoint the place where King Henry raised his standard, the allusion to a place known as 'Goselowe'[9] (formerly Sandeforde) in the *Paston Letters* may point to a small area in St Peter's Street where the king and his household were positioned after they arrived at St Albans. The lengthy negotiations preceding the battle occurred at a barrier near St Peter's Church. Therefore, it is safe to assume that the king, accompanied by his household, were at some point located in St Peter's Street, at a point marked locally by a filled-in water feature (Sandeforde), and not, according to some historians, in the marketplace or opposite Long Butts Lane (Boselawe) – itself a spelling mistake for Goselowe, rightly corrected by C.L. Kingsford in his edition of the *Paston Letters*.

St Peter's Church marked the northern extent of medieval St Albans and, with its extensive grounds and churchyard abutting the top of St Peter's Street, it was the next largest church

29 St Peter's Church, where most of the dead were interred after the battle. (Author's Collection)

after the abbey. Significantly, it is mentioned in contemporary documents and local tradition as the principal burial ground where casualties from both battles of St Albans were interred. The parish church was one of three churches built by Abbot Ulsinus when he laid out the market town in AD 948, and doubtless, it was here, rather than at the abbey, that the pious Henry VI convened before the battle. Above St Peter's was a medieval manor house called Hall Place (Edmund Westby's house), which has a traditional link with the king as the place he visited before the battle. Although local tradition cannot be fully corroborated (especially the claim that Henry stayed here the night before the battle, when he was, in fact, camped at Watford on the night of 21 May), the above evidence does at least confirm that King Henry was initially much further north of the market area than previously thought. That he did not occupy the marketplace with his troops during negotiations before the battle is a feature of the *Fastolf Relation* mentioned in the next chapter.

At the northern end of the town, at Stone Cross, the road from St Albans eventually turned left from Bowgate to leave the confines of the medieval town below Barnet Wood (now Bernards Heath). Here, one branch of the road continued to Sandridge, and the other turned northwest towards Luton, the latter route being the king's intended line of march to Leicester. If the Yorkist army had not confronted the royal host at St Albans, then the itinerary expected and condoned by the Duke of Buckingham would no doubt have followed this course. After a few hours rest (enough time for the king and his entourage to dine), there is every reason to believe that the royal party would have spent the next night, 22 May, at Luton and not St Albans. Therefore, according to the evidence, it is more likely that it was in the St Peter's Church area, and not in the marketplace, that the king initially 'pygth [pitched] his banner'[10] immediately before the battle; the secondary location of Henry and his household being the site of Goselowe/ Sandeforde. According to the evidence, Goselawe could also denote an actual place name, and we may alternatively describe this as a terrain feature (now lost to history) known as Goose Hill, Goselawe being originally derived from the old English *hlaw* meaning hill, mound or tumulus.

However, it is apparent that after the opposing forces had sighted each other on the morning of 22 May, the key areas of occupation were as follows:

The Yorkist Army

1. All of York's contingents were situated in the vicinity of the Key Field to the east of St Albans, and these troops had been waiting for the king to arrive there since at least seven

o'clock that morning. The slightly elevated position of Key Field meant that the Yorkists could view the royal advance towards St Albans, occupy the London road, and command the Tonman Ditch defences, such as they were. Clearly, the Duke of York did not dare order any of his troops into the town for fear of them becoming uncontrollable, and this restraining action on the perimeter of the town also gave the appearance that the Yorkists were not deliberately blocking King Henry's path or seeming antagonistic towards him. There is also the possibility that some of the Yorkist contingents may have been fronted by rudimentary artillery, 'guns and other'.[11] However, there is no evidence that these were used to bombard the town. Indeed, it would have been foolish for the Yorkists to do so.

The King's Army

1. Evidently, the king and his followers had decided to put some distance between themselves and the abbey precincts once they had entered St Albans. At the northern end of the town, and in St Peter's Street, there was ample space to marshal a small army, and it was here and near the parish church of St Peter that, during negotiations, a 'barrier' was manned by some of the king's troops. According to the evidence, this northerly position was where the various heralds rode back and forth on their diplomatic missions immediately before the battle, and no doubt the king was not very far from these preliminary talks and close to a possible escape route north if his life was in danger.

2. There is also ample evidence to support the theory that a second division of the king's men was positioned in St Albans marketplace. This detachment deliberately blocked the possibility of a Yorkist advance up St Peter's Street from the south, and it was probably these men who

erected the barriers (barricades) across two (possibly three) of the main routes into the centre of the town: namely, at the top of Holywell Hill and at the junction of Shropshire Lane, and near the Castle Inn. Any full-scale advance by the Yorkist army would have been immediately spotted from the clock tower, and the curfew bell tolled to warn the rest of the army if any of these positions were compromised.

3. Before hostilities commenced, and indeed while negotiations were still taking place, we are told that elements of both armies had already begun to skirmish with each other. It is, therefore, apparent that some royal contingents were already manoeuvring and taking independent action with or without their superiors' blessing – clearly the most significant point to discuss when considering how and why the first battle of St Albans began. Apparently, some royal troops were situated near the Tonman Ditch and in the 'town backsides', with the intention firstly of guarding the approaches to the town and secondly to act as skirmishers. However, it is thought these men would have quickly dispersed as the Yorkists 'battles' advanced.

Other Forces

1. It is known that Mowbray herald was with the Duke of York at St Albans and conducted negotiations on his behalf before the battle began. He likely retired to a safer place after talks with the king broke down, although we have no eyewitness statement to the contrary. It is also known that several 'interested parties' were also in the vicinity – namely the Duke of Norfolk (Mowbray herald's master), the Earl of Shrewsbury, Lord Cromwell and Sir Thomas Stanley.[12] This is confirmed by the *Fastolf Relation*, which seems to be a verified and impartial source from a witness who heard from the king that other armed forces 'backing York', or waiting for a

favourable outcome, were close by. These nobles were served by messengers, heralds and the like, including the document's author. Therefore, the battle of St Albans was as much about politics as fighting. Other men had a stake in the outcome, although significant contingents raised by Somerset before the battle were likely too late to participate at St Albans and do not feature in contemporary sources.

Without doubt, the most overlooked aspect of the battle of St Albans has been the respective arrivals of the opposing armies and, consequently, the all-important factor of who commanded the town's defences. However prominent (or insignificant) the Tonman Ditch was in 1455, the fact remains that at least three independent sources claim that the Yorkist army was in the best position to capture this before the arrival of the king's forces that morning. According to the *Stow Relation* in the *Paston Letters*, 'the aforesaid Duke of York abiding in the field aforesaid [Key Field] from seven of the clock in the morning till it

30 The abbey gatehouse where, traditionally, Abbot Whethamstede viewed the battle. (Author's Collection)

was almost ten'[13] had obviously arrived outside the town well
before the king's host. The *Fastolf Relation* has it that 'the king
our sovereign lord arrived at the town of St Albans by eleven
[or at the earliest nine] in the morning',[14] a notable source, given
that this was eyewitness evidence. In this account, the approach
of the Duke of York can be taken both ways. But it is most
likely that because the duke had already placed his troops in the
villages near St Albans on the night of 21 May (according to
Davies' Chronicle), it was he, and not the king, who was in the
better position to advance on the town and capture its defences
at first light. The king's march from Watford that morning was
timed to coordinate with his pre-arranged itinerary of arriving
at St Albans in time for dinner. Therefore, since most sources
state that the battle began at ten o'clock, and *Davies' Chronicle*
reports that the king arrived at 'Saint Albans about nine of the
clock',[15] it follows that there was ample time for York to position his troops for whatever action he deemed prudent. C.A.J.
Armstrong's pioneering account of the battle also supports the
claim that the Yorkist army arrived at St Albans before the king,
stating that *Davies' Chronicle* was 'by far the most independent',[16]
and royalist account of the battle, while correctly stating that
Hertfordshire was a county where the Duke of York enjoyed
some influence. Therefore, unless an unlikely night march of
8 1/2 miles was attempted from Watford, it is more probable
that the king arrived at St Albans at least two hours after the
Duke of York's army.

However, upon seeing the Yorkist troops stationed in Key
Field, the Duke of Buckingham was undaunted. Apart from
his obvious surprise, the town could be fortified, and the roads
were not blocked by Yorkists. Therefore, he decided to put some
distance between him and the rebels, taking up quarters at the
northern end of St Peter's Street near the church of the same
name. York allowed him to do this since his main aim was to
negotiate Somerset's capture (backed by force) and to this end, he
had an impartial herald on hand to convey messages to the king.

Leaving a detachment of troops in the marketplace to protect his rear and placing the remainder of his men at the barrier near St Peter's Church, it is likely that Buckingham (with or without the king's advice) gave the demoted Duke of Somerset command of the former detachment. All that remained now was for Buckingham to play for time until the promised royalist reinforcements arrived at St Albans, although it is apparent from his messages to York that he had no idea where these forces were or if they would fight. Buckingham's initial plan was undoubtedly to conduct a similar deception to that worked against the Duke of York at Dartford or one that might appeal to his loyalty and frustrate his will to attack due to overwhelming odds. It was a dangerous royal gamble destined to fail due to the double-edged sword of complacency and mistrust, and one whose bloodthirsty echo would reverberate across the pages of British history.

Five

'I Shall Destroy Them, Every Mother's Son'

The history of 'The first journey [battle] of Saint Albans'[1] has come down to us through the survival of several independent accounts written soon after the event. These newsletters, private correspondence and chronicles were examined and noted by C.A.J. Armstrong in the first comprehensive study of the battle, published in 1960, and included in the May edition of the *Bulletin of the Institute of Historical Research*. Entitled 'Politics and the Battle of St Albans',[2] Armstrong's work provided new insights into the battle and touched upon some aspects of the negotiations not previously covered elsewhere. As with any ground-breaking research, subsequent accounts of the battle owe much to Armstrong's work. However, my reassessment of St Albans differs from the standard because it focuses mainly on the military aspects of the encounter and the battlefield anatomy. The resulting research explains why several inconsistencies have been misunderstood and perpetuated by historians, and it offers a new scenario concerning the deaths of the Duke of Somerset, the Earl of Northumberland and Lord Clifford, who were slain during the fighting.

Another important work that embraces the battle's politics and opens a window into official documents is an article by M.A. Hicks. In his 'Propaganda and the First Battle of St Albans', published by *Nottingham Medieval Studies* in 2000,[3] Armstrong's work is taken a stage further, and the possibility of a Yorkist cover-up after the battle becomes strikingly obvious. Hicks also lends weight to the claim that the battle of St Albans was the first major battle of the civil wars and not simply a skirmish in the street.

By bringing the military aspects into greater focus, it is hoped that my work adds another link to the chain by addressing the ongoing debate of who was responsible for causing the fighting, who initiated the resulting blood feud, and, more importantly, how official government documents covered up cold-blooded crimes. Clearly, if the truth about the battle had been exposed by the defeated in the council chamber soon after the fighting had ended, the next bout of warfare would have occurred much earlier than at Blore Heath in 1459. Indeed, it is much to the credit of the survivors of St Albans and the bereaved families of the nobles slain there that a hostile reaction was deferred for so long.

31 Milanese sallet helmet, 1440–1450. (© The Board of Trustees of the Armouries)

As with any significant historical event, there are conflict-
ing accounts about what occurred on Thursday, 22 May 1455.
Indeed, some carefully prepared propaganda was disseminated,
chiefly by the Yorkists, soon after the battle ended. The subsequent smokescreen helped to distort the truth about the battle
in favour of the Duke of York and his supporters and place the
blame for the whole episode squarely on the shoulders of the
Duke of Somerset, then dead, and some of his followers who
were still in hiding. This 'official' Yorkist propaganda was contained in the *Parliamentary Pardon*, a document enacted at the
session of parliament dated 9–31 July 1455, the significance of
which is fully covered by Armstrong and Hicks in their respective works. Armstrong's opening paragraph of 'Politics and the
Battle of St Albans' lists the five main contemporary sources he
used to trace the events of 22 May and the way they differed
in content:

> Battles are the commonest subject matter for newsletters in
> the later Middle Ages; and because of the number of newslet-
> ters reporting the first battle of St Albans it should be the best
> known of the Wars of the Roses. Taken together these news-
> letters form a substantial body of evidence and require some
> individual examination. For ease of reference, they will be
> designated arbitrarily as follows: 'Stow Relation', 'Phillipps
> Relation', 'Letter to the Archbishop of Ravenna', 'Dijon
> Relation', and 'Fastolf Relation'.[4]

Armstrong explains in detail these essential sources in his work.
However, for ease of use and reference, here are the main points
and conclusions he made about the cornerstones of his research:

1. *Stow Relation* (Appendix 1). Printed by John Stow in 1580,
   from an original text not greatly dissimilar to a contemporary manuscript among the Stoner papers. The Stow
   edition has a longer casualty list and is fuller than the Stoner

account regarding the king's clemency towards the defeated. It is reasonably accurate in local detail, but the pamphlet was biased in favour of the Yorkists, and sadly its date is unknown. However, the last event mentioned is the decision to summon parliament on 9 July, with writs being sealed on 26 May 1455, therefore, it is contemporary with the battle.

2. *Phillipps Relation* (Appendix 2). Published by J. Gairdner in the *Paston Letters* from an original document in the Phillipps collection, now in the British Library. It was sent to one of the Paston family, or perhaps to Sir John Fastolf, and the account again favours the Yorkist side, placing the responsibility for the battle on specific individuals who fought for the king, namely, 'The Lord Clifford, Ralph Percy, Thorpe, Tresham and Joseph'.[5] It was written between late Friday evening, 23 May, and the following Thursday, 29 May, the last recorded event being the king's return to London at six o'clock in the evening on the former. The battle is spoken of as taking place on the 'Thursday before', and interestingly, the Duke of Somerset is not named as one of the 'solicitors and causers of the field'[6] in this account.

3. *Letter to the Archbishop of Ravenna* (Appendix 3). From the *Calendar of State Papers in Milan,* this account is only helpful to date the battle and convey the interest felt on the continent regarding the outcome of the feud between the dukes of Somerset and York. However, the postscript, written on 3 June 1455, gives important information regarding the manner of Somerset's death and the reaction of King Henry to the Yorkist pardon. It is dated from Bruges on 31 May 1455.

4. *Dijon Relation.* See translation from original French (Appendix 4). Published by Boudot from a manuscript in the *Archives de la Cote d'Or* at Dijon. This version, described by Armstrong, was a copy of an original document finished on Tuesday, 27 May (probably in England), as indicated by the allusion to the disappearance of the Earl of Wiltshire. It does

not trace the developments of the battle from the Yorkist point of view; therefore, it may be construed as being biased towards the royalists. Its author is unknown.

5. *Fastolf Relation*. See translation from original French (Appendix 5). An English newsletter which was in the collection of William Worcester, who served Sir John Fastolf as a secretary and councillor. The letter was written by a servant of Fastolf, who he referred to as *mon tres honnoure seigneur et maistre* on the reverse of the last sheet.[7] There is no doubt that the author was an eyewitness to the events immediately before the battle, and his preoccupation with titles and the duties of heralds suggests that he was a pursuivant of Sir John Fastolf, probably attached to Mowbray herald (herald to the Duke of Norfolk). Clearly, the newsletter was composed by someone accompanying the Yorkist army who finished writing his account somewhere other than the battlefield, given that it contains no details of the actual fighting in the town. The letter also represents the earliest dispatch to leave St Albans before the fighting commenced and is highly important regarding local knowledge and unbiased opinion.

Following on from the earliest contemporary accounts of the battle is the version of events chronicled by John Whethamstede, Abbot of St Albans, who was on the spot to record the events in his home town (Appendix 6). However, as previously stated, Whethamstede was generally unconvincing in his rendering of history and, along with his habit of putting words into the mouths of the protagonists, he probably did not actually see what occurred just outside his precinct walls on the day in question. No doubt, Whethamstede played an active, if self-interested, part in the aftermath of the battle, but clearly, the important concern from a military standpoint is that the actual fighting is not covered by him – although he could have spoken to an eyewitness. As regards other contemporary sources, *Giles' Chronicle*, written between 1450 and 1455, also fails to include the battle from a royalist perspective. And as for the remainder of the chronicles, Armstrong only mentions the brief account by Thomas Gascoigne (1404–58), a Chancellor of Oxford University, who wrote within three years of the battle.[8]

As for later accounts of St Albans, they clearly cannot be dismissed out of hand, even though some included misinterpretations inherited from the original newsletters written days and, in some cases, hours after the event. In fact, the two chronicles known as *Davies' Chronicle* and *Gregory's Chronicle*, both written before 1471, describe some events during the battle that are not included elsewhere, and the chronicle described by C.L. Kingsford as the *Great Chronicle*, or the *London Chronicle*, contains evidence that clearly states who was responsible for opening the hostilities. The portion of the *London Chronicle* recording 'The first field of Saint Albans' and dated 'Anno xxxiii'[9] of King Henry's reign, is therefore wholly contemporary and, although the battle was later given its title by another writer (presumably after the second battle was fought in 1461), the details recording the part played by the Earl of Warwick are particularly scathing and pro-royalist in tone.

No doubt, all the above sources contain essential clues as to what occurred on the day in question, but the key to unlocking what set of circumstances caused the transition from mediation to violence at St Albans centres more on the personalities, suspicions, persuasions and ambitions of the nobles under the Duke of York's command. Two very different aims were pursued by the Yorkists after the negotiations before the battle were abruptly interrupted, and to follow this situation through, we must adopt the stance of neutral observers. In short, we must balance the biased source material, and disentangle the facts from not only what was included in the above accounts but also from what was left out.

We have no way of knowing what the weather was like on Thursday, 22 May 1455, but given that none of the letters or chronicles mention adverse conditions, we can assume that the

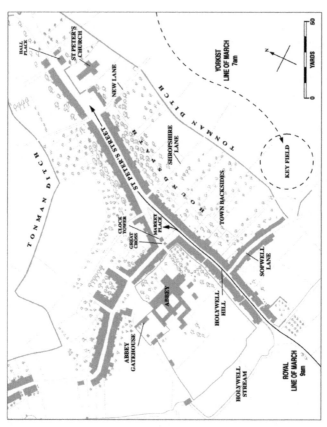

32 *The first battle of St Albans, 1455. Approach marches on the morning of 22 May. (Author's Collection)*

morning to the early afternoon was clear and temperate. Sunrise was about seven o'clock at that time of year, and it has been documented that the king's host had marched over 8 miles to reach St Albans that morning. On the other hand, the Yorkists had been in position in the Key Field since approximately seven o'clock, and doubtless, the 3,000 men under York's command had taken breakfast in camp or the surrounding countryside. Given the time of the king's arrival, there was no reason why the Tonman Ditch would not have been defended by Yorkist soldiers. Most of these were more than likely standing down in Key Field, waiting for the king and his entourage to appear from the south. Therefore, it is supposed that the king's men were about to eat once they had reached St Albans, although they may have foraged on the march from Watford. In both cases, however, it should be noted that neither side would have gained any significant advantage from ingesting more than the other, and doubtless, the 2,000 men in the king's host would not have gone hungry in the town while negotiations were taking place at the barriers.

As regards the Yorkist version of events, the *Stow Relation* is adamant that once the king arrived at St Albans, he 'pighte [pitched] his banner at a place called Goselowe in Saint Peter's Street, which place afore time passed was called Sandeforthe, and commanded in strong wise to keep the wards and barriers of the same town'.[10] The *Phillipps Relation* also clearly states (with blatant Yorkist bias) that 'The inony [enemy's] battle was in the marketplace and the kings standard was pight [pitched], the king being present with these lords, whose names follow ... '[11] It is, therefore, more than likely that before negotiations began, King Henry and his household men were in the open somewhere in St Peter's Street and that at least some of his men were ordered to guard the approaches to the town as a precautionary measure. As C.A.J. Armstrong noted, the above events are closely linked and may be tarnished with half-truths regarding what was said during the negotiations. However, aside from being outwardly

hostile towards the 'enemy battle' in the marketplace, all the
above statements of fact are no doubt authentic. Likewise, the
way the Duke of York marshalled his army in the fields around
St Albans can be ascertained. The writer of *Davies' Chronicle*
believes York's stance was in no respect passive, in that 'they [the
Yorkists] besieged the town about, and sent to the king beseeching him that he would send out unto them their mortal enemy,
Edmund Duke of Somerset'.[12]

Given that it was not possible for 2,000 of the king's men
to maintain the defence of the whole eastern perimeter of
the town, the above orders given by the king (or the Duke of
Buckingham) indicate that some royal troops were ordered to
advance along the approaches to the town towards the waiting
Yorkists. Despite everything, it was not known precisely what
York's intentions were, aside from his well-known open hostility towards Somerset. Therefore, we may ask whether it would
have been prudent for the king to appear negligent or submis-
sive when faced with the threat of an army embattled nearby. In
reply to this offensive manoeuvre, the Yorkist soldiers, according to the *Fastolf Relation*, 'did not enter the town of St Albans,
but remained in attendance near the town, within a crossbow's
shot'[13] – a clear indication that before ten o'clock in the morning the Yorkist contingents were still under orders and had been
primarily charged with holding the Tonman Ditch perimeter.

As for royalists within the town, it was at this point that a
herald was dispatched to the Duke of York. Although only the
writer of the *Fastolf Relation* records in detail the names and
duties of all the various heralds at St Albans, this information
is presented in a uniquely unbiased way, wholly in keeping
with a report by a neutral observer. It is also interesting to note
how the tone of the dialogue (and the seriousness of the situation changed) after each successive message was received and
dispatched back to its master. If taken one stage further, it is
apparent that on the royalist side at least, political alliances and
veiled threats helped intensify the talks considerably, while

a conflict of interests and a marked topographical split in the king's forces are exposed to view. Following the *Fastolf Relation* and using the official dialogue offered in the *Stow Relation* as verification, it is, therefore, possible to give a unique and detailed interpretation of what took place before the fighting began. As stated earlier, the *Stow Relation* was publicised by the Yorkists after the battle of St Albans had been won, and it is reminiscent of the *Parliamentary Pardon* – the Yorkists' official acquittal for what occurred there. However, the remonstrations of the Duke of York and the replies from the 'king' are consistent with how other sources[14] viewed York's motives and how the duke never concealed his intention of using force if Somerset was not released into his custody. In the *Stow Relation*, the tone of the royal replies to York's various demands had to be made to sound both official, on the one hand, and defamatory, on the other, to those (namely Somerset) who the Yorkists said, had concealed and perverted their earlier messages. Apart from some leading nobles and those who had become casualties at St Albans, most, including the king himself, were still alive after the event; therefore, at least the gist of Yorkist propaganda had to sound authentic and not insulting to the king, or the story of what occurred there would simply not hold water.

33 Ballock dagger, 1400–1500, excavated from the Thames. (© The Board of Trustees of the Armouries)

However, a more reliable source of information was supplied by the officials whose job was to deliver and receive

important messages between contending forces on the battlefield. Incontestable proof of the words spoken at St Albans is
key to our understanding of why the battle occurred, and this is
supplied by the testimony of the military heralds and their pur-
suivants who were present on 22 May 1455.

The duties of fifteenth-century heralds echoed what their
predecessors had done before them, although we may wonder
what their job entailed. Aside from their more well-documented
appearances at state events, heraldic courts, ceremonials, tour-
naments and the like, military heralds were called upon to
deliver messages between warring parties and nations. They
also recorded battles in heraldic literature, arranged ransoms
and numbered those who were killed, especially the nobility.
Overall casualties were estimated, but they were verified by
other heralds and appeared in letters and official documentation.
Heralds even arranged for the dead to be buried or transported
to nearby churches. Most heralds and 'Kings of Arms' served a
specific master, essentially the king, or a named noble who gave
them a name, sometimes denoting their areas of influence. And,
although contemporary evidence for the civil wars is limited, for
St Albans, there is a detailed record of their involvement thanks
to a pursuivant employed by Sir John Fastolf.

As a notable example of a fifteenth-century herald at work,
John Smert (Smart) was Garter King of Arms from April 1450
until he died in 1478, but due to a lack of evidence surrounding his
whereabouts, it is not known if he was present at St Albans in 1455.
However, we know that Smart was the son-in-law of William
Bruges, the Garter King of Arms who held the title before him,
and therefore he may have been attending the king, although there
is no proof of this from any source. Smart's parentage is unknown,
but he owned land in Mitcheldean, Gloucestershire, and his family
may have been from that county. He was probably the 'Guyenne
pursuivant' sent to Burgundy in 1444 and on various diplomatic
missions to France after this date. Smart was employed at £40 a
year in 1462 and acted as an emissary in Scotland and Burgundy,

where he attended the marriage of Princess Margaret to Charles the Bold in 1468. 'Mr Garter Smart', is also mentioned in Edward IV's 1475 muster, along with other heralds who sailed to France with the king. And he was the herald sent to defy King Louis before Edward IV sailed with his invasion force, although the king achieved little in the way of military success.[15]

Apart from specific diplomatic tasks, the main preoccupation of heralds in the Middle Ages was controlling the art of heraldry and recording coats of arms for hereditary reasons. Therefore, it is understandable why heralds took an intense interest in battles and casualties like those incurred at St Albans. Heralds were essentially non-combatants and swore to tell the truth and live clean lives. They were known for their impartiality and the exacting nature of their work. However, the fact that they avoided actual violence like the plague is one reason the narrative of Fastolf's man breaks off at a point where staying on the battlefield might have proved hazardous to an official whose job was only to observe and record.

However, aside from the obvious restrictions, the *Fastolf Relation*, written by an unnamed herald or pursuivant, includes unique information concerning who conducted the various attempts to avert bloodshed at St Albans. The evidence proves the meetings were difficult, and this provides fascinating reading from an on-the-spot eyewitness to the negotiations, who was eager to record the actual words spoken by the various parties and even clarification if their messages were unclear.

On 22 May, according to Fastolf's pursuivant, he was stationed in the Key Field with the Yorkists, and it was clearly Somerset who sought to intimidate the Duke of York first:

[And] the Duke of Somerset sent Lesparre, pursuivant of arms [of] my lord Duke of Exeter, to the said Duke of York to command him in the name and on behalf of the king, our lord, that he and all his company should quit at once and withdraw, on pain of their allegiance and breach of honour, and all being false to the king, our lord. And as soon as the said pursuivant was gone, once more came before my lord of York, Buckingham the herald, and in his company Joyeulx, pursuivant to my lord of Bonville, and they delivered the same message and order as had done pursuivant Lesparre. Thereupon, my lord of York ordered the herald and pursuivant to swear upon their duty, to say and declare to him whether this order was spoken by the king, our lord, himself, and whether they had come upon his explicit orders. And they answered that they had not, and that my lord of Buckingham and my lord of Somerset had sent them to say they were coming from before the king, our lord, having received this order from him. To which my lord [York] answered, 'tell the king, our lord, and his cousin Buckingham, that I have come here to settle my petitions and requests, and do loyal service to the king, our lord. And if I knew any in my company who would want to act to the contrary, I would punish him myself, as an example to others.'[16]

Given that the order for the Yorkists to depart was delivered by the pursuivant of the absent Duke of Exeter (the latter also known as *Dominus de Sparre*), and accepting the fact that Exeter had previously been the partner of Lord Egremont (a mortal enemy of the Nevilles), it takes little imagination to conceive what that message must have meant to the earls of Warwick and Salisbury. However, aside from the obvious challenge to York and his allies, using both inferred and apparent threats, what occurred next was highly peculiar and lacked coordination. Indeed, why did Buckingham herald and Joyeulx (Bonville's pursuivant) arrive before York bearing the same message as before? What caused this strange repetition to occur? Clearly, the message was the same from both Somerset and Buckingham, but surely it was Buckingham and not Somerset who was in overall command of the king's forces at St Albans? A situation that suggests there was either a lack of communication between

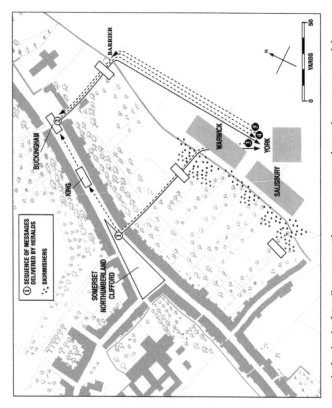

34 The first battle of St Albans, 1455. The opening positions during the negotiations and the preliminary skirmishing. (Author's Collection)

the two dukes in the town or that, in fact, the two messages were
sent out from different locations by mistake.

Given Somerset's dangerous position and previous demo-
tion in favour of Buckingham, the first message sent to York
was doubtless an attempt to assert some of his authority; after
all, neither the writer of the *Fastolf Relation* nor the Duke of
York had any idea that Somerset had been replaced. Even York
was confused by the similar communications and asked for
clarification from the heralds as to whether these were actually the king's words or those of the lords acting on his behalf.
Evidently, after hearing the truth, York decided to take an
equally threatening measure of his own and bring to Somerset
and Buckingham's attention that the Yorkists had reinforcements close at hand. However, instead of using his personal
herald to deliver a message to the king, the duke, according to
the *Fastolf Relation*,

> had Mowbray, herald of my lord of Norfolk, called at once
> and bade him go before the king our lord, to tell him that he
> commended himself and his noble and good grace, as humbly
> as any man could do, to his sovereign lord, as well as to all the
> lords in his company. And he beseeched and implored him,
> very humbly, that it might please his kind grace to grant him
> the petitions, requests and demands that he had in the past sent
> to him, by my lord of Fauconberg and others in his company.[17]

York's humble request to the king via Mowbray herald was, in
fact, a repetition of his many earlier pleas for justice, first used
at Dartford and, more recently, carried to the king by various
messengers, including Lord Fauconberg, who were with the
royalists in the town. However, much stronger language was
used by the Duke of York in the *Stow Relation,* and although
this account was Yorkist propaganda after the event, the tone,
as pointed out by Armstrong, could be a truthful record of the
message carried to the king by Mowbray herald:

The words in writing by the Duke of York to the king.

Please it unto your excellent grace, Richard, Duke of York, to take him as your true liegeman and humble subject. And to consider and tender at the reverence of God and in the way of charity, the true intent of my coming and to be a good and gracious sovereign unto me and all other your true liegemen, which that with all their power and might will be ready to live and die with you in your right and to do all things as shall like your majesty royal to command us, if it be to the worship of the crown of England and the welfare of this your noble realm. Moreover, gracious lord, please it unto your majesty royal of your great goodness and rightwiseness to incline your will to hear and feel the rightwise part of us your true subjects and liegemen. First praying and beseeching to our sovereign Christ Jesus, of his high and mighty power, to give the virtue of prudence and that through the mediation and prayer of that glorious martyr Saint Alban give you very knowledge of our truths, and to know the intent of our assembling at this time, for God that is in heaven knoweth our intent is rightful and true. And therefore, we pray unto that mighty lord these words, *Domine sis clipeus defensionis nostræ.* Wherefore, gracious lord, please it your majesty royal to deliver such as we will accuse, and they to have like as they have deserved, and this done, you [will] be honourably worshipped as most rightful king and our true governor. And if we should now at this time be promised, as afore this time is not unknown have been promises broken which hath been full faithfully promised, and thereupon great oaths sworn, we will not now cease for no such promises nor other till we have them which have deserved death, or else we will die therefore.[18]

Undoubtedly, the treachery at Dartford and how Somerset had manufactured York's submission to the king were primary concerns of all those nobles who witnessed the debacle firsthand, including the Nevilles, who had acted as mediators between the two parties. However, as York watched Mowbray herald gallop towards the town to negotiate with the same men who had decided his fate at Dartford, it must have been apparent to all the Yorkist lords that this might become a repeat performance or, worse, a misrepresentation of the duke's words to the king. However, the *Fastolf Relation* is explicit that Duke Richard's message was delivered to King Henry in person:

> After these things being said to the king our lord, by Mowbray herald, he answered that he had not seen these petitions, and bade him go to my lord of Buckingham saying that he had entrusted him for this day to give answer to all matters that should be answered in his name. Likewise, when Mowbray came before my lord of Buckingham and said and declared his full message, my lord of Buckingham answered to him that it was true that the king our lord had not seen these petitions and requests yet and that he himself would soon show them in diligence to the king, our lord, and would send the answer made to them back to my lord of York by Buckingham herald.[19]

According to this important evidence, York's various petitions and requests had not been handed to the king after all. Buckingham knew this was the case because he had been entrusted with the king's authority in place of Somerset. However, if this is true, and there is no reason to doubt its authenticity, why had York's previous petitions been concealed from the king, and why had York's messengers, including Lord Fauconberg, not persisted in their errand to exonerate his kinsmen from committing treason? Obviously, the king was so shocked by Mowbray herald's words that he instantly questioned their secrecy with Buckingham. Therefore, the answer to this confusion is tantalisingly simple and in keeping with how Buckingham had acted on the march to St Albans – namely, he was in charge and was playing for time. And this

35 Garter stall plate of William Neville, Lord Fauconberg, who was caught on the side opposing the rest of his family during the battle. (Courtesy of Geoffrey Wheeler)

is doubly evident in Buckingham's words to Mowbray herald when he spoke to him at the barrier located somewhere near St Peter's Church,

> [Buckingham said] 'You will commend me to my brothers-in-law, York and Salisbury, to my nephew Warwick, and his brother Norfolk, in case he should be in their company, as you say he is nearby, that is to say that they can clearly be seen, since the king is present, and they will see his own person and banner on the field, as they withdraw to Barnet or Hatfield, for one night, waiting for some appointment to be made, or one or two men of state and honour to be sent before one to speak with them.' Thereupon the herald asked him, 'My lord, please you bid me something else for this time?' and he [Buckingham] answered: 'Yes, I want you to commend me to my brother Norfolk and tell him that we are so next of kin

that if he had a daughter and I had one, we would not marry each other's daughter without a licence from the Pope, and furthermore, he married my sister, that I beseech him to have out of his heart all melancholy thoughts, wrath, and anger for this time, and the king will be grateful to him, and take him into better grace.' This being said, Mowbray herald asked him [Buckingham] again: 'My lord, please you bid me more to say before my lords,' and he [Buckingham] answered: 'Yes, we want everyone to know that we have come here to support no one, nor for any other cause else, but to be in the company of the king, our lord, as we are rightfully bound to, and as is meet.' Thereupon the herald took his leave and returned before my lord of York to whom he delivered his report, as afore stated.[20]

Buckingham was, therefore, fearful that the Duke of Norfolk and his contingents might arrive in the vicinity at any moment. Given that he had no direct intelligence, he wished York to depart and conduct negotiations from a less threatening position, obviously referring to family ties for no other reason than to dissuade Norfolk, via his herald, from supporting the Yorkist cause. However, the *Stow Relation* is unique in providing a more forceful royal reply to York's demands, and this pro-Yorkist version of events reveals just as much as it conceals. Interestingly, in this account, the words spoken by the king, this time, appear to be from the mouth of an archetypal medieval monarch whose intention was to punish traitors rather than negotiate with them:

The answer by the king to the Duke of York.
I, King Henry, charge and command that no manner persons of what degree, estate or condition that ever he be, abide not but that they avoid the field and nought to be so hardy to make resistance against me in my own realm. For I shall know what traitor dare be so bold to raise any people in my own land, where through I am in great distress and heaviness.

Be that faith I owe unto Saint Edward and unto the crown
of England, I shall destroy them every mother's son. And
they [will] be hanged, drawn and quartered that maybe taken
afterwards of them in example to make all such traitors to
beware for to make any rising of people within my own land
and so traitorously to abide their king and governor. And for
a conclusion, rather than they shall have any lord that here is
with me at this time, I shall this day for their sake in this quarrel myself live and die.[21]

These words were obviously intended not only to caution the
Duke of York but also to strike terror into the hearts of all those
men who were prepared to support him.

However, the truth is that the whole of the *Stow Relation* may
be nothing more than Yorkist propaganda intended to support
the story that important messages were concealed from the king
by Somerset and others. As for the Duke of York, this left him
with no other course of action but to extract his enemy by force.
Either way, York's efforts to respond to the king 'in person' was
proving utterly useless. Nerves were reaching breaking point,
suspicions were running high in both camps, and clearly, all
York's men were aware by now that the king's standard was defi-
antly 'pight' in the town. In short, each man knew that he would
be prosecuted as a traitor if he attacked. Nonetheless, despite
the threat delivered by Buckingham, York was still prepared to
negotiate. According to the *Fastolf Relation*,

my lord of York immediately sent back Mowbray herald, for
a second time, before my lord of Buckingham, begging him
to be willing to go before the king our lord in order to get an
answer to his requests and petitions. Thereupon my lord of
Buckingham answered to the herald that he would with all
possible dispatch send his answer by his herald Buckingham
to my lord of York, which he never did. Likewise, because the
answer was not sent along, the company of my lord of York

was made uneasy, saying, that it was only a delay, which is the reason why my lord of York sent back Mowbray for a third time, before my lord of Buckingham, asking him to answer his petitions, with no more delay. And when Mowbray herald came to the barriere [barrier] of the town of St Albans, which is near the town parish church, he found there, Sir Richard Harrington, Bertin Entwistle and John Hanford knights, Breknok squire and John Swythman who asked the herald what he wanted. And he answered that he wanted to speak to my lord of Buckingham. And they said to him that he would instantly speak with him, and they sent him before my lord of Buckingham, who immediately ordered the master of his household and a knight called Sir Thomas Fynderne to go before Mowbray herald. On his arrival Mowbray told him the reason why he had come. Thereupon he returned to my lord of Buckingham and kept the herald waiting till they came back. After going to my lord of Buckingham, he [Fynderne] returned before the herald and told him that my lord of Buckingham had been before the king our lord and was not decided to give them any answer. Thereupon the herald took his leave.[22]

Clearly, confusion and veiled threats were the order of the day, and aside from what was written in the *Stow Relation* regarding the handing over of Somerset, all of York's frustrations appear to have stemmed from the fact that his petitions and requests were not being delivered to the king in person. He neither knew whether Somerset was coercing the king nor whether Buckingham was deliberately stalling for time. Messages had been delivered to York in the king's name but not from him personally. In fact, on three separate occasions, Buckingham had prevented negotiations from proceeding further, and in the end, he had even resorted to using other intermediaries like Sir Thomas Fynderne to act as go-betweens when Mowbray herald arrived at the town barrier near St Peter's Church. Buckingham's

36 Seal of Humphrey
Stafford, Duke of
Buckingham. (Courtesy of
Geoffrey Wheeler)

ill-advised delay and his warnings to both the absent Duke of
Norfolk and the frustrated Duke of York (especially his request
that the Yorkists withdraw their troops to Barnet or Hatfield for
the night) must have rankled with York's pride and the Nevilles
patience. In short, all the above restrictions, and the inference
that royalist reinforcements might be close at hand, caused York
to act more forcefully. The frustration that he must have felt,
given that the Dartford affair was still a recent memory, likely
put him in no doubt that the king was yet again being poorly
served by his councillors. The negotiations were at a crisis point,
and because of this, there was now only one course of action
open to York. He must seek out the king personally or risk
being misunderstood and charged with treason again.

As Mowbray herald returned with his report from the direction of St Peter's Church for the last time, 'he found my lord of
York and all his company coming towards the town of St Albans,
and the herald gave the answer to my lord of York. Thereupon
[York] replied, 'therefore we must do what we can do.'[23]

Six

'A Warwick! A Warwick!'

According to the not wholly impartial *Dijon Relation*, the first battle of St Albans began 'on the stroke of ten hours in the morning'.[1] In the *Stow* and *Phillipps Relation*, there is agreement that fighting took place between eleven and twelve o'clock, while the former states that the Duke of York waited in Key Field 'from seven of the clock in the morning until it was almost ten of the clock without any stroke smitten on either part'.[2] Therefore, the sources agree on approximate timings, given that other chronologies of the period are rarely so detailed. However, the evidence also indicates that at least one hour is not accounted for, which upon investigation, extends the duration of the battle and explains when the fighting at St Albans actually began.

Before ten o'clock, the sources indicate that neither side was involved in hostilities and that negotiations were in progress. But did some fighting occur between ten and eleven o'clock (the missing hour)? Was perfect discipline maintained between the two sides while the heralds rode back and forth with their messages? What exactly happened in that crucial hour, and at what point did the main assault on St Albans begin? Thankfully

the *Dijon Relation* provides the answer, claiming that some skirmishing occurred while both sides tried to avert bloodshed. But
was this violence triggered by some event, or was the armed
bickering inevitable, considering the rivalry and proximity of
the two sides?

Evidently, during that morning, there had been various troop
deployments, not only to capture ground from which an attack
might be launched but also to occupy areas that might be better
defended or from which negotiations might be conducted.
No doubt Yorkist soldiers were, due to their early arrival at
St Albans, in command of the Tonman Ditch perimeter and its
three eastern crossing points: Sopwell Lane, Shropshire Lane and
New Lane (Cock Lane). It is also documented that some of the
king's men had been ordered to keep both the wards and the barriers of St Albans secure soon after their arrival at nine o'clock
– a clearly mandatory move, given the importance of the king's
safety and the fact that there was a 'rebel' army only a crossbow
shot away. Similarly, there was a third troop movement that
morning by the royalists towards the northern end of the town
and the St Peter's Church barrier where, according to the *Fastolf
Relation*, Mowbray herald met with the king's men and then the
Duke of York, who later advanced towards this position.

On seeing the embattled Yorkists advancing with banners displayed, the writer of the *Fastolf Relation* probably considered that
negotiations had broken down already, hence the duke's advance.
However, this account breaks off at the critical moment, leaving
us guessing what York meant by his words, 'therefore we must
do what we can do'.[3] Although we may be confident that the
duke meant to seek out the king using force, if necessary, it is a
great pity that the author of the *Fastolf Relation* did not witness
the battle first-hand. However, York's advance from Key Field
is documented by this vital source, and we may be sure that the
duke had already decided, before Mowbray herald's return, that
his peaceable attempts to remove Somerset were over. Indeed,
York's frustrations are abundantly clear by his pre-emptive

advance, and this time, unlike at Dartford, he meant to seek out the king personally, no matter what the cost.

But could something else have prompted York's impetuous advance from Key Field? Had a council of war with the Nevilles condoned an escalation? Were some Yorkist soldiers already edging across the Tonman Ditch while the Duke of York advanced his banners towards St Peter's Church? Was York acting irrationally, as he was wont to do later in his career, by deserting his camp in Key Field and seeking out his enemies without thinking about what might happen? Or had the Yorkists planned a concerted attack between them if negotiations failed, born out of all the frustrations and rivalries of the previous months and years? Evidently, what must now be considered, in conjunction with all the above evidence, are the actions of the Neville contingents and what, if anything, dictated their strategy while negotiations were taking place. Interestingly, the vital lost hour of that fateful morning in May reveals important differences between the Duke of York trying to seek justice, and the ambitions of a new breed of overmighty nobles bent on local survival and revenge at any price.

Firstly, it will be remembered that there had been a long build-up of mutual antagonism and conflict between the Neville and Percy families, the start of which can be traced back to 1453. As discussed, a disparity of wealth and power between the two houses had caused significant outbreaks of violence when the younger Percys took matters into their own hands. The threatening behaviour of Lord Egremont and Sir Richard Percy, who sought to re-establish a degree of Percy autonomy in the north, escalated the conflict. After Heworth Moor, Sir John Neville and his brother Thomas responded by attacking several Percy manors in Yorkshire, and because of the friction between their rival retainers, violence and disorder had flared up in several parts of the county. Law and order broke down further when Henry VI collapsed in 1453, and the failure to curb the disturbances in the north was a crisis the government was slow to address. Another bloodier confrontation at Stamford Bridge was the result of this non-intervention by York acting as protector. However, by 1454 the northern conflict had widened, drawing in the dukes of York and Exeter, and by January of the same year when the king recovered, it was apparent that York and the Neville earls of Salisbury and Warwick had come together as allies following the release of the Duke of Somerset from the Tower. It is also apparent that another private feud between Somerset and Warwick regarding disputed land in Glamorgan had forced the latter to side with York, although before this, Warwick had shown his hand at Topcliffe, where another major battle with the Percys was narrowly avoided. Add to this the fact that York had also sided with the Nevilles when he tried to curb their rivalry with the Percys, and tempers were more than likely at breaking point at St Albans despite York's efforts to mediate with the king.

Therefore, the two main factions that were later to feature so predominantly in the civil wars had been formed long before the first battle of St Albans began, and although, miraculously, northern feuding had remained isolated, it was abundantly clear to both sides that nothing had been settled. As fate would have it, the next encounter between the Nevilles and the Percys would be in the streets of St Albans. Indeed, according to two important sources, the no-man's-land between the town and the Tonman Ditch, known later as the 'town backsides', was already becoming a battleground where long-standing arguments were being contested at the point of a sword. Incredibly, and likely contrary to York's wishes, skirmishing had broken out here while negotiations were taking place, and the *Dijon Relation* is adamant that this had started well before the herald from the king (or Somerset) had arrived to deliver his first scathing message to the Duke of York:

> The reply that was made from the king's side to the said Duke
> of York was that he [the king] was unaware that there were any
> traitors about him were it not for the Duke of York himself who

37 *Richard Neville, Earl of Warwick, from a Victorian glass window at Cardiff Castle. (Courtesy of Geoffrey Wheeler)*

had risen against the crown. And even before this reply came to the Duke of York there began a skirmish before the town by one side and the other. And thus, when the Duke of York had [received] the aforesaid reply the battle became more violent and both sides with banners displayed began to fight.[4]

The above timings give the impression that the main battle began soon after the two messages had been delivered, one to one side and one to the other, which, according to the most authentic version of events described in the *Fastolf Relation*, was certainly not the case. However, the same preliminary skirmishing is also revealed in an independent English source, which incidentally does not attempt to conceal the name of the man who instigated it. According to the *London Chronicle*, after he arrived at St Albans, the king,

> sent certain of his lords desiring him [York] to keep the peace and to depart, but in conclusion while they were treating of the peace, the Earl of Warwick with the march men and others entered the other end of the town and fought against the king's party.[5]

The fact that the Earl of Warwick is named at all regarding this seemingly unchivalrous behaviour is bad enough. However, the implication that his men then assaulted the 'king's party' is undoubtedly wrong and against York's apparent wish to negotiate the release of Somerset into his custody. If this is true, who decided to launch an attack at the other end of the town? What had caused the apparent escalation from skirmishing into an all-out assault, and were both sides drawn into a major conflict by chance or had a coordinated attack been planned right from the start?

From a chronicler or herald's point of view, it may not have been possible to distinguish between these two modes of warfare. Clearly, the timings of Warwick's actions could have been drawn together by the above authors to form a more concise and newsworthy account of the battle at their leisure. Warwick's command of the assault on the town marks him out as the instigator of the battle, although the skirmishing beforehand had evidently started much earlier while negotiations were still progressing. With both sides occupying the town backsides, it is perhaps not surprising that trouble started early that morning, and in this respect, the two opposing forces of Neville and Percy certainly had the opportunity, and the willingness, to mark out their local enemies and set about them with weapons. Under these circumstances, an escalation of private feuding would have been too complicated for either side to control, both nobles and their retainers quite clearly recognising the fact that here was a battleground where they could right the wrongs of the two previous years of rivalry. The fact that Lesparre, the herald of the hated Duke of Exeter, had ominously made his presence known in association with the Duke of Somerset probably did not help matters. Since advertising his authority as Somerset's envoy in the Yorkist camp, it is hardly likely that Warwick welcomed the association of Exeter with Somerset, his enemy in Glamorgan. However, aside from testing York's patience and the Nevilles' powers of restraint, the arrival of Lesparre would no doubt have inadvertently triggered another, far greater concern within the Yorkist command, which was undoubtedly the real reason why the preliminary skirmishing occurred.

Unlike at Dartford, where York had appeared isolated, at St Albans approximately two-thirds of his army consisted of contingents supplied by the Nevilles. This was undoubtedly a great asset and a significant drawback, chiefly because the Nevilles and the Percys had been caught on opposing sides. The catalyst certainly caused an unstable powder keg of emotions to boil over, and in the end, this must have threatened York and Neville unity. As the various heralds rode back and forth with messages containing warnings of attainder, veiled threats and delaying tactics, the Nevilles and Percys were hardly likely to ignore their chequered past, and the nearness of both sides undoubtedly caused their troops to act impulsively. Therefore, the preliminary skirmishing and ultimately, the main battle that arose from this disunity were as much the result of the polarisation between the Yorkist commanders as the continuation of the Neville and Percy feud. However, far from curbing the actions of his northern allies, York aimed to capture the king's attention, which is why on his last mission, Mowbray herald found Duke Richard and his men advancing towards the northern end of the town. Confident that the skirmishing before St Albans was now beyond his control, and being vehemently contested by the Nevilles and Percys, the actions of York, by comparison, were clearly directed towards protecting the king from the resulting lawlessness. This undoubtedly left the Nevilles with a free hand to pursue their feud against their local enemies, and by acting independently of York's wishes, they nearly lost him the battle.

What of the king's men while all this skirmishing was going on? The Duke of Somerset was no doubt feeling increasingly isolated by the appointment of Buckingham as constable. However, the dispatch of separate heralds into the Yorkist camp indicates that Somerset still enjoyed some influence over the king. Buckingham too, on York's insistence, spoke on behalf of Henry VI, and we may wonder whether both these messages were royal words or if they instead betrayed the feelings, and the fears, of his two chief advisors who had barricaded themselves within the town.

Evidently, the roads into St Albans were barred at some point, but not, according to contemporary accounts, in the way most historians describe. Indeed, according to three accounts, temporary barricades were thrown up across the streets as a precaution against attack. We may conjecture that these barricades had been erected after royalist soldiers had been ordered to guard the approaches to the town. Undoubtedly, the barriers that Whethamstede mentions were put into position once skirmishing began. As to where these were erected, there is no historical or topographical evidence, apart from a brief statement in the *Fastolf Relation* that one was positioned near St Peter's Church. However, we may confidently argue that, due to what occurred when these barriers were attacked, these obstructions were not contiguous with the Tonman Ditch but instead positioned between the houses at the top of Holywell Hill, across Shropshire Lane, abutting the wall of the Castle Inn, and most likely at the end of New Lane, additionally fortifying a more substantial barrier or gate further down the road. This latter section of the perimeter was where Mowbray herald arrived on his last mission to the Duke of Buckingham. Therefore, given its unusual reference in the *Fastolf Relation*, it may have been the only permanent town barrier still serviceable in a much-dilapidated defensive cordon.

Due to the absence of unbiased evidence from the royalist side, a complete picture of how the king's army was positioned cannot be formed. However, according to the evidence so far described, the following facts would have had little bearing on later Yorkist propaganda and, therefore, may have some foundation in truth:

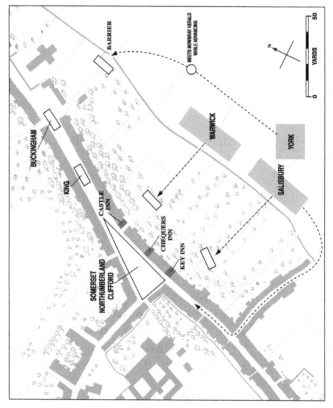

38 The first battle of St Albans, 1455. Movements of the Yorkist forces. (Author's Collection)

1. The king and his household men had taken up position in St Peter's Street somewhere between the parish church and St Albans marketplace, at a location described as Goselowe or Sandeforthe. Before this, Henry was 'in the place of Edmond Westby, hundreder of the said town of Saint Albans',[6] and no doubt later was encouraged to stand beside the royal standard, which that day was carried variously by Lord Sudeley, Steward of the Household, James Butler, Earl of Wiltshire, and Sir Philip Wentworth. Moreover, a statement in *Gregory's Chronicle* that 'King Harry was in harness his own proper person'[7] gives credence to the fact that Henry was armed during the battle, wearing a harness (armour plate), and that he was not just carrying a prayer book for protection.

2. Thomas Lord Clifford of Skipton was in command of the 'barriers of the same town'[8] and defended these bravely, according to more than one account of the battle. The notice of Lord Clifford's bravery was, therefore, a postscript to his death in battle and a tribute to his experience as a soldier. Additionally, we may be sure that his command of the barricades at St Albans marketplace was a well-founded Yorkist observation since they were the victors and need not have recorded this for posterity.

3. The whereabouts of various other nobles before the battle is not documented. Therefore, we may suppose that before 'the alarm bell was rung'[9] from the clock tower, warning of an imminent attack, most of these men were still with the king in St Peter's Street, awaiting orders. The Duke of Buckingham may have been positioned near the barrier at St Peter's Church, along with 'Sir Richard Harrington, Bertin Entwistle and John Hanford knights, Breknok squire and John Swythman',[10] as the *Fastolf Relation* indicates that some of these men were used as intermediaries during Mowbray herald's last mission to the town. However, because of the sudden northerly advance of the Duke of York and a surprise split in Yorkist forces, this area must have been reinforced

and, therefore, would have caused a similar division in the king's army when the perimeter of St Albans was breached.

Topographically, the area that the royalists had chosen to defend covered the triangular marketplace and the whole length of St Peter's Street, ending at the parish church. However, it will be remembered that all along this route, there was a jumble of largely unbroken houses and buildings, which, according to sources, hindered movement when battle was joined and could not be breached by the Yorkists during their first assault. Therefore, apart from one or two inevitable gaps between the rows of houses that hugged the eastern side of the marketplace and St Peter's Street, the 2,000 men at Buckingham's disposal would not have been over-extended and could be considered fortunate in their defensive position.

No doubt, the point at which the preliminary skirmishing ended and the main battle began was a confusing affair and difficult to follow even by those involved. Still, the main attack by the Yorkists on the town barriers and their stout defence by the royalists is reflected in the fact that York and the Nevilles could make no headway. According to the *Stow Relation*:

> [the king] hearing of the said duke's coming commanded his host to slay all manner [of] lords, knights, squires, gentlemen and yeomen that might be taken on the party of the aforesaid Duke of York. This done the aforesaid Lord Clifford kept so strongly the barriers of the same town that the aforesaid Duke of York might in no wise with all the power that he had enter nor break into the said town.[11]

Apart from York's advance towards the barrier near St Peter's Church, it is known that 'The Earl of Warwick with the march men and other entered the other end of the town, and fought against the king's party'.[12] And as a result of this manoeuvre, most of the fighting was likely concentrated at the junction of Shropshire Lane and St Peter's Street, with the main action being located near the Castle Inn, which was to feature predominantly in the battle later. Another Neville contingent may have advanced along Sopwell Lane and up Holywell Hill, hoping to break into the marketplace from there. Still, most sources indicate that Lord Clifford and the Earl of Northumberland frustrated these sustained Yorkist attacks in a holding action that seems to have lasted for the best part of an hour. Even with an advantage in numbers, the barricaded streets of the town would not have proved easy to overcome. Borderers armed with the warbow, the most formidable missile weapon of the day, would

39 An English archer during the Wars of the Roses. (Author's Collection)

have had great difficulty targeting defenders ensconced behind
barricades and houses. The only choice left to the Yorkists would
have been to try and break up the defences with hand weapons
whilst trying to stave off the enemy who lacked archers.

A significant fact of the battle is that the king's men were not
armed with the warbow, since Henry's entourage mainly comprised nobles and men at arms. It is also true that most of the
defenders, and indeed their men at arms, were not wearing a
full complement of armour, the nature of their wounds proving that some were not wearing helmets nor gauntlets during
the street-fighting. However, the Yorkist attack might have been
permanently thwarted if it had not been for one enterprising
soldier in Warwick's ranks. Both the *Stow* and *Phillipps Relation*
give an account of who made the next attack and what part of
the town it was directed against. The writers also describe why
the assault succeeded when the battle was developing into a
stalemate. The *Stow Relation* states that:

> The Earl of Warwick knowing thereof [the Yorkist impasse]
> took and gathered his men together with him and broke in
> by the garden side into the said town between the Sign of the
> Key and the Chequer in Halywell Street. And anon as they
> were within the said town, they blew up trumpets and cried
> with a loud voice 'A Warwick! A Warwick!' that marvel it was
> to here. And until that time the aforesaid Duke of York might
> never have entered into the town. And then with strong hand
> they broke up the barriers and mightily fought.[13]

In the *Phillipps Relation*, there is no doubt which soldier led this
assault and achieved the Yorkist breakthrough, although the
author points out it had nothing to do with the Earl of Warwick:

> And Sir Robert Ocle [Ogle] took 600 men of the Marches
> and took the marketplace [before] any man was [aware]; then
> the alarm bell was rung, and every man fled to harness, for at

that time every man was out of their array, and they joined
battle anon; and it was done within the [half] hour.[14]

The detail and time spent by the authors of the *Stow* and
Phillipps Relation explaining this action proves a certain amount
of local knowledge was known by them about St Albans.

When describing the covert action behind the houses lining
the marketplace, both the above writers make the point that
someone other than the Duke of York was responsible for
breaking the stalemate at the barriers. After the battle, the Earl
of Warwick was made Captain of the Calais Garrison, the only
English standing army abroad, and the very mention of his
name in conjunction with the turning point of the battle gives
the impression that the younger Neville earl was the instigator
of the assault. However, the generalship of Warwick throughout the later civil wars was flawed on numerous occasions,
especially at the second battle of St Albans in 1461. Therefore,
it would be wrong to give him full credit for making the
breakthrough possible. We must also remember that the *Stow
Relation* formed a significant part of Yorkist propaganda after
the event, and as such, it is not surprising that Ogle's attack,
with 600 men of the Marches, was not recorded in this official Yorkist source. After the battle, Sir Robert Ogle received
no reward for his action at St Albans, and he was not raised to
the peerage until the reign of Edward IV. Nevertheless, we can
be sure that he led the assault on the marketplace after a gap
between the houses (or between the two inns) had been found.
Ordering his troops to exploit this alley or breach in the royalist defences, he turned the tide of the battle in the Yorkists'
favour, a manoeuvre which Warwick probably knew about but
failed to recognise in any major way.

Davies' Chronicle also states that Ogle and his men 'broke
down violently houses and pales on the east side of the town,
and entered into Saint Peter's Street slaying all those that with-
stood them,'[15] and the *Dijon Relation* makes it clear that:

they took and blockaded the marketplace of the said town and part of [Warwick's] people found themselves in the middle of it and in this manner began to fight the one party against the other. However, because the place was small few of the combatants could set to work there and matters reached such a great extremity that four of those who were of the king's bodyguard were killed by arrows in his presence.[16]

Packed full of local knowledge, the above accounts of the fight for the marketplace vividly describe firstly the shock of Ogle's attack; secondly, the fact that the area became suddenly filled with masses of men; and, thirdly, that the king and his household troops were suddenly drawn into the fighting. Obstacles, including market stalls, buildings and barricades, hemmed in both sides' troops, and this would have considerably heightened the confusion of the street-fighting. Also, now that the king had ventured or had been encouraged to move closer to the action, the situation suddenly became far more critical for the royalists.

Why had King Henry been allowed to take up such a vulnerable position? Was the move intentional so that the Yorkists could see the king's standard advertising the dire consequences of treason? Or were the royalist commanders now in a desperate position and, throwing caution to the wind, decided to risk the king's safety to ensure their own survival? Much to the dismay of the royalists, the reaction to the king's arrival had the reverse effect on Sir Robert Ogle's mindset, and, despite the apparent show of majesty in the crammed marketplace, his archers began indiscriminately to let loose flights of arrows into the crowd before them.

At this point in the battle, because the king's men were now beset on two fronts, the barricades were of no further use and were quickly abandoned by the royalists. Both in the marketplace and at the barrier near St Peter's Church, the tide of battle suddenly turned in favour of the Yorkists and, chiefly, the Nevilles. The fight now centred on the very heart of St Albans. With

York's men swarming down the broad thoroughfare of St Peter's Street, it would only have been a few minutes before the market-place was a confused mass of men fighting for their lives. Abbot Whethamstede later recorded a convincing description of the slaughter which ensued when the barricades collapsed, and more of the Neville contingents streamed into the town:

> They [the Yorkists] soon sounded the trumpet and rushed into the middle of St Peter's Street, breaking down the barriers until they had the king's battleline in front of them. They fought each other for a short space of time so fiercely that here you would have seen one man lying with his brain struck out, here another with his arm cut off, there a third with his throat cut, there a fourth with his chest pierced, and the whole place beyond filled with the corpses of the slain, on this side and that and everywhere in every direction. And so powerfully at the time was shield driven back by shield and targe by targe, threatening sword by sword, foot by foot and weapon-point by weapon-point that for a time the outcome was in doubt to which side victory would yield, and the dice of fate was unclear enough.[17]

Whethamstede's report, supporting the theory that the town barricades were makeshift and not permanent fixtures, may well have been prompted by what he saw in the streets immediately after the battle ended. As previously explained, his graphic descriptions of wounds, severed limbs, and heads beaten to pulp support the claims that most of the king's men did not have time to arm themselves properly or strap on their helmets before battle commenced.

According to *Davies' Chronicle*, the king and most of his household were now present and fighting in St Peter's Street and the market area. Their lack of defensive equipment clearly disadvantaged them, but it is highly likely that, at first, they made some impact in the confined space available to them. Evidently,

King Henry took no part in this hand-to-hand fighting due to his apparent hatred of violence. However, it is recorded in the *Phillipps Relation* that the king was wearing his armour, and other commentators state that he was vehemently against the Yorkists and their petitions to remove the Duke of Somerset, to the point of wanting to kill them, 'every mother's son'. Although we cannot be sure of the integrity of this remark, men like Somerset and Buckingham clearly thought that any danger to the king's person was minimal when weighed against what could occur if royal eyes were averted. Given that Henry did not arrive in the marketplace until after the defences were breached, it is probable that the royalist nobles thought it imperative to protect themselves with a more tangible symbol of sovereignty. To this end, *Davies' Chronicle* states the king arrived from the direction of St Albans Abbey, and although sources say that Henry did not lodge here before the battle, we can well imagine that the king's entrance into the marketplace would have been masked by confusion and after the event may have been impossible to relate with any certainty.

However, regardless of the danger and the direction of the king's approach, with his banner displayed and his household men in attendance, Henry was at some point directed towards the worst of the fighting,

> and Duke Edmund [Somerset] with him, and the Duke of Buckingham, the Earl of Northumberland, and the Lord Clifford and the Lord Sudeley bearing the king's banner, [and] the king that stood under his banner was hurt in the neck with an arrow.[18]

Another account says that 'the king himself was struck by an arrow in the shoulder, but it penetrated only a little of the flesh'.[19] Several other sources support the claim that the king's injury was a notable occurrence and one that might have easily caused his death. However, the opinionated Abbot Whethamstede does

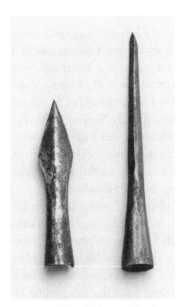

40 *Long and short bodkin arrowheads.*
(© The Board of Trustees of the Armouries)

not mention Henry's wound, which begs the question whether the injury occurred. The fact that Yorkist sources mention it, hence supporting the claims of a near catastrophe, helped their propaganda succeed against the Duke of Somerset and his supporters in the later *Parliamentary Pardon*, and this may suggest that the injury did occur, but it was only a flesh wound. Clearly, an inch or so difference in the trajectory of the arrow's flight would have been disastrous to both sides and the kingdom. If Henry had been struck cleanly in the neck by an arrow or even through his mail collar (standard), the result would have proved fatal and beyond any attempted battlefield surgery. Therefore, considering all the above sources, and indeed bearing in mind what occurred next, we may be sure that the king was only slightly injured in the fight and that his wound was caused either by a ricocheting arrow or by one that pierced the king's shoulder armour (pauldron), thus lessening the impact and therefore the force of penetration.

However, at this point, the clarity of the battle begins to blur in Yorkist propaganda. With the Duke of York's men bearing down upon the marketplace from the northern end of St Peter's Street and all exits barred from the east by Neville contingents, any one source cannot verify the next few minutes of the battle. As with all attempts at reconstruction, there are alternative scenarios, and the final phase of the first battle of St Albans is no exception. Indeed, the killings that occurred in full view of those

who fought may have been perpetrated in the heat and confusion of battle by chance or, indeed, by design. In short, the end
of the fighting can be taken two ways due to a 'cover-up' later
made official by parliament in favour of the Yorkist lords. Some
sources are clear about what occurred in the streets of St Albans
as midday approached, while others, mainly Yorkist, note that
casualties occurred in a more unrecorded and haphazard way.
The truth must lie somewhere between the official Yorkist
pardon and the views of those more unbiased chroniclers who
may have had little to gain from promoting a falsehood.

With the wounded king standing forlornly beneath his
banner, his faithful household men would have closed ranks
around him, and many were killed trying to protect Henry
from further injury. Lord Sudeley, the first of his household to
bear his banner, was hit in the face by an arrow, we are told,
and the Duke of Buckingham shared a similar fate, while all
around them, a writhing mass of pushing bodies, clashing
weapons and cries for help confused the issue. No doubt the
king's banner was picked up after Sudeley's fall, and this was
probably recovered by either the Earl of Wiltshire or Sir Philip
Wentworth, who were both later held responsible for casting
the banner down again and fleeing from the scene. However,
it is clear from casualty reports that the king's household men
fought bravely for some minutes until it was apparent that all
was lost. Fighting for their lives under a canopy of flailing steel
and falling arrows, it was only a matter of minutes before the
unrelenting Yorkists butchered every royalist in sight, including the King of England. And it was at this point that Henry's
banner, the rallying point of all English armies, vanished from
sight. According to *Gregory's Chronicle*:

> The Earl of Wiltshire bore the king's banner that day in the
> battle, for he was at that time named but Sir James Ormond,
> and this said James set the king's banner against a house end
> and fought manly with his heels, for he was a feared of losing

41 Glass depicting the arms of
James Butler, Earl of Wiltshire,
at Ockwells Manor. (Courtesy of
Geoffrey Wheeler)

his beauty, for he was named the fairest knight of this land.[20]

According to sources, the Earl of Wiltshire threw off what armour he had on, ran from the market-place into the abbey and, disguising himself as a monk, made a lucky escape while the fighting still raged. Other men, including Sir Philip Wentworth, also decided to flee St Albans, along with many of the king's men who were being beaten back, running into houses or trying to extricate themselves from the thicket of stabbing weapons which were multiplying by the minute. Pushed both backwards and side-ways across the street, there would have been no escape from the mêlée, apart from seeking cover in buildings or cutting a hole through the Yorkists to the western end of the marketplace, where two roads were still open and unaffected by the fighting. Even the Duke of Buckingham, who had now sustained three arrow wounds, most likely limped away at this point and fled to the abbey and the sanctuary it offered. It is no wonder that the king, alone and unprotected, suffered another bout of insanity soon after the battle and never fully recovered from the trauma of his ordeal. The fighting at St Albans may have been responsible for his well-known revulsion of the sight of blood, which stayed with him for the rest of his unhappy life.

According to the *Dijon Relation*, while confusion still ruled in the streets, the Duke of York 'gave orders that the king should be taken and drawn out of the throng and put in the abbey in safety and thus it was done.'[21] However, a different story was related by John Whethamstede, who, after lamenting the 'softness' of the king's troops, goes on to state that,

> the king, however, seeing that his men were either turned in flight or dead on the field, and that he was standing under his standard without any protection, without hope or relief, on the suggestion of a few who said that he should flee from the face of the bow, and escape from the dangers of the arrows, which kept flying about his head more thickly than snowflakes, took himself off to the tiny dwelling of a tanner and there stayed with his men, until the Duke of York came and greeted him.[22]

If the king was rushed into a nearby house out of harm's way, what price the rest of the king's men still fighting in the street and faced with a gathering tide of Yorkist soldiers, all eager to capitalise on their victory? Evidently, Whethamstede's statement infers that York had nothing to do with the king's removal to safety, as it seems that now he was free to exact his revenge on his rival, the Duke of Somerset, who had also taken refuge in a nearby building. The largely unbiased *Dijon Relation* gives a complete and graphic account of what occurred inside and outside the Castle Inn, located at the junction of Shropshire Lane and St Peter's Street, as the battle moved into its final murderous phase:

> And at last, when they had fought for the space of three hours, the king's party seeing themselves to have the worst of it broke on one wing and began to flee, and the Duke of Somerset retreated within an inn to save himself and hid. Which things seen by those of the said Duke of York's party

[they] incontinent beset the said house all about. And there the Duke of York gave orders that the king should be taken and drawn out of the throng and put in the abbey in safety and thus it was done. And in this abbey took refuge also with him the Duke of Buckingham who was very badly wounded by three arrows. And incontinent this done [the Yorkists] began to fight Somerset and his men who were in this place within the inn and defended themselves valiantly. And in the end after the doors were broken down the Duke of Somerset seeing that he had no other remedy took council with his men about coming out and did so, as a result of which incontinent he and all his people were surrounded by the Duke of York's men. And after some were stricken down and the Duke of Somerset had killed four of them with his own hand, it is said, he was felled to the ground with an axe and incontinent being so wounded in several places that there he ended his life.[23]

According to *Davies' Chronicle,* it was said that the Duke of Somerset had heard a 'fantastic' prophecy that he would some-day die under a castle, and as a result, he had avoided going to Windsor, dreading that the prediction might come true, 'but at Saint Albans there was a hostelry having the sign of a castle, and before that hostelry he was slain'.[24]

Clearly, the *Dijon Relation* makes much of this episode as the climax not only to the battle but also to the feud between York and Somerset. Likewise, Somerset's death is also mentioned in the letter to the Archbishop of Ravenna, underlining the fact that York's ultimate ambition was to kill his rival, with him being unceremoniously dragged out of the mêlée and formally beheaded for his crimes. Therefore, as far as foreign commentators were concerned, York had exacted personal revenge on his rival to the extent of removing the king from the battle so that this might be done more privately. The Duke of Somerset probably realised that if the Yorkists captured him, there would be no mercy anyway, and thus made a fighting exit from the

Castle Inn with the vain hope that Henry might be on hand to save him. Therefore, 'with [Somerset's] death the battle ceased at once, and without loss of time, the Duke of York went to kneel before the king and ask his pardon for himself and his followers, as they had not done this in order to inflict any hurt upon his majesty, but in order to have Somerset'.[25]

After the event, and in keeping with Yorkist propaganda, Somerset was attacked for his conduct in general. In *Gregory's Chronicle*, for example, the case against the duke was particularly slanderous in stating that the people felt that 'the Duke of Somerset was worthy to suffer that death by so much that he brought King Harry at Clarendon beside Salisbury and there he took his great sickness',[26] implying that Somerset might have maltreated the king in some way in 1453 or even have caused his illness. Unfortunately, much like the *Stow* and *Phillipps Relations*, *Gregory's Chronicle* fails to mention who was personally responsible for killing Somerset outside the Castle Inn. The episode is

42 *Memorial plaque to the Duke of Somerset on the corner of Shropshire Lane and St Peter's Street. (Author's Collection)*

glossed over impeccably by Yorkist sources, which prefer to list
Somerset among the casualties of the battle, along with other
nobles such as the Earl of Northumberland and Lord Clifford.
Essentially, Somerset's death was seen by foreign sources as the
culmination of private feuding and by at least one English com-
mentator as retribution for his crimes. That York purposely
sought out the Duke of Somerset, cornered him in the street,
and then killed him with his own hand is one way to view
the event. However, all the evidence proves that there may be
another, more plausible scenario linked with the deaths of the
Earl of Northumberland and Lord Clifford.

It will be remembered that Lord Clifford had commanded at
the 'barres' with great courage during the attack on the town.
This incident is enlarged upon by a chronicler who knew the
Clifford family well, having been in the service of the Earl of
Northumberland in the days of his father, Henry Percy (nick-
named 'Hotspur'), who died at the battle of Shrewsbury in 1403.
John Hardyng had been a soldier at this battle and later wrote a
History of Britain in the reign of Edward IV. Although his writing
is clearly biased in favour of the Yorkists at this time, he left this
interesting description of the battle of St Albans, which poses a
whole host of questions regarding the deaths of Somerset and
those nobles whom the Nevilles saw as their enemies:

> They [the Yorkists] were put by from all their good intent,
> And strange were hold after many a day,
> To the thirty year and three by whole consent,
> At Saint Albans then upon the Thursday,
> Accompted then next afore Whitsunday,
> They slew the Duke Edmund [then]of Somerset,
> For cause he had the realms weal so let.
>
> The Earl [then] of Northumberland was there,
> Of sudden chance drawn forth with the king,
> And slain unknown by any man there were,

The Lord Clifford, ever busy in working,
At the bars them met sore fighting,
Was slain that day upon his own assault,
A such men said it was his own default.

The Earl of Wiltshire with five hundred men,
Fled from the king full fast that time away,
The Duke of Buckingham was hurt there then,
The king they took and saved in good array.[27]

Thomas Gascoigne's pro-Yorkist remark that the Duke of Somerset was slain and that several other of the duke's supporters, such as Northumberland and Lord Clifford, were unintentionally killed, adds weight to Hardyng's interpretation. However, against this evidence, we must also consider that the Nevilles posed an overriding threat to Yorkist strategy and remember that they had instigated the battle in the first place. John Hardyng implies that Clifford fell at the barricades leading an ill-advised assault, that Northumberland was slain by an unknown hand, and that the Duke of Somerset was 'justifiably' killed by the Yorkists because he had mismanaged the kingdom. In this apology, Hardyng was clearly aiming to please the current regime and particularly to encourage Edward IV to raise all England, and particularly the north, against Edward's mortal enemies, the Scots. Therefore, elements of partiality were undoubtedly included in Hardyng's work. The Earl of Northumberland, for example, was certainly not with the king by 'sudden chance' in May 1455, and equally, he was not a bystander during the street-fighting at St Albans. Similarly, Lord Clifford is portrayed in Hardyng's account as causing his own death by leading a suicidal assault on the Yorkist position. It is highly likely that Hardyng fabricated his account of St Albans in favour of the Yorkist court to the extent of leaving out the fact that Somerset, Northumberland and Clifford were not killed by accident but by design.

This alternative viewpoint is hidden deep within Yorkist propaganda and concealed not by what was put into reports after St Albans but by what was left out. Did the Duke of York give explicit orders that King Henry should be removed from danger so that he might freely kill Somerset, or was it that the duke was already dead, along with Northumberland and Clifford, long before York arrived in the marketplace? Faced with this choice, we may either point an accusing finger at York and the Nevilles and conclude that both parties had everything to gain from the deaths of their opposite numbers or suggest that in the heat of battle, the king was taken out of the mêlée with the express purpose of assassinating a select group of nobles. There is no doubt that troops raised by the Neville earls featured predominantly in York's army and that Abbot Whethamstede made much of their role in his account, even to the extent of blaming them for the widespread looting that occurred in his town after the battle had ended. Similarly, among the royalist dead were men from families associated with the Earl of Northumberland, such as Sir John Stapleton, Avery Mauleverer, Ralph Babthorpe and William Curwen, not to mention Lord Clifford – a statement of fact which suggests that some Percy retainers were killed intentionally. Therefore, did the Duke of York have any control over the Nevilles at St Albans? This suggestion seems to have been the case at the beginning of the battle and following the main assault on the barricades. However, York may have lost control over them in favour of rescuing King Henry from the mêlée. In fact, if this is what occurred, then we may absolve York from any direct blame attached to the 'execution' of Somerset since he may not even have been present in the marketplace when he was slain.

According to the *Dijon Relation*, Somerset was killed by 'the Duke of York's men'[28] after York had ordered the removal of Henry from the fighting. Could it be that York returned to the marketplace after removing the king to find Somerset, Northumberland and Clifford already butchered in the street? And if so, did he find his Neville relatives proudly standing over

their bodies, waiting to be congratulated by their faction's leading and most influential member?

Either way, the deed had been done, and in royalist eyes,
it would be later regarded as cold-blooded murder. In the
last throes of royal resistance, three leading members of the
English nobility had been brutally slain, and several others,
including Somerset's son, had been badly injured. According
to the *Stow Relation*:

> And at the same battle of lords of name were hurt: the king
> our sovereign lord in the neck with an arrow, the Duke of
> Buckingham and the Lord Sudeley in the visages with an
> arrow, the Earl of Stafford in the right hand with an arrow,
> the Earl of Dorset [Somerset's son] sore hurt that he might
> not walk, but that he was carried home in a cart, and Sir John
> Wenlock knight in likewise hurt and carried in a chair and
> divers other knights and squires sore hurt. And the substance
> of the king's host [were] despoiled of their harness [armour]
> at their own request and delivery made to the duke's host for
> salvation of their lives. And the Earl of Wiltshire and Thorpe
> with many others fled and cast away their harness in ditches
> and woods.[29]

Awash with blood, bodies, spent arrows and broken weapons,
the streets of St Albans were now in utter confusion. The body
count would be numbered in tens rather than hundreds, but if
one moment can be judged as the start of blood feuding in the
civil wars, then this was indisputably that moment. The feud
and the shadow it would cast across successive generations had
been instigated by ambitious men who had used the politics of
others to satisfy their own needs. To begin with, Neville troops
had not thought twice about skirmishing with the enemy right
under the nose of their commander-in-chief; they had been
oblivious to the fact that once the battle was underway, they
might have killed their king by loosing arrows; they had stood

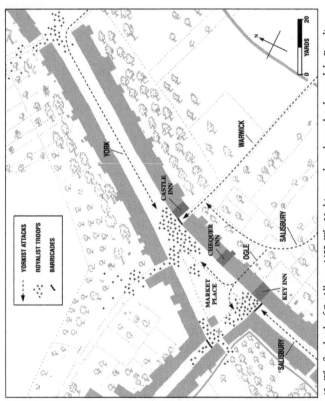

43 The first battle of St Albans, 1455. The Yorkist attack on the marketplace and the Royalist rout. (Author's Collection)

idly by while a portion of the nobility was first targeted and then unchivalrously hacked to death without being offered ransom; and, much like armies on foreign soil, they were now about to loot and ravage an English town in repayment for their ordeal.

If the Duke of York had aimed to arrest his rival Somerset or indeed to execute him for his crimes against Henry and the kingdom, it was certainly not his intention to kill or anger any other members of the nobility. Alienation was the last thing that York hoped to achieve at St Albans, and thus he had, according to Buckingham's intuition, adopted a restrained attitude, entered negotiations and tried to keep his men at a safe distance. However, Buckingham had not bargained how the Nevilles might react to these delaying tactics. In fact, the Nevilles had another agenda due to their feud with the Percys in the north and Somerset in Wales. York's sudden advance was primarily instigated by his predatory Neville allies, whom he had failed to control. His aim of securing the king and, if need be, using force to arrest Somerset was therefore thwarted by his own allies' violent desire to kill their indigenous enemies without mercy – as the Percys had tried to do at Heworth in 1453.

With the king's men in complete rout or being precariously guarded by their captors, the focus now turned from St Albans marketplace to the abbey, where it was said that the Duke of Buckingham and the Earl of Wiltshire had taken refuge. Since the king had also been rushed there in the heat of battle and some of York's men were reported in the vicinity soon after the rout had occurred, it was now imperative that the Yorkists follow up their victory with Henry's capture. The *Dijon Relation* takes up the story and reveals that when he finally had the chance to speak to Henry face to face, York, despite his rebellious actions, behaved like a loyal subject and certainly did not in any way undermine the king's authority:

The battle lasted until two and a half hours after noon and this done the Duke of York's men took themselves to the abbey to kill the Duke of Buckingham and the Treasurer, who is called the Earl of Wiltshire, who had retreated there with the king, but the said Duke of York would not suffer it but sent his herald to the king to inform him that he must choose which he preferred, either to hand over the two lords as prisoners into his hands, or that they should be killed in front of him and to put himself in danger once more. Wherefore the king agreed freely to allow [York] to arrest the said two lords and so he did, in particular the Duke of Buckingham. And when all these things were done the Duke of York entered within the abbey and went before the king's person and there went on his knees to him crying mercy for whatever way he might have offended and for the peril in which he had put his person, and many other good and humble words, showing him that he had not gone against him but against the traitors to his crown, and in the end before the Duke of York went away from there the king pardoned him everything and took him in his good grace.[30]

The actual fighting at St Albans had lasted from about ten o'clock to around midday, but the rout and the point at which the king proclaimed 'that all manner of people should cease of their malice'[31] may have prolonged the struggle into the afternoon. To corroborate this, precise evidence in the *Dijon Relation* states that the battle lasted until half past two. Therefore, some attention must be given to the seriousness of St Albans – and we may be sure that the fighting did not last half an hour, as some historians have claimed. Instead, the struggle must have included at least an hour of skirmishing, followed by a stand-off at the barricades and, thereafter, a more intense bout of street-fighting, in which several events and manoeuvres occurred. The rout, as always, is challenging to calculate regarding time, but the *Dijon Relation* is remarkably precise (and does not use Roman numerals to complicate matters) when describing the cycle of events. Indeed, all the

St Albans 1455

relevant sources make it abundantly clear that the first battle of
St Albans did not deserve to be called a skirmish.

Most modern accounts, except that of C.A.J. Armstrong, are
wildly off the mark, and due to the low casualty figures and the
duration of the fighting, the battle has been misinterpreted. It is
interesting to speculate what might have occurred if contingents
supplied by the Duke of Norfolk, the Earl of Shrewsbury, Lord
Cromwell and Sir Thomas Stanley had participated in the fighting. That they did not arrive in time to fight and waited in the
wings speaks volumes about the perceived seriousness of York's
rivalry with Somerset, not to mention his rebellious intentions.

There is no doubt that contemporaries saw St Albans as a
significant event, not only because York was willing to commit
treason to achieve his aims but also because other nobles, like the
Nevilles, were willing to join him. Due to the merciless nature
of the final moments of the battle, the stripping of bodies and
the despoiling of the dead (according to Abbot Whethamstede)
there could be little hope of a lasting and peaceable settlement
in the future. Localised civil war had been transposed from the
north to the south of England, and nothing would be the same
again. The first battle of St Albans certainly inspired revenge
in the minds of all those sons who had lost their fathers in the
fighting. Additionally, we may speculate that the event placed
a degree of uncertainty and fear in the hearts of some of York's
men, especially those who had re-defined the codes of chivalry
and ransom in a moment of madness and cold-blooded murder.

Seven

The Fate of the Kingdom

It is tempting to speculate what could have happened if Henry VI had been killed at St Albans and the Duke of York, as protector, had taken control of the kingdom. Indeed, the way that the Yorkist border archers had loosed their arrows at the king's standard, and those crowding around it in the restricted marketplace, was wilful and uncontrolled. There is little doubt that the Duke of York would have been furious if he had been present, considering his earlier concern for the king's safety. But as fate would have it, York was likely busy fighting further up St Peter's Street, according to the sources. Proof, if any were needed that Warwick and Salisbury's troops were operating independently and some were totally out of control. In the fog of medieval warfare, any atrocity was possible, and given what could have happened to the King of England, the deaths of Somerset, Northumberland and Lord Clifford would have been secondary.

According to the Victorian historian William Stubbs 'the first battle of St Albans sealed the fate of the kingdom',[1] and indeed, regarding factionalism and how this polarised the

English nobility thereafter, medieval England would never be the same again. Contemporaries did not ignore the seriousness of the battle. And although the reality was partially censored by the Yorkists immediately afterwards, it was seen by many as a national disaster. As for casualties, most chroniclers did not exaggerate their figures, as was the standard practice of the day. Some authors may have even suppressed the actual death toll, certainly regarding lesser ranks, to accord with Yorkist propaganda. Alternatively, a tendency towards lower casualty figures may indicate that specific individuals were sought out and targeted at St Albans instead of being randomly slaughtered. Therefore, the battle's significance should not be underestimated, and how the victors attempted to cover up the truth in official documents like the *Parliamentary Pardon* after the event betrays the seriousness of their actions.

Omitting the remarks of Tudor historians, the highest casualty estimate for the battle is that given in the *Phillipps Relation*, which states that 400 men died in the fighting, 'and as many or more hurt'.[2] In contrast, the lowest estimate is given in the *London Chronicle*, which names three lords and a single knight plus 'twenty-five squires with other people'.[3] However, in most sources, there is a consensus that the death toll was relatively low. As an alternative to the above rather haphazard accounting by writers, the *Stow Relation* provides a much more detailed record of the casualties:

At which fight were slain of lords of name the aforesaid Lord Clifford, the Duke of Somerset and the Earl of Northumberland, Sir Barton Entewsell knight, William Zouche, John Botreaux, Ralph Babthorpe and his son, William Corvin, William Coton, Receiver of the Duchy of Lancaster, Gilbert Faldinger, Reynold Griffyn, John Dawes, Elys Woode, John Eythe, Robert Wodewarde, Gilbert Skarlok and Raufe Willoughby squires, a gentleman of court, Roger Mercrofte, the queen's messenger, Hawkin the king's

porter, Maleners, Padington and William Boteler yeomen
and twenty-five more whose names are not known and
of them that were slain [these were] buried at Saint Albans
forty-eight persons.[4]

A similar casualty list is included in the *Phillipps Relation*, along
with a detailed report of the injured, which echoes the above
in all but overall casualties. Evidently, some of the named individuals in both accounts survived the battle, but unfortunately,
neither source gives a full indication of how many men were
killed on each side – an all-important factor regarding how
ferocious the fighting became and how closely the rout was followed in the afternoon. In the *Dijon Relation,* it is stated that
200 'or thereabouts'[5] were slain at the battle, while *Davies'
Chronicle* put the casualty figure at 'sixty persons of gentlemen
and of other'.[6] A continuation of the *Polychronicon* attests to
140 men killed, while a Paston letter sent by John Crane suggests a figure in the region of 'six score [120]'.[7] In addition to
the above figures, we should also balance the evidence against
a casualty report from the *Register of the Archdeacons of St Albans*,
which lists the names of over forty casualties, all of whom were
buried in the abbey and St Peter's churchyard. However, even
with proportionately lower estimates, the sources vary considerably, therefore, we may never know the actual death toll.
We can hazard a guess that about 100 men died at St Albans,
not accounting for casualties in the rout and those about whom
little or no evidence exists.

As previously stated, contemporaries recorded that several
royalist soldiers sustained arrow wounds during the battle, and
this fact alone may have contributed to a higher casualty rate
in royalist ranks – not to mention the possibility that some of
the injured probably suffered from diseased wounds after the
event. It is known that injuries inflicted by either barbed or
bodkin arrowheads, along with the dirt and fragments of metal
and cloth they introduced to the body and bloodstream, were

44 Sir John Wenlock, was wounded and carried home in a chair from St Albans. (From a modern glass at St Mary's Church, Luton. Courtesy of Geoffrey Wheeler)

wounds that did not heal properly. Indeed, even if some men arrived home safely carrying these injuries and were treated by local physicians, this probably did not ensure their survival from blood poisoning. Therefore, the after-effects of the battle may have filled many local churchyards with gentry and commoners alike. For example, Bertin Entwistle, the veteran soldier from Lancashire who manned the barrier near St Peter's church, was listed among the St Albans dead. However, according to sources, he did not die of his wounds until some days after the battle. Finally interred in St Peter's Church on 28 May, his epitaph was recorded by John Weever more than 150 years later:

> Here lieth Sir Bertin Entwisel knight, who was born in Lancaster shire and was Viscount and Bailiff of Constantin who died the twenty-eighth day of May on whose soul Jesus have mercy.[8]

John Leland, the Tudor antiquary, located Entwistle's memorial under the place of the lectorium of the choir, but nothing now remains of his last resting place apart from a rubbing from sections of his armorial brass (the centre of the body and the left leg), now in possession of the Society of Antiquaries in London.

Also buried in St Peter's Church were Ralph Babthorpe and his son, both mentioned in the above casualty lists, and Thomas Pakington, the sword-bearer of the Earl of Northumberland, who doubtless was cut down along with his master in the marketplace. It is unknown how many other soldiers were buried in St Peter's churchyard, but Weever's statement recording notable burials there has most likely been confused with the larger casualties inflicted at the second battle of St Albans in 1461 when much greater armies were engaged.

All the leading nobles killed during the first battle of St Albans received a proper burial in the abbey church when it was safe to do so, and it is said that some of these bodies were unearthed below the altar of the Lady Chapel, where they had been seen 'in their rusty armour'[9] by workers undertaking floor renovations in the late nineteenth century. However, whether these were the bodies of Somerset, Northumberland and Clifford remain highly conjectural, and since the excavation was not correctly recorded at the time, the written evidence cannot be verified with any certainty.

According to E.B. de Fonblanque, the renowned Percy annalist, the Earl of Northumberland was at some point exhumed from St Albans and reburied in York Minster, where a window showing him along with his wife and children was still extant in 1590. It was either here or in the Percy church of St Denys, also in York, that Northumberland's body was finally interred – neither the first nor the last of his family to be butchered in the civil wars. As for Somerset and Clifford, the *Paston Letters* record that all three nobles were first buried at St Albans, and since a memorial to Lord Clifford once existed in the Lady Chapel, maybe at least two out of the

three royalist nobles may still be interred somewhere inside
the abbey church.

Among the injured royalists who managed to escape the field
was Henry Fylongley, whom the *Phillipps Relation* noted for his
bravery during the battle. Fylongley was a servant of Sir John
Fastolf, and he had been repeatedly 'shot through the arms in
three or four places'[10] – which again attests to the fact that, at least
at the onset of the battle for the marketplace, a hail of arrows had
been indiscriminately unleashed on the royalist troops, with the
hope of causing the maximum amount of confusion and panic.
In a letter written by William Barker to William Worcester in
June 1455, Fylongley was said to be still recovering at his home,
tended by his wife, and it was feared that his injuries would keep
him incapacitated for some time, much to the dismay of his
friends. Whether he fully recovered is unknown, but many like
him did not. An analysis of the casualty lists reveals that the main
cause of injuries and deaths at St Albans was that Yorkist archers shot at the royalist troops while they were massed in such a
confined area. Many of Henry's household men were among the
dead, and this attests to the dangerous situation that developed
around the king's standard when Sir Robert Ogle's men first targeted them with their powerful warbows.

Others of the king's household, afterwards called cowards,
managed to escape the street-fighting long before Somerset,
Northumberland, and Clifford met their deaths, which again
suggests the panic and confusion that resulted from Ogle's attack.
For example, the *Stow Relation* states that the Earl of Wiltshire,
Thomas Thorpe and many others fled the marketplace, casting
away their armour in ditches and woods to speed their escape.
The king's standard was thrown down in a rush to evacuate
the area because royalist troops had no way of replying to the
weight of missiles falling on their exposed position. Add to this
the original surprise of Ogle's breakthrough into the town, and
those royalists who fled the fighting were not faint-hearted but
were responding to a highly alarming situation which could nei-

45 Fifteenth-century hand-and-a-half sword, possibly English. (© The Board of Trustees of the Armouries)

ther be counteracted nor sustained with the weapons available to them.

Notably, the *Register of the Archdeacons of St Albans* recorded that most of the casualties were located to the north, in St Peter's ward, which then extended south from the parish church to a point bisecting the marketplace. This area obviously included the whole length of St Peter's Street, the area around the Castle Inn, the junction of Shropshire Lane and a portion of the shambles, which not only confirms contemporary accounts of the fighting but also suggests that it was here in the marketplace where most of the royalists were shot at by Ogle's northern archers. Interestingly, the parish boundary can still be seen marked on a wooden lintel between the houses lining the east side of what is now Chequer Street. And it was likely here in the marketplace, where most of the uncontrolled looting and pillaging occurred after the battle.

As discussed previously, Abbot Whethamstede of St Albans related an 'eyewitness' account of the final stages of the fighting in his chronicle, although his *narrative* must be approached with some caution:

> At last, however, by some terror sent from heaven, or breath of madness implanted or innate, turning their backs they [the king's men] fled in great numbers – nay, the greater part, on the king's side, running about through the gardens and fields, the brambles and thickets, the hedges and woods, sought for themselves places and hideouts where they could

best lurk and conceal themselves until the storm of the battle had stopped.[11]

Whethamstede then goes on to record the pillage carried out by the Yorkist troops, who were predominantly north-erners, and according to the abbot's principals, thugs of the worst kind:

> Meantime, while the Duke of York was consoling the king, and comforting him, the victors were left idle, and being too eager and avaricious, passed their time with pillage, plun-der and rapine, incapable of restraining their hands either at home among their neighbours or outside among enemies. They were all, for the most part, of the northerly parts of the kingdom, and therefore, although stronger in arms and more ready for war, [were] also used to the spilling of blood ... they turned their hands to plunder, their fingers to pillaging, sparing not king nor peer nor [commoner] nor knight, nor any other man at whose house plunder might be found. And thus, one man, robbed of his golden vase ... another man, robbed of his horse and arms, was forced to abandon his own home, weaponless, poor and on foot, miserable less from the theft than from the shame and derision that followed him by his own people. And a third man, relieved of all the gold and silver in his purse or money pouch, was forced to beg borrowed money to convey him to his people, but he was happy in this, that he had escaped so, with no worse damage in that furious uproar. And so far, increased the strength and violence of this despoliation and rapine, that rumour even reached the monastery that the thieves would reach there and despoil it.[12]

Indeed, it is hard to believe that Whethamstede exaggerated the sack of St Albans even though his history is prone to certain falsehoods and religious asides. Instead, it is more than likely that the abbot witnessed the aftermath of the battle, and considering the reports of the fighting, he genuinely feared for his enclave, which, according to him, was saved from the looting Yorkist soldiers by the miraculous intervention of St Alban himself! However, his pleas for the burial of the dead on both sides seems genuine enough:

> The duke [of York], moved to piety by the abbot's words, put away the rancour and gall of his disposition, and consented most graciously that their bodies be entombed; and more, he vehemently entreated the abbot to take special care over their burial. This permission granted, the abbot quickly sent out monks and servants to bear the bodies back to the church, where they might be received with honour; and later, having performed the funeral obsequies, in the Chapel of the Blessed Virgin there was made the place of their tomb. And therefore, the three lords already mentioned were also entombed [in the abbey], and placed in lineal order of their dignity, according to state, rank and honour, and all men rejoiced together over this who were accustomed to applaud and sing praises to deeds of charity, clemency and piety. [13]

The deaths of leading nobles and members of the king's household, the indiscriminate pillage of the town by Yorkist troops and the capture of King Henry by a faction of the nobility whose aim had been to rid the country of a corrupt regime were events that had to be condoned by the victors. However, the Nevilles had complicated the issue by also killing their local enemies – a calamity that was evidently not foreseen before the fighting began. How were these 'murders' to be condoned by the Duke of York? With the king in a position to be manipulated once more, could York both console the injured Henry and accord with those royalists who had been, in Yorkist eyes, caught on the wrong side of the fence? How would the Yorkists deal with the families of Somerset, Northumberland and Clifford, all of whom had sons waiting in the wings to avenge their father's deaths? Judging by how the Yorkists changed their story after reaching London, it seems that their propaganda evolved out of many attempts at fabrication. The resulting *Parliamentary Pardon* would merely postpone the inevitable blood feuding, which would again surface in 1459, despite the efforts of King Henry, who, in his own indomitable way, sought to bring about a peaceful settlement.

As stated earlier, St Albans was the most important of the first battles of the civil wars. However, York had made his peace with the king in the sanctity of St Albans Abbey, and it was much to Henry's credit that order was restored in the town thereafter. Thus far, York had exorcised the gut-wrenching humiliation of Dartford, but at a high price. Many contemporaries would have understood his quarrel with the Duke of Somerset and the reason behind his apparent 'execution' at St Albans, but who, apart from the Nevilles, would be willing to condone the 'murders' of Northumberland and Clifford and the deaths of many of the king's household men?

After spending the remainder of Thursday, 22 May, in his apartments within the great abbey of St Albans, Henry was conducted to Westminster, where he arrived at six o'clock the following day. With York riding on the king's right and Salisbury on his left, accompanied by Warwick ahead, bearing the sword of state, appearances were boldly maintained in a public procession that same evening. It was important that Henry should not appear to the populace as a Yorkist prisoner, even though the king may have privately thought differently about the whole affair. However, the tensions between York and the king reached a new climax at St Pauls on Whitsunday, when Henry insisted that the duke, not the archbishop, should place the crown on his head – a clear reminder of his sanctity to all who stood witness. Indeed, from this point on, the king appears to have distanced himself from his keepers, and after writs were sent out on 26 May to summon parliament, Henry

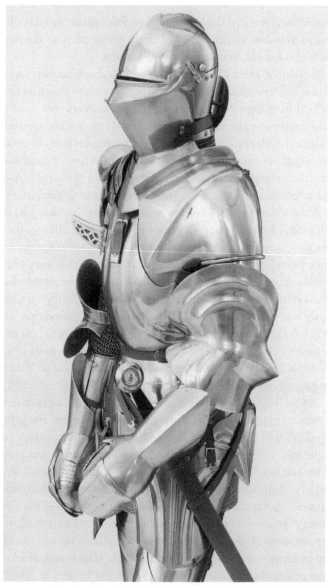

46 Composite 'harness', c.1453, in the style of Milan, typical of that worn by gentry during the Wars of the Roses. (© The Board of Trustees of the Armouries)

immediately vacated the bishop of London's palace and travelled
first to Windsor and then to Hertford, presumably to shut out
the traumatic events which had befallen him.

Soon after, Henry seems to have required at least two weeks
of medical treatment, and although he was seen to function nor-
mally during the next parliament, the threat of another bout of
deep depression placed a tremendous strain on Yorkist security.
Ultimately, Henry's continued instability and inability to retain
the mantle of kingship would bring about renewed factionalism, the emergence of Queen Margaret as a political leader,
and a renewal of hostilities. However, regarding the battle of
St Albans, *Gregory's Chronicle* maintained that 'the king let all
this matter be in a dormon a great and a long time after ... for it
was no season to treat of peace, for some were well content and
some [were] evil pleased'[14] with York's action. This uneasy peace
was also noted in a letter written from Bruges to the Archbishop
of Ravenna in 1455, in which the gravity of Henry's melancholy was so pronounced that the writer proclaimed that 'the
king has forbidden anyone to speak about it [the battle] on pain
of death'.[15] No doubt all this uncertainty, and the need to re-
establish Yorkist respectability, made the first phase of Yorkist
propaganda more difficult to initiate.

Before convening parliament, York needed to grasp firm
government control. Therefore, he took for himself the privi-
leged office of Constable of England; Archbishop Bourchier was
requested to retain the Great Seal, and the treasury was given
to his brother, Viscount Bourchier. Salisbury and Warwick were
already joint wardens of the West March towards Scotland,
but now this appointment was confirmed to them for the next
twenty years – a situation which, in conjunction with the
appointment of Warwick as Captain of Calais, confirms Neville
pre-eminence after the battle of St Albans, which was, after all,
won primarily by their support. In fact, the houses of Neville
and Bourchier were the most striking aspect of Yorkist favouritism. Precious few rewards were given to nobles or gentry

for their military service at St Albans, apart from six named individuals, and the likelihood of an act of resumption in the forthcoming parliament further dictated the need for restraint. In short, York's hands were tied by his need to restore normal political life. His need for former royalists, some of whom had been badly injured in the battle, to 'come in … and draw the line'[16] with him, and with those of his party who had opposed them across the barricades, was to be a constant feature in his forthcoming propaganda. With this thought in mind, men like the Duke of Buckingham, Sir John Wenlock, and even the Earl of Dorset, Somerset's son, were to be 'forgiven' for their part in the battle, along with those ambivalent peers who had stood idly by on the sidelines awaiting a result. To avoid political isolation, York had to balance his actions with his desire to retain loyal support, and although the Nevilles and Bourchiers must have felt well satisfied with their scoop of vacant offices and titles, men such as Lord Clinton, Lord Cobham and Sir Robert Ogle paid the price of York's restricted favouritism.

All now awaited the calling of parliament, which assembled as planned on 9 July 1455, giving the Yorkists ample time to prepare speeches favourable to themselves and detrimental to the Duke of Somerset and his followers. Attendance at Westminster was average, but conspicuous by their absence were the Duke of Exeter and Henry Beaufort, the new Duke of Somerset (the latter still in Warwick's close custody since the Yorkists had returned to London). By all accounts, Somerset's young heir was inconsolable – and was doubtless more offended when he heard that the opening sermon of parliament blamed the first battle of St Albans wholly on his father and two of his followers, Thomas Thorpe and William Joseph. It was stated that these three had misled the king into thinking that York, Warwick and Salisbury had gathered their forces with rebellious intent. The first part of King Henry's speech, probably delivered by Archbishop Bourchier, then described how Somerset had used the king's power to further his feud with York. Next, the two

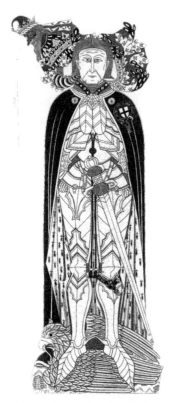

47 *Brass of Henry Bourchier, Earl of Essex, Little Easton Church, Essex. (© The Board of Trustees of the Armouries)*

letters written by the Yorkists before the battle were read out, and the archbishop assured the commons that York, Warwick and Salisbury had met the king at St Albans as loyal vassals and had taken great pains to clarify their honourable intentions before the battle commenced.

Jean-Philippe Genet is one of the few historians to have analysed sections of the parliamentary speeches. In his opinion, the two letters sent to the king before the battle of St Albans had not been altered or concocted for the speech's sake. Genet pointed out that the tone of the letters was one of extreme piety and loyalty and that they were included in parliament as concrete proof that rebellion had never been York's intent.[17] Apart from this, many at Westminster that day, including the king, would have immediately noticed if the letters had been changed in any biased way. Henry's speech went on to state that he was in no doubt of the Yorkists' loyalty and that if he had seen the letters before the battle, which he said he had not, he would have trusted their contents and acted upon them. Thus, by casting Somerset as a traitor and the king as misinformed, the battle of St Albans became a loyal action, not a Yorkist insurgency. The closing declaration of the *Parliamentary Pardon* decreed:

We therefore considering the premises, declare ... our said cousins and all those persons who came with them in their fellowship to the said town of St Albans, the said twenty-second day, and all other persons who ... helped them, our true and faithful liegemen ... And that none of our said cousins, the Duke of York, and the earls of Warwick and Salisbury, nor any of the said persons coming or being with them, nor any of their ... helpers ... be impeached, sued, vexed, grieved, hurt or molested in any wise in their bodies, lands, or goods, for anything supposed or claimed to have been done to or against our persons, crown, or dignity.[18]

There then followed an oath of allegiance to the king and a ritual signing of the document by those present, in this case, thirty-three lords temporal and twenty-seven lords spiritual. In effect, by putting pressure on the king to accept their prepared speeches, which promised the hope of peace and unity in England, the Yorkists had pandered to the king's dearest wishes. By agreeing to the above, Henry again became the puppet of corrupt councillors – this time York and the Nevilles. He had proved to be as malleable as ever, even regarding his memory of events immediately before and during the battle, by willingly agreeing to the 'lawful' killings of three of his highest-ranking nobles. The parliamentary proceedings closed on 31 July, with the declaration of a general pardon for all offences committed before 8 July, the earliest recipients being Lord Egremont and his brother on 6 August and the infamous Duke of Exeter a few days later. York's need to heal the wounds of St Albans was great indeed, considering the activities of the troublemakers. But for the moment, York had succeeded in concealing the transgressions of his allies and further blood feuding.

The *Parliamentary Pardon* stifled the fierce recriminations that might have surfaced after the battle, but the bill had not been without its problems in the making. In the *Phillipps Relation*, written soon after St Albans and well before parliament sat on

9 July, responsibility for the battle was placed squarely on the shoulders of Lord Clifford, Ralph Percy (a younger son of the Earl of Northumberland), Thomas Thorpe, Thomas Tresham and William Joseph. This blacklist was eventually changed in parliament to add Somerset in place of Clifford and to remove the names of those whom York wished to placate. Tresham and Joseph, it may be supposed, had fled like Thorpe from St Albans and were easy targets to blame next to those killed in battle. However, it was also crucial for the Yorkists not to blame the conflict on the heirs of those killed, and thus the final list of traitors was not finalised until it had been decided that individuals, such as the new Earl of Northumberland (then Lord Poynings) and John Lord Clifford, had been reconciled with York.

Another incident that probably hastened the need for the naming of scapegoats was the action of Lord Cromwell, who had not fought at St Albans but seemed paranoid about how the Yorkist indictment might implicate him. While parliament was in session on 17 July, Cromwell suddenly, without notice, excused himself to the king 'of all the stirring or moving of the male journey of Saint Albans', and on hearing of this, Warwick hastened to court, swearing that Cromwell was a liar and that he was the 'beginner of all that journey'.[19] Cromwell was so alarmed by Warwick's revealing outburst that he immediately begged the Earl of Shrewsbury to come to Charing Cross for his protection. Proclamations against bearing arms were issued, but after that, the Yorkists travelled daily to Westminster armed to the teeth, their barges stuffed with weapons and men at arms. It was the shape of things to come, and even though the incident between Warwick and Cromwell was isolated and had more to do with the apportioning of property rights than of blame for the battle, the *Parliamentary Pardon* was no safeguard for a bill which it was said that only a few days afterwards, 'many a man grudged full sore now it is passed.'[20]

Evidently, the Yorkist lords compiled their speeches intending to limit damage, but their words only postponed the factionalism that was later to cause so much unrest. With men like Archbishop Bourchier and, later, Sir John Wenlock as Yorkist speakers, their propaganda may have sounded wholly convincing to both Lords and Commons. It may have seemed acceptable to many who wished to avoid further strife. However, the fact that Somerset had been punished for his crimes on the battlefield changed nothing regarding who ruled England. Parliament was not always in session, and soon it was clear that the king was, yet again, incapable of ruling the country. And eventually, a bill which decided that York would have to be appointed protector for a second term of office was witnessed by the king at Westminster on 19 November 1455:

> We, considering the petition of the commons and the infirmity with which it has pleased the Most High Saviour to visit our person, an affliction which hinders us from the actual execution of the protection and defence of the realm and of the Church of England, and considering that if we are troubled with numerous matters of business, the speed of our recovery will be impaired, and reposing full confidence in the circumspection and industry of our most dear cousin Richard Duke of York. By the advice and assent of the lords spiritual and temporal and the assent of the commons of our realm of England, assembled in our present parliament, ordain and constitute our cousin to be protector and defender and our principal councillor of our realm of England and of the Church of England.[21]

Renewing his allegiance to essentially a hollow crown, York again assumed the mantle of kingly authority. How patient he was, and how his desire for the throne must have increased when Henry's frailty and inability to rule the kingdom was tested by further local unrest. With a renewed feud in the West

Country in full swing, this time between Lord Bonville and the Earl of Devon, and more brewing elsewhere in the kingdom, the Yorkists yet again established themselves in government and tried to maintain order. However, as in the past, the pretence of strong kingship was not enough to stop aristocratic violence in the provinces. In Bonville and Devon's case, their family feud reached new heights of seriousness during October and December 1455, proving that local feuding between rival nobles was again becoming an everyday fact of life.

From the beginning of October 1455, Thomas Courtenay, Earl of Devon and his sons had completely disrupted all ordered life in Exeter and the surrounding countryside. On 22 October, Courtenay's son, Thomas, assembled a band of ruffians and ransacked the manor of Nicholas Radford at Upcott. The elderly retainer of Lord Bonville was tricked out of his bed and murdered in cold blood. A mock trial was set for the day after to accuse him of trumped-up charges, but his death became the curtain-raiser for a series of military operations that resulted in tit-for-tat raiding like that experienced previously in the north between the Nevilles and Percys. York's appointment as protector the same November changed nothing in the West Country. Having acquired the authority to put down the disturbances, York showed no great haste in using his powers where they were most needed. A deciding battle was inevitable between the rival families, and this took place at Clyst near Exeter on 15 December 1455.

After an intermittent siege of Powderham Castle, the Earl of Devon 'departed out of the city [of Exeter] with his people into the field by Clyst and there bickered and fought with the Lord Bonville and his people and put them to flight'.[22] According to the archaeological evidence, it was a bloody affair, as when Clyst Heath was first cut through by the plough in 1800, many bones were uncovered (although another battle had been fought on the same field in 1549 to complicate matters).[23] However, the Earl of

48 Halberd, fifteenth century, with a single-edged blade. (© The Board of Trustees of the Armouries)

Devon's army was said to be huge by the standards of the day. Still, when Bonville informed the Duke of York of his plight at Clyst, the Courteney's courage deserted them. When the earl was finally arrested after sacking the Bonville town of Shute, he was sent to the Tower, although his custody did not last long. In February 1456, with the king in slightly better health, York was formally discharged from his duties as protector and Devon was freed. It was to be a repeat of 1454 for York, and the unrelenting cycle of fortune and adversity left him and his supporters once more out in the cold and vulnerable to attack.

As for foreign correspondents in the aftermath of St Albans, views of the battle and its consequences were mixed and, as usual, filled with bias and mistakes. In a letter from Bruges to the Archbishop of Ravenna, the writer was extremely partisan and remarked that the Yorkists had done an outstanding job at St Albans:

> They [the king's men] went armed because they suspected that the Duke of York would also go there with men at arms. That day they travelled 20 miles to the abbey of St Albans. On the 22nd the king set out to continue his journey, but when they were outside the town they were immediately attacked by York's men, and many perished on both sides. The Duke of Somerset was taken and forthwith beheaded. With his death the battle ceased at once and, without loss of time, the Duke of York went to kneel before the king and ask pardon for

himself and his followers, as they had not done this in order to inflict any hurt upon His Majesty, but in order to have Somerset. Accordingly, the king pardoned them, and on the 23rd the king and York and all returned to London. On the 24th they made a solemn procession, and now peace reigns … The Duke of York has the government, and the people are very pleased at this.[24]

London was certainly a hotbed of Yorkist support, which in the end forced the queen to remove her husband from the unfriendly atmosphere in the city to the Midlands, where the court remained and ruled England for the next four years. At a council meeting at Coventry on 16 October, the king's household, led now by Margaret, staged a coup. The chancellor and the privy seal were dismissed, leaving York and the Nevilles further isolated. Then, on 5 November, the Duke of Exeter and the new Duke of Somerset, aided by the Earl of Shrewsbury, attempted to ambush the Earl of Warwick on his way to London. An attack on the Duke of York followed soon after, this time at Coventry, and by the following year, it seemed that the Yorkists were in mortal danger. Had it not been for King Henry, it is highly likely that at some point, the Duke of York and his allies would have been assassinated, probably by those men who had lost fathers in the streets of St Albans. However, it appeared that the king believed achieving a negotiated settlement between the various parties was still possible. And to this end, he arranged a meeting in January 1458 to address 'various matters' yet unresolved.

A reconciliation was proposed in London. However, nothing was resolved at the so-called 'Love Day' of 16 March, when King Henry blundered and once again overlooked issues of much deeper significance. With hundreds of armed retainers in London and men like Lord Egremont and the Duke of Exeter loose in the city, it was no surprise that the charade did little to alleviate personal tensions and the desire for vengeance. In fact, the assembly of lords and the pretence of harmony precipitated the onset of more mistrust and ill feeling. In the resulting council meeting, called to make financial amends for St Albans, the terms of arbitration were firstly that the Yorkists would pay compensation to the families who had suffered by their hands at St Albans, and secondly that a perpetual memorial for the slain would be built in the abbey church, also at the Yorkists' cost. In theory, the Duke of York was to pay some 5,000 marks in compensation, made out in tallies yet to be issued. A deal was also struck whereby York could export wool to pay for his share of the endowment, terms that were hardly a penance for his part in rebellion and the premeditated 'murders' of Somerset, Northumberland and Clifford.

However, potentially far more costly for York was the promise to settle land in lieu of compensation, but again the terms of honouring such an agreement would be lengthy and were soon be overtaken by events. Guilty as charged, York and the Nevilles had barely paid the first instalment of their blood money when, in 1459 Henry yet again misjudged the situation. A complete reversal of fortunes followed later that same year when a council at Coventry advised the king that the Yorkists should be charged with treason for causing 'the execrable and most detestable deed by them done at Saint Albans'.[25]

Significantly, the two contending factions that later met in the next bout of civil war had seen their families' shed their blood in the streets of St Albans. The Yorkist transgressions there had been resurrected in public for all to see, and now it was their turn to pay with their lives for the deaths of Somerset, Northumberland and Clifford. Worse still, a new and more dangerous enemy had been made in Margaret, King Henry's queen, and, with the sons of those killed at St Albans crying out for vengeance, it was soon apparent that Margaret's political intentions were strengthened and built on much firmer foundations than her pious husband. In fact, she aimed to destroy York, the Nevilles, and all who supported them, no matter what additional damage this might inflict on her adopted country.

Her son's future would be the clarion call to arms for all loyal 'Lancastrians' to unite behind, and apart from those nobles who had lost family members at St Albans, these supporters included the chief instigators of the civil wars – the Duke of Exeter, Lord Egremont and Lord Cromwell.

To explain this further, two months after the battle at St Albans it will be remembered that the Earl of Warwick had sworn to the king that it was Cromwell alone who caused the fighting there, which may at first seems strange. However, if one harkens back to the Heworth incident in 1453, all the evidence proves that Warwick was, in fact, correct in his assumptions. His knowledge of the Percy and Neville dispute inflamed by the machinations of the Duke of Exeter and Lord Egremont may have struck a chord in 1455 with Warwick when Cromwell was seen to delay his arrival in the streets of St Albans. His loyalty to King Henry was well known, but his affiliations to the Yorkist cause were also significant. Therefore, Cromwell may have been hedging his bets in 1455, and like other nobles, he waited in the wings to see who the victor might be. He may also have wished the Yorkist lords dead so that his landed ambitions might continue unrestrained without Warwick and his father.

Therefore, the quarrel between Warwick and Cromwell in the king's presence was a significant event in the aftermath of St Albans. A report of it featured in the *Paston Letters,* which may have been common knowledge, and this did not help the king's ongoing attempts to restore peace in the kingdom afterwards.[26] In fact, the dispute was so profound that Cromwell sought the protection of the Earl of Shrewsbury against Warwick, and later, after Cromwell died in 1456, tensions between the parties were still running high, especially amongst the wounded element of the Lancastrian party. The council's decision at Coventry to charge the Yorkist lords with treason directly resulted from Queen Margaret's own bid to protect the king and her son the prince, and this overt action, in turn, opened the floodgates to continue hostilities.

In response to the royal mandate forced on the king at Coventry, York called upon the Nevilles again to support him, this time by concentrating at Ludlow. But after a positive result at the battle of Blore Heath and a disastrous encounter with the king at Ludford Bridge, the Yorkist lords were forced into exile in Calais and Ireland. Queen Margaret's emergence as a formidable leader and the chief protector of her son had added new credibility to the Lancastrian cause by pushing York into another corner. After his return to England in 1460, the Yorkist victory at Northampton and the death of Lord Egremont, York tried to usurp the crown, although his desire to be accepted by his followers failed. The throne was an ambition that York never realised, even though an act of 'accord' had been struck with the king that York's heirs would succeed him after his death.

On a bitterly cold December day in 1460 near Wakefield, Duke Richard was tricked, surrounded and butchered by a Lancastrian force under the command of the 'new' Duke of Somerset, Earl of Northumberland and Lord Clifford. The Duke of Exeter was also a witness to York's final 'execution' from politics, and the wheel of fortune turned once more in the queen's favour and her newfound power behind the throne.

The battle of Wakefield also sealed the fate of many of the Duke of York's principal adherents, including his son, the Earl of Rutland, who was killed in the rout, and the Earl of Salisbury who suffered execution at Pontefract Castle after being captured. It was left to the Earl of Warwick and York's son Edward of March to pursue their fathers' killers as the civil war raged on. The result was further bloodletting, and this would eventually prove fatal for the Percys, the Cliffords and the Beauforts. In fact, Edward almost extinguished the male line of the Beauforts and seriously injured the fortunes and lives of the Percys and the Cliffords in the next act of mass violence played out in a grim Yorkshire snowstorm.

After the bloodbath of Towton in 1461, the renegade Duke of Exeter escaped into Scotland, where he continued to threaten

49 The fields below Sandal Castle where the Duke of York was slain at the battle of Wakefield in December 1460. (Author's Collection)

the Yorkist regime. After fighting at the battle of Barnet in 1471, this time for the taciturn Earl of Warwick against Edward IV, he was wounded and left for dead on the battlefield. That he survived Barnet was a miracle, and although his later imprisonment by the Yorkists was guaranteed, he somehow managed to volunteer his services to Edward IV when he invaded France in 1475.

However, Exeter's association with the king was to be short lived. On the return voyage to England, the duke was allegedly thrown overboard, probably on the orders of Edward, who, no doubt, recalled Exeter's chequered past as one of the chief instigators of unrest in the north and, therefore, a 'beginner' of the first battle at St Albans.

Crucially, St Albans marked the continuation of one feud and the beginning of another far more significant problem for English kings. Before Thursday, 22 May 1455, feuding English families and localised rebellion had been isolated. After the battle, political life would become secondary to violence and battlefield murder. However, it is a mistake to think that the first battle of St Albans produced an immediate slide into anarchy and a long winter of discontent. In fact, the encounter had far more dangerous and long-lasting consequences regarding the way other battles were fought from then on. When hostilities and local feuding continued after 1455, the memory of St Albans caused a greater willingness to resort to violent action and execution rather than mediation. After all, mediation had failed spectacularly before the battle of St Albans and was to prevent successful arbitration between York and Lancaster for at least thirty-five years. Also, the battle ended the traditional chivalric practice of ransoming prisoners of war and, worse, the struggle it initiated caused a genuine fear in succeeding generations that the same thing could happen all over again. What more significant consequences could there be than a battle where the actual psychology of the combatants changed the course of history?

For many historians, the 'short scuffle in the street' at St Albans was seen as a precursor or side-show to the civil wars that followed, but as I have proved, the battle was far from a precursor to all out warfare, as were the other 'minor' battles that preceded it. Even the struggle at Clyst after St Albans had its local and national consequences, and it is hoped that this work re-classifies such battles of the 1450s as part of a chain of events, rather than one incident that changed the course of British history.

Appendix 1

The Stow Relation

Bellum apud Seynt Albons (Battle at St Albans).

Be it known and had in mind that on the twenty-first day of May in the thirty-fourth year of the reign of King Harry the Sixth, our sovereign lord king took his journey from Westminster toward Saint Albans, and rested at Watford all night; and on the morrow he came to Saint Albans, and with him in his party assembled under his banner the Duke of Buckingham, the Duke of Somerset, the Earl of Pembroke, the Earl of Northumberland, the Earl of Devonshire, the Earl of Stafford, the Earl of Dorset, the Earl of Wiltshire, the Lord Clifford, the Lord Dudley, the Lord Berners, the Lord Roos, with other diverse knights, squires, and other gentlemen and yeomen to the number of ii^{ml} [2,000] and more. And upon the twenty-second day of the said month above rehearsed assembled the Duke of York, and with him came in company the Earl of Salisbury, the Earl of Warwick with diverse knights and squires unto their party into the field, called the Key Field, beside Saint Albans. Furthermore, our

said sovereign lord the king, hearing and knowing of the said
duke's comyng with other lords aforesaid, pygth [pitched] his
banner at the place called Boslawe [Goslawe] in Saint Peter's
Street, which place was called afore time past Sandeforde, and
commanded the ward and barriers to be kept in strong wise;
for the said Duke of York abiding in the field aforesaid from
seven of the clock in the morning till it was almost ten without any stroke smitten on either party. The said duke sent to
the king our sovereign lord, by the advice of his council,
praying and seeking him to take him as his true man and
humble subject; and to consider and to tender at the reverence of Almighty God, and in way of charity the true intent
of his coming – to be a good and gracious sovereign lord to
his liegemen, which with all their power and might would be
ready at all times to live and die with him in his right. And to
what thing it should like his majesty royal to command them,
if it be his worship, keeping right of the crown and welfare of
the land; 'Moreover, gracious lord, please it your Majesty
Royal of your great goodness and rightwiseness to incline
your will to hear and feel the rightwise party of us your subjects and liegemen; first, praying and beseeching to our Lord
Jesus of his high and mighty power to give unto you virtue
and prudence, and that through the mediation of the glorious
martyr Saint Alban to give you very knowledge to know the
intent of our assembling at this time; for God that is [in]
Heaven knoweth than our intent is rightful and true. And
therefore, we pray unto Almighty Lord Jesus these words –
Domine sis clipeus defensionis nostræ. Wherefore, gracious lord,
please it your High Majesty to deliver such as we will accuse,
and they too have like, as they have deserved and done, and
you to be honourable and worshiped as most rightful king
and our governor. For and we shall now at this time be promised, as afore this time is not unknown, of promises broken
which full faith fully hath ben promised, and there upon great
others made, we will not now cease for none such promises,

surety, nor other, till we have them which have deserved
death, or else we [will] die therefore.' And to that answered
the king our sovereign lord, and said: 'I, King Harry, charge
and command that no manner of person, of what degree, or
state, or condition who ever he be, abide not, but void the
field, and not be so hardy to make any resistance against me in
my own realm; for I shall know what traitor dare be so bold
to raise a people in my own land, where through I am in great
disease and heaviness. And by the faith that I owe to Saint
Edward and to the crown of England, I shall destroy them
every mother's son, and they be hanged, and drawn, and
quartered, that may be taken afterward, of them to have
example to all such traitors to beware to make any such rising
of people within my land, and so traitor-like to abide her king
and governor. And, for a conclusion, rather then they shall
have any lord here with me at this time, I shall this day, for her
sake, and in this quarrel myself live or die.' Which answer
came to the Duke of York, who, by the advice of the lords of
his council, said unto them these words: 'The king our sovereign lord will not be reformed at our beseeching nor prayer,
nor will not understand the intent that we come hither and
assembled afore and gathered at this time; but only this full
purpose, and there is no other way but that he will with all his
power pursue us, and if been taken, to give us a shameful
death, losing our livelihood and goods, and our heirs shamed
forever. And therefore, seeing it will be no other wise but that
we shall utterly die, better it is for us to die in the field than
cowardly to be put to a great rebuke and a shameful death;
moreover, considering in what peril England stands in at this
hour, therefore every man help to help power for the right
thereof, to redress the mischief that now reigns, and to acquit
us like men in this quarrel; preying to that lord that as king of
glory, that reigns in the kingdom celestial, to keep us and save
us this day in our right, and through the help of his holy grace
we may be made strong to withstand the great abominable

and cruel malice of them that purpose fully to destroy us with shameful death. We, therefore, lord, prey to thee to be our comfort and defender, saying the words aforesaid, *Domine sis clipeus defensionis nostræ.*' And when this was said, the said Duke of York, and the said Earl of Salisbury, and the Earl of Warwick, between eleven and twelve of the clock at noon, they broke into the town in three diverse places and several places of the aforesaid street. The king being then in the place of Edmund Westby, hundreder of the said town of Saint Albans, commanded to slay all manner men of lords, knights, and squires, and men that might be taken of the aforesaid Duke of York. This done, the aforesaid Lord Clifford kept strongly the barriers that the said Duke of York might not in anywise, with all the power that he had, enter nor break into the town. The Earl of Warwick, knowing thereof, took and gathered his men together and ferociously brake in by the garden sides between the sign of the Key and the sign of the Chequer in Holywell Street; and anon as they were within the town, suddenly they blew up trumpets, and set a cry with a shout and a great voice, 'A Warwick! A Warwick! A Warwick!' and unto that time the Duke of York might never have entered into the town; and they with strong hand kept it, and mightily fought together, and anon, forth with after the breaking in, they set on them manfully. And as of lords of name were slain the Lord Clifford, the Duke of Somerset, the Earl of Northumberland, Sir Bartram Entwistle, knight; and of men of court, William Zouch, John Batryaux, Ralph of Babthorpe and his son, William Corbyn, squires; William Cotton, Receiver of the Duchy of Lancaster; Gilbert Starbrok, squire; Malmer Pagentoun, William Butler, yeomen; Roger Mercroft, the king's messenger; Halyn, the king's porter; Ralf Willerby; and twenty-five more, which their names be not yet known. And of them that been slain forty-eight [were] buried in Saint Albans. And at this same time were hurt lords of name – the kyng, our sovereign Lord,

in the neck with an arrow; the Duke of Buckingham, with an
arrow in the visage; the Lord of Stafford in the hand, with an
arrow; the Lord of Dorset, sore hurt that he might not walk,
but he was carried home in a cart; and Wenlock, knight, in
likewise in a cart sore hurt; and other diverse knights and
squires sore hurt. The Earl of Wiltshire, Thorpe, and many
other fled, and left their harness behind them cowardly, and
the substance of the king's party were despoiled of horse and
harness. This done, the said lords, that is to say, the Duke of
York, the Earl of Salisbury, the Earl of Warwick, came to the
king, our sovereign lord, and on their knees be sought him of
grace and forgiveness of that they had done in his presence,
and be sought him of his highness to take them as his true
liegemen, saying that they never [intended] to hurt his own
person, and therefore [the] king our sovereign lord took them
to grace, and so desired them to cease their people, and that
there should no more harm be done; and they obeyed his
commandment, and let make a cry in the kings name that all
manner of people should cease and not [be] so hardy to strike
any stroke more after the proclamation of the cry; and so
ceased the said battle, *Deo gratias*.

And on the morrow the kyng and the said duke, with other
certain lords, came into the bishops of London, and there
kept residence with joy and solemnity, concluding to hold the
parliament at London, the ninth day of July next coming.

Reprinted from *Archaeologia*, Vol. xx, p. 519. From a record kept
in the Tower of London in 1822. J. Gairdner, ed., Stow Relation,
The Paston Letters, Vol. 3, 1904, pp. 25–9.

Appendix 2

The Phillipps Relation

The solicitors and causers of the field taking at Saint Albans their names shown hereafter:

The Lord Clifford.
Ralph Percy.
Thorpe.
Tresham and Joseph.

The inony [*enemy's*] battle was in the marketplace, and the king's standard was pight [pitched], the king being present with these lords, whose names follow:

The Duke of Buckingham. The Duke of Somerset. The Earl Devonshire. The Earl of Northumberland. The Earl Stafford. The Earl Dorset. The Lord Clifford. The Lord Roos.	With many knights and squires, to the number in all fought that day iii^{ml} [3,000], and it was done on Thursday last past betwixt eleven and twelve at midday.

The names of the lords that were on the other party shown hereafter:

The Duke of York. The Earl of Salisbury. The Earl of Warwick. The Lord Clinton. Sir Robert Ocle [Ogle].	With many others, to the number of v^{ml} [5,000] men.

And Sir Robert Ocle [Ogle] took vi^c [600] men of the Marches, and took the marketplace [before] any man was [aware]; then the alarm bell was rung, and every man [fled] to harness, for at that time every man was out of their array, and they joined battle anon; and it was done within di [*one half*] hour, and there were slain the men whose names follow:

The Duke of Somerset. The Earl Northumberland. The Lord Clifford The Lord Clinton. Sir Bartyn at Wessyll [Entwistle]. Babthorpe and his son. Cotton, Receiver of the Duchy. Gryphet, Usher of Hall. Herry Loweys. William Regmayde. John Rawlins. Asple. Harpour, Yeoman of the Crown.	With many other men, to the number of iv^c [400], and as many or more hurt. The king was hurt with an arrow in the neck. The Duke of Buckingham hurt and fled into the abbey. The Earl Devonshire hurt. The Earl Stafford and Dorset greatly hurt. Fylongley fought manly and was shot though the arms in three or four places.

The Duke of Norfolk came a day after the journey was done with vi^{ml} [6,000] men.
And the Erle of Oxford also.

The Earl of Shrewsbury. Lord Cromwell. And Sir Thomas Stanley.	with x^{ml} [10,000] men were coming.

The king with all the lords came to London to Westminster on Friday, at six of clock at after noon, and [in] London went a general procession the same day.

From MS. Phillipps, 9735, No. 278. J. Gairdner, ed., Stow Relation, *The Paston Letters*, Vol. 3, 1904, pp. 29–30.

Appendix 3

State Papers of Milan

Copy of part of a letter written on 31 May from Bruges to the Archbishop of Ravenna (Bartolomeo Roverella).

We left London on the 27 May and at that time there was nothing new; my lord of Somerset ruled as usual. Subsequently I learned here yesterday, by letters which came straight from Sandwich to Dunkirk, that fresh disturbances broke out in England a few days after my departure. A great part of the nobles have been in conflict, and the Duke of Somerset, the Earl of Northumberland and my lord of Clifford are slain, with many other lords and knights on both sides. The Duke of Somerset's son, who presented the collars of the king, was mortally wounded; my lord of Buckingham and his son are hurt. The Duke of York has done this, with his followers. On the 24th he entered London and made a solemn procession to St Pauls. They say he has demanded pardon from the king for himself and his men and will have it. He will take up the government again, and some think that the affairs of that kingdom will now take a turn for the better. If that be the case, we can put up with this inconvenience. No one comes from Calais as the passages are guarded. We should hear further particulars from merchants, messengers and those who come. I send your lordship these particulars, as you will be glad to hear them even though the news seems unpleasant.

Postscript on the 3rd of June.

I have further news of the battle in England brought by one who came here from Calais. They say that on the 21 of May the king left Westminster with many lords, including the Duke of Somerset, to hold a council at Leicester (*a le cestre*), eight miles (*sic*) from London. They went armed because they suspected that the Duke of York would also go there with men at arms. That day they travelled twenty miles to the abbey of St. Albans. On the 22nd the king set out to continue his journey, but when they were outside the town they were immediately attacked by York's men, and many perished on both sides. The Duke of Somerset was taken and forthwith beheaded. With his death the battle ceased at once and, without loss of time, the Duke of York went to kneel before the king and ask pardon for himself and his followers, as they had not done this in order to inflict any hurt upon his Majesty, but in order to have Somerset. Accordingly, the king pardoned them, and on the 23rd the king and York returned to London. On the 24th they made a solemn procession, and now peace reigns. The king has forbidden anyone to speak about it [the battle] upon pain of death (*il Re ha mandato Bando a pena di vita, non se ne parli*). The Duke of York has the government, and the people are very pleased with this (*il duca de Jorlz ha il governo et li popoli se ne tengono molto contenti*).

A.B. Hinds, ed., *Calendar of State Papers and Manuscripts in the Archives and Collections of Milan 1385–1618*, 1912, pp. 16–17 (Italian).

Appendix 4

The Dijon Relation

When the Duke of Somerset and those who were of his party then being in the City of London, heard that the Duke of York and many other lords in his company were advancing against them with a force of 5,000 men, and when he considered what he had done against the Duke of York and that he was also in very bad odour with the people of London, he came to the conclusion that he should not remain in the City of London for fear that the people would fall on him the moment he [York] arrived. For which cause he persuaded the king to sally forth against the said Duke of York and his other enemies, their opponents, and hastily gathered the said third day after the feast of the Ascension up to 3,500 persons and on the 21st day of May in the morning they issued out of London and went to lodge twenty miles away from there at a little village where there is an abbey called St Albans, near the which village at less than half a day's march their enemies were lodged. These, when they knew of the king's coming, immediately approached him and also the 22nd day of the said month very early the king sent a herald to the Duke of

York to know the cause for which he had come there with
so many men and that it seemed to the king something quite
new that he, the duke, should be rising against him, the king.
The reply made was that he [York] was not coming against
him thus, [he] was always ready to do him obedience but he
well intended in one way or another to have the traitors who
were about him so that they should be punished, and that in
case he could not have them with good will and fair consent,
he intended in any case to have them by force. The reply that
was made from the king's side to the said Duke of York was
that he [the king] was unaware that there were any traitors
about him were it not for the Duke of York himself who had
risen against the crown. And even before this reply came to
the Duke of York there began a skirmish before the village
by one side and the other. And thus, when the Duke of York
had the aforesaid reply, the battle became more violent and
both sides with banners displayed began to fight. And first
the Duke of York's men incontinently approached the village
and set a good guard at all the ways about and entered in with
such great force that incontinent they took and blockaded the
marketplace of the said village and part of his people found
themselves in the middle of it and in this manner began to
fight the one party against the other. The battle began on the
stroke of ten hours in the morning but because the place was
small, few of the combatants could set to work there and matters reach such a great extremity that four of those who were
of the king's bodyguard were killed by arrows in his presence
and the king himself was struck by an arrow in the shoulder,
but it penetrated only a little of the flesh. At last, when they
had fought for the space of three hours the king's party seeing
themselves to have the worst of it broke on one wing and
began to flee and the Duke of Somerset retreated within an
inn to save himself and hid. Which things seen by those of
the said Duke of York [they] incontinent beset the said house
all about. And there the Duke of York gave orders that the

king should be taken and drawn out of the throng and put in
the abbey for safety and thus it was done. And in this abbey
took refuge also with him the Duke of Buckingham who was
very badly wounded by three arrows. And incontinent this
done [they] began to fight Somerset and his men who were in
this place within the inn and defended themselves valiantly.
And in the end after the doors were broken down the Duke
of Somerset seeing that he had no other remedy took council with his men about coming out and did so, as a result of
which incontinent he and all his people were surrounded by
the Duke of York's men. And after some were stricken down
and the Duke of Somerset had killed four of them with his
own hand, it is said, he was felled to the ground with an axe
and incontinent being so wounded in several places that there
he ended his life. And while the Duke of Somerset made this
defence at the inn others of his party who remained outside
all the time fought against those of the Duke of York so that
three lords died there on Somerset's side, that is to say the
Earl of Northumberland, Lord Clifford, which was a great
pity for he was a brave man, and Sir Richard Harrington also
a noble knight and a brave man and many other gentlemen
and esquires as many of one party as the other so that in all
there died 200 persons or thereabouts. The battle lasted until
two and a half hours after noon and this done the Duke of
York's men took themselves to the abbey to kill the Duke
of Buckingham and the treasurer, who is called the Earl of
Wiltshire, who had retreated there with the king, but the
said Duke of York would not suffer it but sent his herald to
the king to inform him that he must choose which he preferred, either to hand over the two lords as prisoners into his
hands, or that they should be killed in front of him and to
put himself in danger once more. Wherefore the king agreed
freely to allow him to arrest the said two lords and so he did,
in particular the Duke of Buckingham. The treasurer could
not be found for disguising himself he fled in a monk's habit

and even now the 27th May no one knows where he has gone. And when all these things were done the Duke of York entered within the abbey and went before the king's person and there went on his knees to him crying mercy for whatever way he might have offended and for the peril in which he had put his person and many other good and humble words, showing him that he had not gone against him but against the traitors to his crown, and in the end before the Duke of York went away from there the king pardoned him everything and took him in his good grace, and this day the king, the Duke of York and all the other lords came to London where they have been received with great joy and solemn procession. And the said Duke of York will now be without contradiction the first after the king and will have the government of all. God give him grace to carry out his tasks well and have pity on the souls of sinners. Amen.

The Dijon Relation, Archives de la Cote d'Or, Dijon, B.11942, no.258 (French).

The Fastolf Relation

The first 'journey' [battle of] Saint Albans.

On Thursday the 22nd day of May, just before the day of Whitsun [Pentecost], the 33rd year of the reign of our sovereign lord, Henry VI, after the conquest of England, the king our sovereign lord arrived at the town of St Albans by eleven [or nine] in the morning, and in his company were my lords the dukes of Buckingham and Somerset, my lords the earls of Pembroke, of Stafford, of Dorset, of Northumberland, of Devonshire and of Wiltshire, the lords of Roos, Clifford, Berners, Sudeley and Fauconberg, master John Ormond, Sir Richard Harrington, controller of the King's household, Sir Bertin Entwistle, John Hanford and William Lucy, knights, and several [many?] others.

(Item) Likewise, on the same day, at more or less the same time, arrived near the town of St Albans, my lord the Duke of York, and in his company were my lords the earls of Warwick and Salisbury, and several knights and bannerets, bachelor esquires and several others. They did not enter the town of

St Albans, but remained in attendance near the town, within a crossbow's shot.

(Item) Likewise, as soon as the Duke of Somerset had knowledge of my lord of York's approach near the place, the aforementioned Duke of Somerset sent Lesparre pursuivant of arms to my lord Duke of Exeter to the said Duke of York, to command him in the name and on behalf of the king, our lord, that he and all his company should quit at once and withdraw, on pain of their allegiance and breach of honour, and all being false to the king, our lord. And as soon as the said pursuivant was gone, once more came before my lord of York, Buckingham the herald, and in his company Joyeulx, pursuivant to my lord of Bonville and they delivered the same message and order, as had done pursuivant Lesparre. Thereupon, my lord of York ordered the herald and pursuivant to swear upon their duty, to say and declare to him whether this order was spoken by the king, our lord, himself, and whether they had come upon his explicit orders. And they answered that they had not and that my lord of Buckingham and my lord of Somerset had sent them to say they were coming from before the king our lord having received this order from him. To which my lord answered: 'Tell the king our lord and his cousin Buckingham that I have come here to settle my petitions and requests, and do loyal service to the king, our lord. And if I knew any in my company who would want to act to the contrary, I would punish him myself, as an example to the others.'

(Item) Likewise, my lord of York had Mowbray, herald of my lord the Duke of Norfolk, called at once and bade him go before the king our lord, to tell him that he commended himself and his noble and good grace, as humbly as any man could do, to his sovereign lord, as well as to all the lords in his company. And he was beseeching and imploring him, very humbly, that if might please his kind grace to grant him the petitions, requests and demands that he had in the past sent to him, by my lord of Fauconberg and others in his company.

(Item) Likewise, these things being said to the king our lord, by Mowbray herald, he answered that he had not seen these petitions, and bade him go to my lord of Buckingham saying that he had entrusted him for this day to give answer to all matters that should be answered in his name.

(Item) Likewise, when Mowbray came before my lord of Buckingham and said and declared his full message, my lord of Buckingham answered to him that it was true that the king our lord had not seen the petitions and requests yet and that he himself, would soon show them in diligence to the king, our lord, and would send the answer made to them back to my lord of York by Buckingham herald, saying then this to Mowbray herald, 'You will commend me to my brothers-in-law, York and Salisbury, to my nephew Warwick, and his brother Norfolk, in case he should be in their company, as you say he is nearby, that is to say that they can clearly be seen, since the king is present, and they will see his own person and banner on the field, as they withdraw to Barnet or Hatfield, for one night, waiting for some appointment to be made, or one or two men of state and honour to be sent before one to speak with them.' Thereupon the herald asked him, 'My lord, please you bid me something else for this time,' and he answered: 'Yes, I want you to commend me to my brother Norfolk and tell him that we are so next of kin that if he had a daughter and I had one, we would not marry each other's daughter without a licence from the Pope, and furthermore, he married my sister. That I beseech him to have out of his heart all melancholy thoughts, wrath, and anger for this time, and the king will be grateful to him, and take him into better grace.' This being said, Mowbray herald asked him again, 'My lord, please you bid me more to say before my lords.' And he answered, 'Yes, we want everyone to know that we have come here to support no one, nor for any other cause else, but to be in the company of the king, our lord, as we are right-fully bound to, and as is meet.' Thereupon the herald took his leave and returned before my lord of York to whom he delivered his report, as afore stated.

(Item) Likewise, my lord of York immediately sent back Mowbray herald, for a second time, before my lord of Buckingham, begging him to be willing to go before the king our lord, in order to get an answer to his requests and petitions. Thereupon my lord of Buckingham answered to the herald that he would with all possible dispatch send his answer by his herald Buckingham, to my lord of York, which he never did.

(Item) Likewise, because the answer was not sent along, the company of my lord of York was made uneasy, saying, that it was only a delay. It is the reason why my lord of York sent back Mowbray for a third time, before my lord of Buckingham, asking him to answer his petitions, with no more delay. And when Mowbray herald came to the gate [*barriere*: barrier, bar] of the town of St Albans, which is near the town parish church, he found there, Sir Richard Harrington, Bertin Entwistle and John Hanford knights, Breknok squire and John Swythman who asked the herald what he wanted. And he answered that he wanted to speak to my lord of Buckingham. And they said to him that he would instantly speak with him, and they sent him before my lord of Buckingham, who immediately ordered the master of his household and a knight called Sir Thomas Fynderne to go before Mowbray herald.

On his arrival Mowbray told him the reason why he had come. Thereupon they returned to my lord of Buckingham and kept the herald waiting till they came back. After going to my lord of Buckingham, they returned before the herald and told him that my lord of Buckingham had been before the king our lord, who was not decided to give them any answer. Thereupon the herald took his leave. As he returned, he found my lord of York and all his company coming towards the town of St Albans and the herald gave the answer to my lord of York. Thereupon he [York] replied, 'Therefore we must do what we can do.' Thereupon they made their way towards the town etc.

Fastolf Relation, College of Arms, *Arundel MS.* 48, folio 342 (translated from the French).

Whethamstede's *Registrum*

After an invented speech given by the Duke of York, he and his allies, the earls of Warwick and Salisbury, take up position in Key Field to the east of St Albans. Abbot John Whethamstede gives his account of the battle in which he speaks of himself in the third person:

> Meanwhile, while they [the Yorkists] halted for their discussion, the king, informed of their arrival, sent the Duke of Buckingham to them, and he asked them whether their arrival was peaceful, or arising from some other opposite intention. They all answered the same thing, saying, 'We are faithful liegemen of the king, we intend him no evil, nor have we come here for this reason, to do him any harm. Only let there be given to us that evil man who has lost Normandy, who has neglected Gascony, and who has led and misled this kingdom of England to this wretched state. Let that man be given to us, and we shall return again peacefully without the turmoil of a struggle, or the damaging of peace. But if not, if a refusal be given to us in this our desire, and the king is

unwilling for any reasons now stated to defend him, then he is to know that we would prefer rather to go into the field than to return to our own, our proposal frustrated, without our desired prey.'

The king, informed of their words and desires, and understanding this to be their will rather than reasonable or lawful, chose rather to make trial of the doubtful outcome of battle than to agree either to lose the said duke [of Somerset] or hand him over into the hands of his enemies. Realising this, they [the Yorkists] soon sounded the trumpet and rushed into the middle of St Peter's Street, breaking down the barriers until they had the king's battleline in front of them. They fought each other for a short space of time so fiercely that here you would have seen one man lying with his brain struck out, there another with his arm cut off, there a third with his throat cut, there a fourth with his chest pierced, and the whole place beyond filled with corpses of the slain, on this side and that, and everywhere in every direction. And so powerfully at the time was shield driven back by shield and targe by targe, threatening sword by sword, foot by foot and weapon-point by weapon-point that for a short while the outcome was in doubt as to which side victory would yield, and the dice of fate was unclear enough.

At last, however, by some terror sent from heaven, or breath of madness implanted or innate, turning their backs they [the king's men] fled in great numbers − nay, the greater part, on the king's side, running about through the gardens and fields, the brambles and thickets, the hedges and woods − sought for themselves places and hideouts where they could best lurk and conceal themselves until the storm of the battle was over. Among whom there were some of knightly rank, men of elegant enough appearance in themselves, but more like Paris than Hector in nature. To whom because,

It had been more [gentle] to have lain on a soft bed,
And to have held a tender girl in folded arms,
Than to have loaded their right shoulders with shields or
　　spears,
Or to have supported a helmet on their flattened hair.

So pursuing softness rather than service, and more often fre-
quenting the park than the combat of the next battle, they
abandoned the king in the field, and even sought out-of-the-
way places to hide in for themselves. There were also others
from the king's household, or palace, who all, as they were
clothed for [more] gentle activities, thus from the softness
of their spirit shuddering away from the sight of blood, took
themselves from the field lest they should see its spilling.
There were moreover even a third group, from the eastern
region of the kingdom who, because of their origin were
softer than the rest, and more tender, according to that saying
of the poet,

Whatever faces the eastern regions, and the warmth of the
　　kingdom,
The mildness of the sky softens their spirits.

So, struck by the spirit of fear, they left the king alone on the
field, and they fled from him in the same way as sheep or small
lambs are accustomed to fleeing from the shepherd when they
have seen a wolf coming. The king, seeing that almost all his
men had either turned to flight or were slain on the battlefield, and that he stood with no guard under his own banner,
with no hope of relief, at the suggestion of the few men who
remained that he should flee before the bows and avoid the
peril of the arrows that flew dense as snowflakes around his
head, removed himself to the meagre hospitality of a certain
[trader's] cottage, where he remained with his men, until such
time as the Duke of York came to him, and with these words

he greeted and comforted him. 'Rejoice, illustrious king, and may these men rejoice also who stand about you, all you lords. Now that evil slanderer [Somerset] has been thrown down, he who night and day would accuse me and my brothers – I mean these lords here present with me – in your sight, your majesty. And therefore, by the grace of God, that man who had a just cause against him has been proven victor, and that impious enemy for his wickedness has come to great ruin. Rejoice therefore, for his downfall is like another hanging of Aman in the opinion of the common people. All now rejoice together at this downfall, just as formerly the Jews delighted at the hanging of their greatest enemy. Rejoice further, that this downfall will pacify the common people throughout your kingdom. And indeed, he was detested of children and youths, of maidens and wives, and also by all others of all sexes and ages, so that wherever he walked or rode by the common roads in the City of London, or anywhere, they would call down curses upon him, and would curse him according to the imprecation of the Psalm, in this way:

May his days be few, may his children be orphans, may his wife be a widow, and may his name be remembered no more.

Rejoice therefore, prince, rejoice, for that curse has trickled like water into his flesh, like oil into his blood. Rejoice further that this downfall will raise you to the heights of honour, higher than you have ever risen yet while he whispered in your ear. I am, and always was, and all my followers are and were your faithful, indeed, your most faithful liegemen, and we will always remain, as much as any man, while flesh is wedded to spirit and spirit rules flesh, or if you prefer while will is subject to reason, your most ready servants, in advance or retreat, proceeding at the nod and nomination of your royal self.'

And having said these things, [the Duke of York] led him out with all due reverence from that humble cottage and led him first to the bier then to his chambers, and there made him remain for all that day. And in the morning, he led him to London, where in the Bishop's Palace lodging was prepared for him, and there he made him remain throughout the ensuing Pentecost, continually, for all that sacred week, attended in all things by the two aforementioned earls, impeding his obsequies and reverential observances. And this was the beginning, middle and end of that battle.

Meantime, while the Duke of York was consoling the king, and comforting him, the victors were left idle, and being too eager and avaricious, passed their time with pillage, plunder and rapine, incapable of restraining their hands either at home among their neighbours or outside among enemies. They were all, for the most part, of the northerly parts of the kingdom, and therefore, although stronger in arms and more ready to war, [were] also used to the spilling of blood, according to this metre:

He who is born with the northern hoarfrost in his veins,
[Is] indomitable in war, and Death's lover.

Nevertheless, because that people are more penurious than pecunious, having more an abundance of peas and barley, wheat and grain, than of rich purple dyes, or ebony, or ivory, or Tyrian cloth, or gold, or silver, upon coming to a place so much more opulent and sumptuous, that is the southern regions of the kingdom, they turned their hands to plunder, their fingers to pillaging, sparing not king nor peer nor [commoner] nor knight, nor any other man at whose house plunder might be found. And thus, one man, robbed of his golden vase, thought like Prince Agathocles to eat from clay plates and drink from earthenware vessels, or from cups of mean price and little renown. Another man, robbed of his

horse and arms, was forced to abandon his own home, weap-
onless, poor and on foot, miserable less from the theft than
from the shame and derision that followed him to his own
people. And a third man, relieved of all the gold and silver
in his purse or money pouch, was forced to beg borrowed
money to convey him to his people, but he was happy in this,
that he had escaped so, with no worse damage in that furious uproar. And so far, increased the strength and violence
of this despoliation and rapine, that rumour even reached the
monastery that the thieves would reach there and despoil it.
And that voice was true and faithful, and so it would have
happened save that Saint Alban valourously donned his arms
and set his shield against the enemies of his church. With that
knight and martyr defending her, his church remained safe,
to the extent that it was later found to be free of any despoliation or heavy cost of goods.

The said battle being over, and the victory achieved
through the favour of Mars by the Duke of York's side
having been reported, what followed was dolorous indeed
and brought tears to the eyes of the beholders. The corpses
of the slain lay scattered about in great number at every street
corner, nor did any man wish, for fear of raising the anger
of the said Duke, to prepare ditches to bury them. Among
them lay the bodies of three illustrious lords; the body, that
is, of Lord Edmund Beaufort, Duke of Somerset, the body
of Lord Henry Percy, Earl of Northumberland, and the body
of Lord Thomas Clifford, Earl of Clifford. For fear of the
aforementioned duke, no man dared to touch these corpses or
to perform pious obsequies over them, because the said lords
were so odious to him. The abbot hearing this, and remem-
bering well the actions of Tobias, went boldly before the
person of the duke and intrepidly spoke to him in this way:
'Good and illustrious prince. Many and many a quality are
laudable in a prince, but it is believed to be no small virtue
after victory to spare the vanquished, rather than to wield

the sword of vengeance further against them. Trojan Aeneas
was certainly praised in these terms, and Achilles the Greek.
Also, the Roman general Julius who, upon seeing the head
of Pompey, his enemy, is said to have been moved to compassion, even to tears. Therefore, may you too be moved to
compassion, good prince, on the vanquished and conquered,
or more, the overthrown and the slaughtered. I say not your
enemies and adversaries, but indeed, your cousins, your com-
patriots, your kin; and command their bodies to be gathered
away as cannot be denied them by the compassion not only of
any Christian man, but of the meanest and lowest man of all.
To rage further against them after their death is not proper,
nor the act of a generous mind. Rather it is bestial, brutish, or
wolfish. We read it written:

Let the wolf and the filthy bear worry the dying,
Just as all the other creatures of the lower orders of beasts.
And also, the greater a man is, the more his anger may be calmed,
Nor is a generous mind easily moved.
For the noble man asks nothing but the palm of victory,
And all his desire is won when his enemy falls.

For today, prince, you have the palm, you have the victory,
you have all that your soul desired as regards their persons. For
today let your rage be calmed therefore, nor let it vent itself
any further against their bodies, when so many men passing by and seeing them lying there in that way are moved to
compassion. Indeed, they [Somerset and his men] lie now in
the most despicable way, despoiled of their arms, denuded of
their clothes, with nothing at all to cover them; and to cause
them to lie any longer is not the deed of a pious prince but
truly of a tyrant like Creon who, due to a similar deed, was
believed by the Duke Theseus to be visiting a similar torture
on the dead. Pious victory, prince, becomes rather impious
savagery where it is not followed by compassion. More dam-

nable than laudable is that victor who in triumph persists too
far and knows not afterwards how to return his sword to its
scabbard, nor restrain the spirit of vengeance. Therefore, that
your victory may be known as pious and your triumph as
laudable, in the work of benignity, goodness and clemency,
in the work of charity, piety and compassion, in any works
that may be pleasing to the angels, welcome to man, and dear
to God, in order that it may be worthy of eternal reward, may
the soul of a prince be touched by that sincere piety which
raises princes above men, that they might aspire to be equal
with God, according to this saying,

The great clemency of God raises our lowly clemency.

And, by that same piety, to the removal of their bodies into
their tombs may you graciously give your consent.'

   Therefore, the duke, moved to piety by the abbot's words,
put away the rancour and gall of his disposition, and con-
sented most graciously that their bodies be entombed; and
more, he vehemently entreated the abbot to take special care
over the burial. This permission granted, the abbot quickly
sent out monks and servants to bear the bodies back to the
church, where they might be received with honour; and later,
having performed the funeral obsequies, in the Chapel of the
Blessed Virgin there was made the place of their tomb.

   And therefore, the three lords already mentioned were also
entombed, and placed in lineal order of their dignity, according to state, rank and honour; and all men rejoiced together
over this who were accustomed to applaud and sing praises to
deeds of charity, clemency and piety; and truly such a scene
would sadden only those who are wicked and impious and
desire especially to pursue vengeance beyond the natural term
of life. And of these lords, and of their place of burial, there
was written a short verse in this way:

Those whom Mars, whom Mars' savage fate and sister,
Struck down through war and slaughtered in the middle of
    the city,
Death has entombed them here like these men;
And after their death he has given them eternal peace.
He is the one who stands in the centre, without whom no
    man can aspire to rest.
Here a quarrel, there a fight. Death is takes a man's arms and
    lays them down.
Death, fate, and Mars, who scattered these lords.

John Whethamstede, *Registrum Abbatiae Johannis Whethamstede Secundae*, ed., H.T. Riley, Vol.1, 1872–3, pp. 167–78 (Latin).

Appendix 7

The Parliamentary Pardon

The official Yorkist pardon, granted in 1455, blamed the first battle of St Albans wholly on the late Edmund Duke of Somerset, Thomas Thorpe and William Joseph. The *Rotuli Parliamentorum* provides a good example of early Yorkist propaganda that absolved the Duke of York and the Nevilles who were clearly responsible for rebelling against the king. Principally the pardon focuses on the Yorkist letters of 'innocence' supposedly concealed from Henry VI prior to the battle by named individuals. However, dates and times are skewed, and no doubt, the king is speaking through the parliament record after being pressured to reach an accord with the victors:

> The which letters either to us, or to the said most reverend father in God sent, or the content thereof, or any copy or copies of them, were never opened or declared unto us, afore the coming of our said cousins to the side of the town of St Albans, the twenty-second day of May last passed, we then being within the same town, but from us to that time kept by the said Edmund, Thomas, and William. Howbeit that we

now understand and know certainly, that the said most reverend father in God, incontinent after the reception and sight of
the said letters to him brought, sent us the same, which were
to us presented at Kilburn by John Saye, the twenty-first day
of May aforesaid, about ten of the clock of the same day afore
noon, by Thomas Manning clerk, there then received, and by
him and the said Edmund, Thomas, and William, there then
read as we for certain be informed. And that the said letters to
us from our said cousins sent, were to us presented at Watford
by master William Willeflete, the twenty-second day of
May aforesaid, about eleven of the clock in the morning,
and by the Earl of Devonshire by our commandment there
then received, and by the said Edmund, Thomas Thorpe and
William Joseph, from our hearing kept to us undeclared, unto
the said coming of our said cousins to the side of the town of
St Albans aforesaid. And the said twenty-second day, our said
cousins hearing of our being in the said town of St Albans,
came there desiring in full lowly wise to have had knowledge
of our intent and pleasure of their demeaning, touching the
matter in their said letters, to us by them the said twenty-
second day afore sent, and to come to our presence to declare
them as it is specified; where unto about twelve of the clock
of that same day, by the advice of the said Edmund, Thomas
Thorpe, and William Joseph, it was as we conceived without
our knowledge answered unto them, that then we had not
seen the same letters; where upon our said cousins deeming
as we now conceive and understand the truth, that the same
letters should be by the said Edmund, Thomas Thorpe and
William Joseph, that were then there about us kept from us,
to the intent that we should not know the truth and faithful disposition of the same our cousins toward us and our
estate, preferred themselves to enter the same town, to come
to our presence for their declaration. And the said Edmund,
Thomas Thorpe, and William Joseph, with a great multitude of people to them assembled, defensibly arrayed, to the

intent to let our cousins to come to our presence, and them to destroy and flee, openly saying and calling them false traitors to us, and that they should die as traitors, then and therefore assaulted our said cousins as they entered the said town, in which assault it happened the said Edmund, the said twenty-second day, at the said town of St Albans was slain; and at the coming of our said cousins to our presence, they and all that came with them, put them in as notable, humble and true devoir and acquittal in their allegiance to our said person, and the surety and safeguard thereof, and also to our said estate in the duty and obedience that they owe unto us, as ever did any liegemen to their sovereign lord, approving and showing them of worshipful and honourable devoir therein our true and faithful liegemen, whose faith and truth therefore at that time was, and is to us undoubted, and to all men it ought to be. We therefore considering the promises, declare, repute, accept, hold and approve our said cousins, and all those persons that came with them in their fellowship to the said town of St Albans, the said twenty-second day, and all other persons that they or any of them have assisted, stirred, helped, comforted or counselled, our true and faithful liegemen; and will that through all our said realm by all our people of the same, they and each of them before taken, reputed, accepted, holden and approved. And over that, we will and grant by the advice of the lords spiritual and temporal, and of all of the commons in this present parliament assembled, and by the authority of the same, that our said cousins, and all of the said persons coming or being in their fellowship, and each of them, their assistors, helpers, stirrers, comforters, and councillors aforesaid, before taken, had and reputed against us and our heirs, and all other men, forever. And that none of our said cousins, the Duke of York, and the earls of Warwick and Salisbury, or none of the said persons coming of being with them, nor none of their said assisters, helpers, stirrers, comforters, or councillors, nor none of any of their heirs, of nor for anything supposed or pretended to be done or against our person, crown or dignity, be impeached, sued, vexed, grieved, hurt or molested, in their bodies, lands or goods, in any wise. And over that, we will by the said advice and authority, that none of our said cousins, nor none of the said persons coming with them to the said town of St Albans, nor none of their said assistors, helpers, stirrers, councillors of comforters, nor none of any of their heirs, or nor for anything that happened the said twenty-second day to befall or be done at the said town of St Albans, be impeached, sued, grieved, vexed, hurt or molested, in their bodies, goods or lands, in any wise.

J. Strachey, ed., *Rotuli Parliamentorum*, Vol. 5, 1783, pp. 281–2.

Notes

Introduction

1 M.A. Hicks, 'The Sources', in *The Wars of the Roses*, ed., A.J. Pollard, 1995, pp. 39–40.

2 S.B. Chrimes, *Lancastrians Yorkists and Henry VII*, 1966, p. xiv.

3 H. Ellis, ed., *Edward Hall's Chronicle*, 1809.

4 Hall relied mainly on the *Brut* and *London Chronicles*. As for oral tradition, veterans of Stoke Field (1487), for example, would have been over 76 years old when he wrote his chronicle.

5 See, A. Gransden, *Historical Writing in England II*, 1982, p. 476.

Chapter One: York and Somerset

1 H. Ellis, ed., *Original Letters Illustrative of English History*, First Series, I, 1827, pp.11–13.

2 Ibid.

3 Dominic Mancini, *The Usurpation of Richard the Third*, ed. C.A.J. Armstrong, second edition, 1969, p. 95. We also now have the benefit of a facial reconstruction of Richard III to compare the resemblance.

4 The text of Blacman's work is printed in *Duo Rerum Anglicarum Scriptores Veteres*, ed., T. Hearne, Vol. 1, 1732, pp. 285–307. See also *Henry the Sixth, a reprint of John Blacman's Memoir,* with translation and notes by M.R. James, 1919.

5 H. Ellis, ed., *The Chronicle of John Hardyng*, 1812, p. 410.

6   C.L. Kingsford, 'Extracts from the first version of Hardyng's Chronicle',
    English Historical Review, 27, 1912, pp. 744–5.

7   John Whethamstede, *Registrum Abbatiae Johannis Whethamstede Secundae*,
    ed. H.T. Riley, Vol.1, 1872–3, pp. 171–3.

8   J. Gairdner, ed., *The Paston Letters*, Vol. 2, 1904, p. 147.

9   J. Gairdner, ed., *Three Fifteenth Century Chronicles*, 1880, p. 94.

10 H. Ellis, ed., *Original Letters Illustrative of English History*, First Series, I,
    1827, pp. 11–13.

11 Ibid.

12 C.L. Kingsford, 'London Chronicle for 1446–1452', *English Historical litera-
    ture in the Fifteenth Century*, 1913, pp. 297–8.

13 J. Strachey, ed., *Rotuli Parliamentorum*, Vol. 5. p. 241.

14 J. Gairdner ed., *The Paston Letters*, Vol. 2, 1904, p. 297.

15 J. Stevenson, ed., 'Annales Rerum Anglicarum' (The Wars of the English
    in France), *Rolls Series*, Vol. 2, 1864, p. 770.

Chapter Two: The Beginning of Sorrows

1   See, A.J. Pollard, *North-Eastern England During the Wars of the Roses*, 1990.

2   Ibid., pp. 244–65.

3   J. Strachey, ed., *Rotuli Parliamentorum*, Vol. 5, 1783, p. 394.

4   J.C. Atkinson, ed., *Cartularium Abbathiae de Whitby*, Vol. 2, 1879, pp. 694–5.

5   R.A. Griffiths, 'Local Rivalries and National Politics: The Percies, the
    Nevilles and The Duke of Exeter', *Speculum*, Vol. XLIII, 4, 1968.

6   Ibid., p. 602.

7   R.L. Storey, *The End of the House of Lancaster*, 1966, p. 131.

8   J. Gairdner, ed., *The Paston Letters*, Vol. 2, 1904, p. 296–7.

9   G.M. Trevelyan, *History of England*, 1945, p. 259.

10 R.A. Griffiths, 'Local Rivalries and National Politics: The Percies, the
    Nevilles and The Duke of Exeter', *Speculum*, Vol. XLIII, 4, 1968, p. 598.

11 J.C. Atkinson, ed., *Cartularium Abbathiae de Whitby*, Vol. 2, 1879, p. 695.

12 R.A. Griffiths, 'Local Rivalries and National Politics: The Percies, the
    Nevilles and The Duke of Exeter', *Speculum*, Vol. XLIII, 4, 1968, p. 622.

13 J.C. Atkinson, ed., *Cartularium Abbathiae de Whitby*, Vol. 2, 1879, p. 695.
    Trinity College, Dublin MS E. 5. 10 f. 187.

14 Oyer and terminer – to hear and determine. A commission issued by the
    sovereign to judges to try cases on assize.

15 See, H.E. Maurer, *Margaret of Anjou*, 2003, pp. 100–1.

16 R. Flenley, ed., 'Bale's Chronicle' in *Six Town Chronicles of England*, 1911,
    p. 141.

17 J. Strachey, ed., *Rotuli Parliamentorum*, Vol. 5, 1783, p. 280.

18 The Dijon Relation, *Archives de la Cote d'Or, Dijon*, B.11942, no. 258
    (French). Letter cited by C.A.J. Armstrong in 'Politics and the Battle of

St Albans, 1455', *Bulletin of the Institute of Historical Research*, Vol. 33, no. 87, 1960, p. 63.

19 M.D. Harris, ed., *The Coventry Leet Book*, E.E.T.S., 1907–13, p. 282.

20 J. Strachey, ed., *Rotuli Parliamentorum*, Vol. 5, 1783, pp. 280–1.

21 Ibid.

Chapter Three: Faith, Allegiance and Duty

1 J. Gairdner, ed., Stow Relation, *The Paston Letters*, Vol. 3, 1904, p. 25.

2 J. Strachey, ed., *Rotuli Parliamentorum*, Vol. 5, 1783, p. 281.

3 Ibid.

4 J.S. Davies, ed., *An English Chronicle of the Reigns of Richard II, Henry IV, Henry V and Henry VI*, 1856, pp. 79–80.

5 Ibid., p. 71.

6 A.B. Hinds, ed., *Calendar of State Papers and Manuscripts existing in the Archives and Collections of Milan*, Vol. 1, 1912, pp. 16–7.

7 J. Gairdner, ed., Phillipps Relation, *The Paston Letters*, Vol. 3, 1904, p. 30.

8 J. Strachey, ed., *Rotuli Parliamentorum*, Vol. 5, 1783, p. 348.

9 J. Gairdner, ed., Phillipps Relation, *The Paston Letters*, Vol. 3, 1904, p. 30.

10 For more on recruitment practices of the period see, A.W. Boardman, *The Medieval Soldier in the Wars of the Roses*, 2022.

11 A.C. Reeves, ed., 'Some of Humphrey Stafford's Military Indentures', *Nottingham Medieval Studies*, Vol.16,1972, p. 91.

12 H.M. Cam, 'The Decline and Fall of English Feudalism', *History*, 25, 1940, p. 225.

13 See, C.A.J. Armstrong, 'Politics and the Battle of St Albans, 1455', *Bulletin of the Institute of Historical Research*, Vol. 33, no. 87, 1960, p. 70.

14 K. Dockray, 'Contemporary and Near-Contemporary Chroniclers: The North of England and the Wars of the Roses, c. 1450–1471', in L. Clark and P. Fleming, eds., *The Fifteenth Century XVIII: Rulers, Regions and Retinues, Essays Presented to A. J. Pollard*, 2020, pp. 65–80. Also see, A.J. Pollard, 'The Northern Retainers of Richard Nevill, Earl of Salisbury', *Northern History*, Vol. 11, 1976.

15 J. Gairdner, ed., Phillipps Relation, *The Paston Letters*, Vol. 3, 1904, p. 30.

16 R.L. Storey, *The End of the House of Lancaster*, 1986, p. 122.

17 J. Nicolson and J.R. Burn, *The History and Antiquities of the Counties of Westmorland and Cumberland*, Vol. 1, 1777, pp. 97–8.

18 For commissions of array see, A.W. Boardman, *The Medieval Soldier in the Wars of the Roses*, 2022, pp. 130–9.

19 A.J. Pollard, *North-Eastern England During the Wars of the Roses*, 1990, p. 264. C.M Fraser, Ogle, Robert, first Baron Ogle (1406–69), *Oxford DNB* online article, 2004.

20 J. Gairdner, ed., Phillipps Relation, *The Paston Letters*, Vol. 3, 1904, p. 30.

Chapter Four: St Albans

1   A.H. Burne, *The Battlefields of England* (consolidated edition), 1996, pp. xi–xii.
2   C. Oman, *The Political History of England, 1377–1485*, 1920, p. 367.
3   H.T. Riley, ed., Gesta Abbatum Monasterii Sancti Albani, *Rolls Series*, Vol. 3, 1867–8, pp. 355–6.
4   Ibid.
5   W. Page, 'The Marian survey of St Albans', *Trans. St Albans and Herts. Architectural and Archaeological Society*, 1893–1902, pp. 8–24.
6   J. Gairdner, ed., Stow Relation, *The Paston Letters*, Vol. 3, 1904, p. 25.
7   Fastolf Relation, College of Arms, *Arundel MS*. 48, folio 341.
8   F.G. Kitton, 'The Old Inns of St Albans' in *Trans. St Albans and Herts. Architectural and Archaeological Society*, 1895–1902, pp. 146–8.
9   See Stow Relation, *Chancery Miscellanea*, PRO, C47/37/3/4-11; also M.L. Kekewich, C. Richmond, A.F. Sutton, L. Visser-Fuchs, J.L. Watts, 'John Vales Book', *The Politics of Fifteenth-Century England*, 1995.
10 J. Gairdner, ed., Stow Relation, *The Paston Letters*, Vol. 3, 1904, p. 25.
11 J. Strachey, ed., *Rotuli Parliamentorum*, Vol. 5, 1783, p. 347.
12 Fastolf Relation, College of Arms, *Arundel MS*. 48, folio 341.
13 J. Gairdner, ed., Stow Relation, *The Paston Letters*, Vol. 3, 1904, p. 25.
14 Fastolf Relation, College of Arms, *Arundel MS*. 48, folio 341.
15 J.S. Davies, ed., *An English Chronicle of the Reigns of Richard II, Henry IV, Henry V, and Henry VI*, 1856, p. 71.
16 C.A.J. Armstrong, 'Politics and the Battle of St Albans, 1455', *Bulletin of the Institute of Historical Research*, Vol. 33, no. 87, 1960, p. 25.

Chapter Five: 'I Shall Destroy Them, Every Mother's Son'

1   Fastolf Relation, College of Arms, *Arundel MS*. 48, folio 341.
2   C.A.J. Armstrong, 'Politics and the Battle of St Albans, 1455', *Bulletin of the Institute of Historical Research*, Vol. 33, no.87, 1960.
3   M.A. Hicks, 'Propaganda and the First Battle of St Albans', *Nottingham Medieval Studies*, Vol. 44, 2000.
4   C.A.J. Armstrong, 'Politics and the Battle of St Albans, 1455', *Bulletin of the Institute of Historical Research*, Vol. 33, no. 87, 1960, p. 1.
5   J. Gairdner, ed., Phillipps Relation, *The Paston Letters*, Vol. 3, 1904, p 29.
6   Ibid.
7   Fastolf Relation, College of Arms, *Arundel MS*. 48, folio 342.
8   C.A.J. Armstrong, 'Politics and the Battle of St Albans, 1455', *Bulletin of the Institute of Historical Research*, Vol. 33, no. 87, 1960, p. 6. See also, W. Pronger, 'Thomas Gascoigne', *English Historical Review*, liii, 1938.

9 A.H. Thomas and I.D. Thornley, eds, *The Great Chronicle of London*, 1983, p. 187.

10 J. Gairdner, ed., Stow Relation, *The Paston Letters*, Vol. 3, 1904, p. 25.

11 J. Gairdner, ed., Phillipps Relation, *The Paston Letters*, Vol. 3, 1904, p. 29.

12 J.S. Davies, ed., *An English Chronicle of the Reigns of Richard II, Henry IV, Henry V, and Henry VI*, 1856, p. 71.

13 Fastolf Relation, College of Arms, *Arundel MS.* 48, folio 341.

14 Namely the Dijon Relation, Thomas Gascoigne, John Whethamstede and *Davies' Chronicle*.

15 F.P. Barnard, ed., *Edward IV's French Expedition of 1474*, 1975, pp. 128–31.

16 Fastolf Relation, College of Arms, *Arundel MS.* 48, folio 341.

17 Ibid.

18 J. Gairdner, ed., Stow Relation, *The Paston Letters*, Vol. 3, 1904, p. 26. See also Stow Relation, *Chancery Miscellanea*, PRO, C47/37/3/4-11 and M.L. Kekewich, C. Richmond, A.F. Sutton, L. Visser-Fuchs, J.L. Watts, *'John Vales Book', The Politics of Fifteenth-Century England*, 1995, p. 191. *Domine sis clipeus defensionis nostræ* (Lord, be the shield of our defence).

19 Fastolf Relation, College of Arms, *Arundel MS.* 48, folio 341.

20 *Ibid.*

21 J. Gairdner, ed., Stow Relation, *The Paston Letters*, Vol. 3, 1904, pp. 26–7. See also Stow Relation, *Chancery Miscellanea*, PRO, C47/37/3/4-11, and M.L. Kekewich, C. Richmond, A.F. Sutton, L. Visser-Fuchs, J.L. Watts, *'John Vales Book', The Politics of Fifteenth-Century England,* 1995, p. 191.

22 Fastolf Relation, College of Arms, *Arundel MS.* 48, folio 342.

23 Ibid.

Chapter six: 'A Warwick! A Warwick!'

1 The Dijon Relation, Archives de la Cote d'Or, Dijon, B.11942, no.258 (French). Cited by C.A.J. Armstrong in 'Politics and the Battle of St Albans, 1455', *Bulletin of the Institute of Historical Research*, Vol. 33, no. 87, 1960, p. 63.

2 J. Gairdner, ed., Stow Relation, *The Paston Letters*, Vol. 3, 1904, p. 25.

3 Fastolf Relation, College of Arms, *Arundel MS.* 48, folio 342.

4 The Dijon Relation, Archives de la Cote d'Or, Dijon, B.11942, no. 258 (French). Cited by C.A.J. Armstrong in 'Politics and the Battle of St Albans, 1455', *Bulletin of the Institute of Historical Research*, Vol. 33, no. 87, 1960, p. 63.

5 A.H. Thomas and I.D. Thornley, eds., *The Great Chronicle of London*, 1983, p. 187.

6 J. Gairdner, ed., Stow Relation, *The Paston Letters*, Vol. 3, 1904, p. 27.

7 J. Gairdner, ed., 'Gregory's Chronicle', *The Historical Collections of a Citizen of London*, 1876, p. 198.

8 J. Gairdner, ed., Stow Relation, *The Paston Letters*, Vol. 3, 1904, p. 28.

9 J. Gairdner, ed., Phillipps Relation, *The Paston Letters*, Vol. 3, 1904, p. 30.

10 Fastolf Relation, College of Arms, *Arundel MS*. 48, folio 342.

11 J. Gairdner, ed., Stow Relation, *The Paston Letters*, Vol. 3, 1904, pp. 27–8.

12 A.H. Thomas and I.D. Thornley, eds., *The Great Chronicle of London*, 1983, p. 187.

13 J. Gairdner, ed., Stow Relation, *The Paston Letters*, Vol. 3, 1904, p. 28.

14 J. Gairdner, ed., Phillipps Relation, *The Paston Letters*, Vol. 3, 1904, p. 30.

15 J.S. Davies, ed., *An English Chronicle of the Reigns of Richard II, Henry IV, Henry V, and Henry VI*, 1856, p. 72.

16 The Dijon Relation, Archives de la Cote d'Or, Dijon, B.11942, no. 258 (French). Cited by C.A.J. Armstrong in 'Politics and the Battle of St Albans, 1455', in *Bulletin of the Institute of Historical Research*, Vol. 33, no. 87, 1960, p. 64.

17 John Whethamstede, *Registrum Abbatiae Johannis Whethamstede Secundae*, ed. H.T. Riley, Vol.1, 1872–3, p. 168.

18 J.S. Davies, ed., *An English Chronicle of the Reigns of Richard II, Henry IV, Henry V, and Henry VI*, 1856, p. 72.

19 The Dijon Relation, Archives de la Cote d'Or, Dijon, B.11942, no. 258 (French). Cited by C.A.J. Armstrong in 'Politics and the Battle of St Albans, 1455', *Bulletin of the Institute of Historical Research*, Vol. 33, no. 87, 1960, p. 64.

20 J. Gairdner, ed., *Gregory's Chronicle*, The Historical Collections of a Citizen of London, 1876, p. 198.

21 The Dijon Relation, Archives de la Cote d'Or, Dijon, B.11942, no. 258 (French). Cited by C.A.J. Armstrong in 'Politics and the Battle of St Albans, 1455', in *Bulletin of the Institute of Historical Research*, Vol. 33, no. 87, 1960, p. 64.

22 John Whethamstede, *Registrum Abbatiae Johannis Whethamstede Secundae*, ed. H.T. Riley, Vol.1, 1872–3, p. 169.

23 The Dijon Relation, Archives de la Cote d'Or, Dijon, B.11942, no. 258 (French). Cited by C.A.J. Armstrong in 'Politics and the Battle of St Albans, 1455', in *Bulletin of the Institute of Historical Research*, Vol. 33, no. 87, 1960, p. 64.

24 J.S. Davies, ed., *An English Chronicle of the Reigns of Richard II, Henry IV, Henry V, and Henry VI*, 1856, p. 72.

25 A.B. Hinds, ed., *Calendar of State Papers and Manuscripts existing in the Archives and Collections of Milan*, Vol. 1, 1912, p. 17.

26 J. Gairdner, ed., *Gregory's Chronicle*, The Historical Collections of a Citizen of London, 1876, pp.198–9.

27 H. Ellis, ed., *The Chronicle of John Hardyng*, 1812, p. 402.

28 The Dijon Relation, Archives de la Cote d'Or, Dijon, B.11942,
     no. 258 (French). Cited by C.A.J. Armstrong in 'Politics and the Battle of
     St Albans, 1455', *Bulletin of the Institute of Historical Research*, Vol. 33, no. 87,
     1960, p. 64.

29 J. Gairdner, ed., Stow Relation, *The Paston Letters*, Vol. 3, 1904, p. 28.

30 The Dijon Relation, Archives de la Cote d'Or, Dijon, B.11942,
     no. 258 (French). Cited by C.A.J. Armstrong in 'Politics and the Battle of
     St Albans, 1455', *Bulletin of the Institute of Historical Research*, Vol. 33, no. 87,
     1960, p. 64.

31 J. Gairdner, ed., Stow Relation, *The Paston Letters*, Vol. 3, 1904, p. 29.

Chapter Seven: The Fate of the Kingdom

1   W. Stubbs, *The Constitutional History of England*, Vol. 3, 1903, p. 176.

2   J. Gairdner, ed., Phillipps Relation, *The Paston Letters*, Vol. 3, 1904, p. 30.

3   N.H. Nicolas, E. Tyrell, eds, *Chronicle of London 1089–1483*, 1827, p. 139.

4   J. Gairdner, ed., Stow Relation, *The Paston Letters*, Vol. 3, 1904, p. 28.

5   The Dijon Relation, Archives de la Cote d'Or, Dijon, B.11942,
     no. 258 (French). Cited by C.A.J. Armstrong in 'Politics and the Battle of
     St Albans, 1455', *Bulletin of the Institute of Historical Research*, Vol. 33, no. 87,
     1960, p. 64.

6   J.S. Davies, ed., *An English Chronicle of the Reigns of Richard II, Henry IV,
     Henry V, and Henry VI*, 1856, p. 72.

7   J. Gairdner, ed., *The Paston Letters*, Vol. 3, 1904, p. 31.

8   W.E. Hampton, *Memorials of the Wars of the Roses*, 1979, p. 87.

9   F. Yeoman, 'Skeletons in Armour', *The Ricardian, Journal of the Richard III
     Society*, no. 28, 1970, p. 8.

10 J. Gairdner, ed., Phillipps Relation, *The Paston Letters*, Vol. 3, 1904, p. 30.

11 John Whethamstede, *Registrum Abbatiae Johannis Whethamstede Secundae*,
     ed. H.T. Riley, Vol.1, 1872–3, p. 168.

12 Ibid., pp. 171–2.

13 Ibid., pp. 175–8.

14 J. Gairdner, ed., *Gregory's Chronicle*, The Historical Collections of a
     Citizen of London, 1876, p. 198.

15 A.B. Hinds, ed., *Calendar of State Papers and Manuscripts existing in the
     Archives and Collections of Milan*, Vol. 1, 1912, p. 17.

16 J. Gairdner, ed., *The Paston Letters*, Vol. 3, 1904, p. 32.

17 Jean-Philippe Genet, 'New Politics or New Language? The words of
     politics in Yorkist and early Tudor England', in *The End of the Middle Ages?
     England in the Fifteenth and Sixteenth Centuries*, ed. J.L. Watts, 1998, p. 52.

18 J. Strachey, ed., *Rotuli Parliamentorum*, Vol. 5, 1783, p. 282.

19 Ibid., p. 280.

20 J. Gairdner, ed., *The Paston Letters*, Vol. 3, 1904, p. 44.

21 T. Rymer, ed., *Foedera*, Vol. 5, 2, 1704–13, p. 64.

22 R.L. Storey, *The End of the House of Lancaster*, 1966, p. 172.

23 Ibid.

24 A.B. Hinds, ed., *Calendar of State Papers and Manuscripts in the Archives and Collections of Milan 1385–1618*, 1912, pp. 16–17.

25 J. Strachey, ed., *Rotuli Parliamentorum*, Vol. 5, 1783, p. 347.

26 J. Gairdner, ed., *The Paston Letters*, Vol. 3, 1904, p. 44.

Bibliography

Primary Sources

C.A.J. Armstrong, ed., *Dominic Mancini, The Usurpation of Richard the Third*, second edition, 1969.

J.C. Atkinson, ed., *Cartularium Abbathiae de Whitby*, II, 1879.

W. Brigg, 'Register of the Archdeacons of St Albans', *The Herts Genealogist and Antiquary*, i, 1895.

J.S. Davies, ed., *An English Chronicle of the Reigns of Richard II, Henry IV, Henry V, and Henry VI*, 1856.

The Dijon Relation, Archives de la Cote d'Or, Dijon, B.11942, no.258 (French). Cited by C.A.J. Armstrong in 'Politics and the Battle of St Albans, 1455', *Bulletin of the Institute of Historical Research*, Vol. 33, no.87, 1960.

H. Ellis, ed., *Original Letters Illustrative of English History*, First Series, I, 1827.

—, *The Chronicle of John Hardyng*, 1812.

—, *Edward Hall's Chronicle*, 1809.

Fastolf Relation, College of Arms, *Arundel MS.* 48, folio 342.

R. Flenley, ed., *Bale's Chronicle*, in *Six Town Chronicles of England*, 1911.

E.B. de Fonblanque, *Annals of the House of Percy*, 1887.

J. Gairdner, ed., *Gregory's Chronicle, The Historical Collections of a Citizen of London*, 1876.

—, Phillipps Relation, *The Paston Letters*, Vol. 3, 1904.

—, Stow Relation and Phillipps Relation in *The Paston Letters*, Vol. 3, 1904.

—, *Three Fifteenth Century Chronicles*, 1880.

M.D. Harris, ed., *The Coventry Leet Book*, E.E.T.S., 1907–13.

T. Hearne, ed., *Duo Rerum Anglicarum Scriptores Veteres*, Vol. 1, 1732.

A.B. Hinds, ed., *Calendar of State Papers and Manuscripts existing in the Archives and Collections of Milan*, Vol. 1, 1912.

C.L. Kingsford, 'Extracts from the first version of Hardyng's Chronicle', in *English Historical Review*, 27, 1912.

—, 'London Chronicle for 1446–1452', *English Historical Literature in the Fifteenth Century*, 1913.

—, ed., *The Stoner Letters*, Camden Society, 3rd Series, xxix, 1919.

N.H. Nicolas, E. Tyrell, eds, *Chronicle of London 1089–1483*, 1827.

W. Pronger, 'Thomas Gascoigne', *English Historical Review*, liii, 1938.

H.T. Riley, ed., *Gesta Abbatum Monasterii Sancti Albani, Rolls Series*, Vol. 3, 1867–8.

—, John Whethamstede, *Registrum Abbatiae Johannis Whethamstede Secundae*, Vol. 1, 1872 –3.

J.E.T. Rogers, ed., Thomas Gascoigne, *Loci e Libro Veritatum*, 1881.

T. Rymer, ed., *Foedera*, Vol. 5, 2, 1704–13.

L.T. Smith, ed., *The Itinerary of John Leland 1535–1543*, 1910.

J. Strachey, ed., *Rotuli Parliamentorum*, Vol. 5, 1783.

A.H. Thomas and I.D. Thornley, eds, *The Great Chronicle of London*, 1983.

J. Weever, *Ancient Funeral Monuments*, 1767.

Secondary Sources

C.T. Allmand, ed., *War, Literature and Politics in the Late Middle Ages*, 1976.

C.A.J. Armstrong, 'Politics and the Battle of St Albans, 1455', *Bulletin of the Institute of Historical Research*, Vol. 33, no.87, 1960.

T. Billings, *St Albans Directory*, 2003.

M. Blatcher, *The Court of the King's Bench, 1450–1550,* 1978.

A.W. Boardman, *The Medieval Soldier in the Wars of the Roses*, 2022.

A.H. Burne, *The Battlefields of England* (consolidated edition), 1996.

F.P. Barnard, ed., *Edward IV's French Expedition of 1474*, 1975.

K. Cameron, *English Place Names*, 1961.

S.B. Crimes, C.D. Ross, R.A. Griffiths, eds, *Fifteenth Century England 1399–1509*, 1995.

—, *Lancastrians, Yorkists and Henry VII*, 1964.

J. Crosland, *Sir John Fastolfe: A Medieval man of Property*, 1970.

K. Dockray, *Henry VI, Margaret of Anjou and the Wars of the Roses*, 2000.

J. Gillingham, *The Wars of the Roses, Peace and Conflict in Fifteenth-Century England*, 1981.

A. Goodman, *The Wars of the Roses*, 1981.

—, *The Wars of the Roses – The Soldier's Experience*, 2005.

A. Gransden, *Historical Writing in England*, ii, 1982.

R.A. Griffiths, *The Reign of King Henry VI*, 1981.

—, 'Local Rivalries and National Politics: The Percies, the Nevilles and the Duke of Exeter, 1452–55', *Speculum*, Vol. XLIII, No.4, October 1968.

—, 'Duke Richard of York's Intentions in 1450', *Journal of Medieval History*, Vol.1, 1976.

B. Grimshaw, *The Entwistle Family*, 1924.

W.E. Hampton, *Memorials of the Wars of the Roses*, 1979.

M.A. Hicks, *Warwick the Kingmaker*, 1998.

—, 'Propaganda and the First Battle of St Albans', *Nottingham Medieval Studies*, Vol.44, 2000.

—, *The Wars of the Roses*, 2012.

P.A. Johnson, *Duke Richard of York, 1411–1460*, 1988.

C.E. Johnston, 'Sir William Oldhall', *English Historical Review*, 25, 1910.

M.K. Jones, 'Somerset, York and the Wars of the Roses', *English Historical Review*, Vol. 14, No 411, April 1989.

M.H. Keen, *Chivalry*, 1984.

M.L. Kekewich, C. Richmond, A.F. Sutton, L. Visser-Fuchs, J.L. Watts, *'John Vales Book', The Politics of Fifteenth-Century England*, 1995.

F.G. Kitton, 'The old inns of St Albans', *Trans. St Albans and Herts. Architectural and Archaeological Society*, new series, i (1895–1902).

J.R. Lander, *The Wars of the Roses*, 1990.

H.M. Lane, 'The male journey of St Albans', *Trans. St Albans and Herts. Architectural and Archaeological Society*, 1931.

M. Lewis, *Richard Duke of York: King by Right*, 2016.

H.E. Maurer, *Margaret of Anjou,* 2003,

K.B. McFarlane, *The Nobility of Later Medieval England*, 1973.

—, 'Bastard Feudalism', *Bulletin of the Institute of Historical Research*, 20, 1943–45.

P.D. McGill, *Heraldic Banners of the Wars of the Roses*, 1990.

C. Munro, ed., *Letters of Queen Margaret of Anjou*, Camden Society, LXXXVI, 1863.

A.R. Myers, ed., *English Historical Documents, 1327–1485*, 1969.

C.W.C. Oman, *The Art of War in the Middle Ages*, 1991.

—, *The Political History of England, 1377–1485*, 1920.

J. Otway-Ruthven, *The King's Secretary and the Signet Office in the Fifteenth Century*, 1939.

W. Page, 'The Marian survey of St Albans', *Trans. St Albans and Herts. Architectural and Archaeological Society*, 1893–1902.

A.J. Pollard, *North-Eastern England During the Wars of the Roses*, 1990.

—, 'Percies, Nevilles and the Wars of the Roses', *History Today*, September 1993.

—, 'The Battle of St Albans 1455', *History Today*, May 2005.

M. Prestwich, *Armies and Warfare in the Middle Ages: The English Experience*, 1996.

J.H. Ramsay, *Lancaster and York*, Vol.1, 1892.

A.C. Reeves, 'Some of Humphrey Stafford's Military Indentures', *Nottingham Medieval Studies*, Vol. 16, 1972.

J.T. Rosenthal, 'The Estates and Finances of Richard Duke of York, 1411–1460', *Studies in Medieval and Renaissance History*, Vol. 2, 1965.

C.L. Scofield, *Life and Reign of Edward IV*, 1923.

R.L. Storey, *The End of the House of Lancaster*, 1966.

—, 'The Wardens of the Marches of England towards Scotland, 1377–1489', *English Historical Review*, No.72, October 1957.

M. Strickland, R. Hardy, *The Great Warbow*, 2003.

W. Stubbs, *The Constitutional History of England*, Vol. 3, 1903.

C.R. Swift, *Historic St Albans*, 1940.

G.M. Trevelyan, *History of England*, 1945.

J.A. Tuck, *Border Warfare: A History of Conflict on the Anglo Scottish Border*, 1979.

J.A. Tuck, A. Goodman, *War and Border Societies in the Middle Ages*, 1992.

J.L. Watts, The *End of the Middle Ages? England in the Fifteenth and Sixteenth Centuries*, 1998.

B. Wolffe, *Henry VI*, 1981.

C.M. Woolgar, *The Great Household in Late Medieval England*, 1999.

F. Yeoman, 'Skeletons in Armour', *The Ricardian, Journal of the Richard III Society*, No.28, 1970.

P. Young, J. Adair, *Hastings to Culloden*, 1979.

Index

References to the battle are given either under specific topics or under 'St Albans'; peers and lords are listed under their family names.

About the Author

Andrew Boardman has written extensively on British military history. In 1992, he formed the Towton Battlefield Society and wrote the first major work about the battle two years later. His special interest is the medieval period, and when a mass grave was unearthed in Towton village in 1996, Andrew was consulted and formed part of the team from Bradford University that investigated it.

He has been a consultant on many TV documentary series for the BBC, Channel 4, Sky One and Yesterday Channel, and lectures on the battles of the Wars of the Roses and related subjects.

To date, Andrew's other non-fiction work includes *The Medieval Soldier in the Wars of the Roses*, *Hotspur: Henry Percy Medieval Rebel*, *Blood Red Roses* and *Towton 1461: The Anatomy of a Battle*. He lives in Yorkshire, writes a weekly newsletter called *History Mondays*, and has recently published two historical novels with military themes.

twitter.com/wotroses
linkedin.com/in/awboardman/
historymondays.substack.com

You may also enjoy...

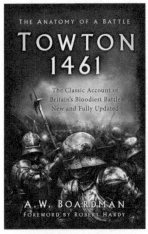

978 0 7509 9897 0

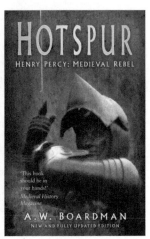

978 1 80399 165 8

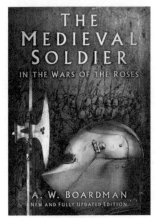

978 1 80399 031 6